P9-CMX-964

Phillips Library
Bethany College

Community Control of Schools

STUDIES IN SOCIAL ECONOMICS

TITLES PUBLISHED

The Doctor Shortage: An Economic Diagnosis
Rashi Fein

Medicare and the Hospitals: Issues and Prospects
Herman Miles Somers and Anne Ramsay Somers

Education and Poverty
Thomas I. Ribich

Social Security: Perspectives for Reform
Joseph A. Pechman, Henry J. Aaron, and Michael K. Taussig

Poverty and Discrimination
Lester C. Thurow

Community Control of Schools
Henry M. Levin, Editor

STUDIES IN SOCIAL ECONOMICS

Community Control of Schools

Henry M. Levin, Editor

Harold W. Pfautz
Mario D. Fantini
Leonard J. Fein
Robert C. Maynard
Marilyn Gittell
Robert F. Lyke
Rhody A. McCoy
Michael H. Moskow & Kenneth McLennan
Anthony Downs
H. Thomas James & Henry M. Levin

THE BROOKINGS INSTITUTION
Washington, D.C.

THE BROOKINGS INSTITUTION
1775 Massachusetts Avenue, N.W.
Washington, D.C. 20036

SBN 8157-5224-5
Library of Congress Catalog Card Number 78-106564

THE BROOKINGS INSTITUTION is an independent organization devoted to nonpartisan research, education, and publication in economics, government, foreign policy, and the social sciences generally. Its principal purposes are to aid in the development of sound public policies and to promote public understanding of issues of national importance.

The Institution was founded on December 8, 1927, to merge the activities of the Institute for Government Research, founded in 1916, the Institute of Economics, founded in 1922, and the Robert Brookings Graduate School of Economics and Government, founded in 1924.

The general administration of the Institution is the responsibility of a self-perpetuating Board of Trustees. The trustees are likewise charged with maintaining the independence of the staff and fostering the most favorable conditions for creative research and education. The immediate direction of the policies, program, and staff of the Institution is vested in the President, assisted by an advisory council chosen from the staff of the Institution.

In publishing a study, the Institution presents it as a competent treatment of a subject worthy of public consideration. The interpretations and conclusions in such publications are those of the author or authors and do not purport to represent the views of the other staff members, officers, or trustees of the Brookings Institution.

Foreword

The failure of big-city schools to provide equal educational opportunity to black Americans and other racial minorities has long been acknowledged by educators and laymen alike. Until recently, it was widely expected that the advent of racial integration and higher educational expenditures would remedy the inequity. Yet, fifteen years after the Supreme Court's desegregation ruling, the schools of our cities remain largely segregated and the prospects of effective integration are diminishing as whites move to the suburbs. Moreover, wherever educational expenditures for schools serving racial minorities have been increased, the results have been less than encouraging, in part because additional dollars have been spent on strategies that have not worked in the past.

Many black Americans have reacted to the frustration by challenging the ability of the city school boards to solve the educational problems of minority students. As an alternative, community groups have increasingly demanded the power to govern the schools serving their children. That is, they seek to decentralize control of the city schools by obtaining the power to elect local governing boards. The sharp and emotional controversy over such community control continues, and the complex educational and social issues it has raised remain unresolved.

In order to clarify these issues, the Brookings Institution sponsored a Conference on the Community School in December 1968. For the conference, experts drawn from a variety of disciplines and experiences prepared ten papers, which became the basis for a two-day discussion of the objectives, politics, and mechanics of community control of big-city schools by some thirty participants. This volume presents the papers, together with an introduction and a summary of the conference discussion by Henry M. Levin, formerly a Brookings staff member and now on the faculty of Stanford University.

Professor Levin acknowledges the assistance of the authors of the papers and other conference participants in the preparation of his introduction and summary. He is also indebted to Joseph A. Pechman, Rashi Fein, and Stephan Michelson for their encouragement and advice in planning the conference and to Miss Nancy Simpson for her administrative help during the early stages of the project. The manuscript was edited by Mrs. Susan Gilbert, with the assistance of Mrs. Evelyn Fisher who checked the numerous factual and bibliographical references. The index was prepared by Florence Robinson.

Michael H. Moskow and Kenneth McLennan received assistance from Daniel R. Fascione and Jack Schwartz of the Office of Research of the School District of Philadelphia in developing the questionnaire and planning the research for their chapter, and from Jerome Staller, Young J. Park, and Stephen Zelinger of the Department of Economics, Temple University, in collecting and analyzing data.

The project was undertaken with the financial support of a grant by the Carnegie Corporation. The research upon which the chapter by Michael H. Moskow and Kenneth McLennan is based was partially supported by a Temple University Manpower Research Institutional Grant from the U.S. Department of Labor.

The views expressed in this book are those of the authors and are not presented as the views of the Carnegie Corporation, the U.S. Department of Labor, or the staff members, officers, or trustees of the Brookings Institution.

KERMIT GORDON
President

September 1969
Washington, D.C.

Contents

Community Control of Schools

HENRY M. LEVIN

Introduction

One of the most controversial recent developments in education is the movement toward community control of the big-city schools. Black Americans across the country have demanded the power to govern those schools that serve black students. There are many indications that this strategy will be employed increasingly by other ethnic minorities—for example, the Mexican-American and Puerto Rican populations residing in urban areas. In response to the demands for community control, several cities have already begun experiments in decentralizing the governance of their schools, while other cities are planning such efforts. Yet the transition from a familiar territory to an uncharted one has raised enormous conceptual and practical issues for the architects of school policy. The Brookings Conference on the Community School brought together experts from the schools, universities, and urban communities to discuss the nature and implications of this recent phenomenon.

In order to place the conference in perspective, it is important to sketch some of the background of the present situation confronting the schools in large cities. Specifically, the demands for community control of these schools can only be fully understood by recognizing the frustrations that black Americans and other racial minorities have experienced in their quest for freedom, equality, and dignity. Two hundred years of slavery have been followed by one hundred years of "freedom," and the black American still remains outside the mainstream of American life. By all standard measures, his welfare is substantially below that of the white American; and statistics on income, employment, life expectancy, housing, and infant mortality all reflect his unenviable position.

The black American has migrated from rural to urban areas seeking opportunity and has worked hard at the jobs that he could get, but the rapid upward mobility that greeted immigrants from other lands has eluded him. In part this is due to his relatively late arrival in the cities, when opportunities for unskilled labor were fast diminishing and the big-city political systems had become established and stabilized without his participation. Thus, he was caged in by the walls of the urban ghetto with housing and job discrimination handicapping his chances of improving his status. Massive discrimination in both the government and the private sector have prevented any semblance of equal human rights for the black man, and while recent attempts have begun to redress these inequalities, progress has been pitifully slow.

Yet the worst condition facing the American black has been his feeling of powerlessness. Because of discriminatory barriers, the black man is unable to fulfill the same high aspirations as his fellow citizens. He is imprisoned in substandard, overpriced ghetto housing, and his choice of jobs is limited. He has neither the occupational or residential mobility nor the political power to counter these disabling conditions. Moreover, his feeling of impotence has been compounded by the failure of those social institutions that were designed to improve his prospects. This frustrating lack of control over his life's circumstances is the most difficult aspect to accept, for without some measure of control over his destiny, his aspirations can never be more than pipe dreams.

Thus the basic problem of the black American is to gain control over his destiny, and in recent years a prospective solution has come into focus. Through racial cohesiveness and self-development the black man intends to liberate himself from racism and to gain equality and dignity. Foremost in this drive is the quest to redirect and reform those institutions that have failed black Americans or, worse, have inflicted injury and further disadvantages on racial minorities. In the black neighborhoods of the large cities the schools have become the first of these institutions to be challenged.

Neither urban educators nor informed laymen dispute that the city schools have failed to help the black American substantially to improve his status. The indictment of the schools is particularly serious because formal education has represented the primary social device for equalizing opportunities among children of different races or social groupings. Yet, while about 75 percent of white males in their late twenties have completed high school, only about 60 percent of nonwhite males in this age bracket have received a high school education. Even among those students who do reach the twelfth grade, the average Negro is about three years behind the average twelfth-grade white in standardized achievement units.

The black American, then, enters his adult life with severe educational deficiencies, and the nature of the schooling experience that is provided for him must share some of the blame for this condition. The average black in the large cities attends a school that is less well-endowed than that attended by whites. For example, teachers in Negro schools have less experience and lower verbal ability than their counterparts in white schools. In addition, schools with black enrollments are more likely to be crowded and to experience shortages of supplies and other materials; and historically they have been characterized by lower expenditures.

But inferior resources are only one way in which the schools handicap the preparation of the ghetto child for a productive life. More destructive to his self-concept and growth is the cultural intolerance reflected by his schooling experience. The materials, curriculum, and teaching methods were developed for the white middle-class child and they have been largely irrelevant to the experiences and special educational requirements of the black child. Thus, the present schools in Negro neighborhoods tend to undermine the identity of the black student by ignoring his cultural heritage. That is, in their noble effort to be "color-blind," the schools have ignored color by demanding that the ghetto child reflect the language patterns, experience, and cultural traits of the white middle class. The city schools have, in effect, forced black students to be captive audiences in a hostile environment—one that did not consider their needs. In this sense, the schools do not reflect the pluralism that is claimed for our society.

Since it is the intention of the blacks to take responsibility for those institutions that mold their lives and the lives of their children, it is no accident that the schools represent the initial focal point. As one of the participants in the Brookings conference noted:

> . . . the schools are rather natural and logical vehicles for a first thrust because they represent the white underbelly of society. They are present. They are constant. They are not something that is hidden in a back room in city hall which you can't reach. The principal of the school is at hand. The teachers are there. So the school is a very tangible instrument around which action can focus.

In addition to the visibility of the schools, there is the widespread notion that in the long run education is a potent power in society and that those who control it control something that is extremely important.

Additional impetus for school decentralization comes from support of the black community's position by a large segment of the white middle class which has also been frustrated with the empty promises, administrative rigidities, lack of responsiveness, and red tape that seem to characterize the city school bureaucracies. Yet the most powerful element underlying the push for radical changes in school governance is that the suggestions of the educational professionals for improving the ghetto schools have generally been ineffective in meeting the problems.

The conventional thinking of the late 1950s and early 1960s suggested that through racially integrating the schools the educational problems of blacks and other minorities would be solved. In most cities, the promises of integration were never fulfilled. Inaction on the issue or, worse yet, the gerrymandering of local attendance districts to prevent meaningful integration created great bitterness among the many blacks whose top priority was racially integrated education. The failure of the city school boards to deliver what they had promised led to much of the present distrust of centralized school boards by minority citizens. Where integration did take place, it tended to be token in nature, with black students placed in different "ability" groups or curricula than white students. Indeed, the U.S. Commission on Civil Rights found that "many Negro students who attend majority-white schools in fact are in majority-Negro classrooms."[1]

[1] *Racial Isolation in the Public Schools*, Vol. 1 (1967), p. 162.

Today, the white middle-class outflow from the cities combined with the black in-migration and the political opposition to bussing and other methods of alleviating de facto school segregation have made large-scale integration an improbable event. Of the twenty cities in the largest metropolitan areas in 1966, ten had Negro majorities among their elementary school enrollments and fifteen had enrollments that were over 30 percent nonwhite. Thus, true school integration would require breaking down traditional political boundaries and incorporating metropolitan school districts that would encompass both city and suburbs. But substantial opposition by suburbanites would probably prevent the implementation of this proposal for the foreseeable future. In the meantime, the inability of the big-city schools to adapt to the special needs of minority students will become the failure to adapt to the needs of a majority of the students, most of whom obtain their schooling in segregated environments. Among seventy-five cities surveyed by the Commission on Civil Rights in 1966, three-quarters of the Negro students in elementary schools were already attending schools whose enrollments were 90 or more percent Negro.

Indeed, many blacks reject integration as a solution not only because it is identified with false promises but also because it has ideological overtones that are an affront to black dignity. As Floyd McKissick has suggested, the view that quality education can only take place in an integrated school seems to be based upon the degrading proposition: "Mix Negroes with Negroes and you get stupidity."

The second approach at improving schools in the black ghetto has been that of compensatory education. During the early 1960s, it became the vogue among educators to refer to the educationally deprived or disadvantaged child. In particular, most urban black children were considered to be disadvantaged because they lacked the home and community environment that stimulated educational motivation, achievement, and the derivation of middle-class attributes. Therefore, additional school resources were to be provided to the disadvantaged child in order to compensate for his deficiencies.

Unfortunately, the record to date for compensatory education is unimpressive. Most compensatory efforts have focused on smaller class sizes and more remedial personnel. The types of teachers, curriculum, school organization, and educational methods that have consistently failed the ghetto child have largely been retained, and little educational progress has been demonstrated. Some school spokesmen have passed off the failures of compensatory programs by asserting that most of these attempts have been underfinanced. Perhaps this is true, but one can certainly question how spending more money on such traditional panaceas as the reduction of class size is going to change the qualitative nature of a basic schooling process that did not have urban black children in mind.

It is clear that the schools as presently constituted have shown little evidence of being able to fulfill the educational needs of the disadvantaged child and, particularly, the black disadvantaged child. Both compensatory education and school integration have witnessed more failures than successes (with the possible exception of preschool programs), and all future plans for improving the education of black children revolve around these two approaches. In a sense, representatives of the black communities are telling the educational professionals and the white community: "You've been given your chance, and our schools have not improved." Blacks now want a chance to solve their own educational problems, and the professionals have not been able to counter these demands with any new alternatives. Instead, the response has been: "Just give us a chance to really provide racially integrated, quality education." For the black community this reply has not only come too late, but it smacks of the same remedies that have not changed the picture in the past. The surge for self-determination combined with the failure of the professionals to prove themselves has made the schools particularly vulnerable. This vulnerability has manifested itself in the increasingly voiced sentiment that the education of blacks can no longer be considered the "white man's burden." The black community has rejected this paternalistic approach and wants to take responsibility for the schooling of its own.

Given the demands for decentralization of the big-city schools, several substantial questions are raised. First, what are the objectives and social implications of community governance of the city schools? The chapters by Harold W. Pfautz, Mario D. Fantini, Leonard J. Fein, and Robert C. Maynard are addressed to this issue. Pfautz discusses the long-run impact of community-governed schools on goals of racial equality and harmony. Fantini suggests the curriculum and other ingredients that might be the focus of community attempts to improve urban schools. Fein examines the universalistic underpinnings of the present schooling approach and contrasts it with a more secular or community-oriented strategy for educating minority Americans. Finally, Maynard links the community school movement to the general surge for black self-determination.

A second concern focuses on the redistribution of power. Specifically, how should decision-making power be redistributed among community representatives, teachers, administrators, students, city school boards, and state governments? Marilyn Gittell discusses the roles of the participants in the changing scenario. Robert F. Lyke examines the factors that seem to explain the lack of response of city school boards to the needs of minority students. Rhody A. McCoy chronicles the formation of the Ocean Hill-Brownsville demonstration school district in New York City. Michael H. Moskow and Kenneth McLennan describe the probable impact of school decentralization on teacher negotiations.

A third problem area is that encompassing the arrangements and procedures that might be established to make decentralization a more effective alternative than the present centrally administered system. Anthony Downs suggests both tenets of evaluation and incentive schemes to improve the operations of urban schools or offer meaningful alternatives to minority children, and H. Thomas James and Henry M. Levin present criteria for financing community schools.

The conference papers that are included in this volume were used as a basis for the two-day Brookings Conference on the Community School. A summary of the conference discussion follows the last chapter.

PART ONE

Social Foundations and Objectives

HAROLD W. PFAUTZ

The Black Community, the Community School, and the Socialization Process: Some Caveats

The American people have a sublime faith in the school. They have traditionally viewed organized education as the one unfailing remedy for every ill to which man is subject. And when faced with any trouble or difficulty they have commonly set their minds at rest sooner or later by an appeal to the school. Today, as social institutions crumble and society is shaken by deep convulsions that threaten its very existence, many persons are proclaiming that education provides the only true road to safety. They are even saying that it should be brought into the service of building a new social order.—George S. Counts and others, The Social Foundations of Education *(Scribner's, 1934), p. 533.*

Social problems, like social facts, do not speak for themselves. But the problematic character of public education today, however obvious it may always have been to professional educators, stems largely from its relation to the race problem. And the current visibility of the problematic character of race relations, however obvious it may have been to concerned social critics, stems, in turn, from the rate of growth of the Negro populations in major cities and the information explosion that has made patently clear *the* American dilemma: the dissociation between creed and conduct.

The scale of big-city educational operations has led to the growth of rigid, centralized bureaucracies for school administration and the development of a professional, client-processing role for teachers. Yet, the central difficulty remains the failure of white Americans to face the problem of race. The inevitable result is that the schools do not function (and have never functioned) for the masses of poor blacks as they have functioned (and continue to function) for the majority of middle-class whites.[1]

Indeed, it is ironic that the concept of the community school should become salient just at the time when daily events continually demonstrate that our cities are, at best, only pseudocommunities. For, when hundreds of thousands of black residents of most of the major cities are functionally outside the dominant polity and social system, it is folly to speak of "community." Moreover, while there are special and unique educational connotations attached to the community school concept, local control (with all its vices and virtues) has been the abiding characteristic of American public school administration. The result today is de facto community schools that almost perfectly reflect the prejudices of the dominant community, and a myriad of research has documented their separate and unequal character, despite the law of the land.

Just as James Baldwin once remarked that "color is not a human or a personal reality; it is a political reality,"[2] education in America has always been an economic and, correlatively, a political problem. Thus, there will be no significant institutional changes in the educational systems without accompanying economic and political changes in society and local communities. This, of course, is why much of the dialogue concerning the community school is political rather than educational in both content and style. The community school concept today is less an idea than an ideology; it has become not only part of the rhetoric but even more significantly a part of the tactics of a social movement; and it is perilous to ignore its status and functions in this regard.

[1] A quarter of a century ago, Warner and his colleagues described how schools, administrators, teachers, and students "serve the social system by keeping down many people who try for higher places. . . . The place of the Negro in our society in many respects is like that of the lower-class white. He has many of the same penalties applied to him and is prevented from enjoying many of the same opportunities as the lower-class white. But there are profound differences between Negroes and lower-class whites which have fundamental consequences for the kind of education provided for them. The problem of race relations is becoming crucial." W. Lloyd Warner, Robert J. Havighurst, and Martin B. Loeb, *Who Shall Be Educated? The Challenge of Unequal Opportunities* (Harper, 1944), pp. xi, xii.

[2] James Baldwin, *The Fire Next Time* (Dial Press, 1963), p. 118.

However symbolically significant education may be in America, however functional it may be in performing the service that the U.S. Commissioner of Education has proposed—"to form a third force for racial equality in the United States"[3]—the public education system cannot do the job by itself. This is true not only because it is an institution, understandably imbued with pervasive and powerfully vested interests, but also because, despite its function to train and socially educate the young, it is essentially a secondary service institution. Moreover, only part of the plight of black Americans is due to educational discrimination. The most recent and extensive study of the determinants of occupational achievement in the United States has shown that

> . . . only about one-fourth of the income gap between Negro and white men can be attributed to the three family characteristics in the basic model [father's education, father's occupation, and number of siblings]. . . . Other major components are due to educational discrimination (unequal education attained by men with equivalent family backgrounds), occupational discrimination (unequal occupational achievements for men with equivalent education and family backgrounds), and economic discrimination (unequal earnings for men in the same kinds of occupations, with the same number of years of schooling, and with equivalent family backgrounds).[4]

This means that no amount of change in the educational system will resolve the racism in the social structures of our communities. Racism, discussed in the *Report of the National Advisory Commission on Civil Disorders* (referred to as the Kerner Report), is characteristically mindless and institutional.

The focal points that best provide insight into the fundamental issues—both ideological and functional—and the future of the community school are the concepts of community and socialization. On the one hand, examination of the nature of community will show the limitations of traditional administrative approaches to the

[3] Harold Howe II, "The Heat in Our Kitchen" (speech delivered at the School Administrators' Conference on The Community School and Integrated, Quality Education, Hotel Roosevelt, New York City, June 18, 1966), p. 2. Published in Harold Howe II, *The Human Frontier: Remarks on Equality in Education* (U.S. Department of Health, Education, and Welfare, 1966).

[4] Otis Dudley Duncan and others, *Socioeconomic Background and Occupational Achievement: Extensions of a Basic Model*, ED 023879 (U.S. Office of Education, Bureau of Research, May 1968), p. 3.

problems of big-city systems of public education as well as provide some estimate of the community status and the potential of the black ghetto to organize and maintain community schools. On the other hand, the community school concept has significant implications regarding the functions of training and socializing the young. Here, concern will be less with "instrumental socialization" (the acquisition of motor or intellectual skills and items of information to be used in enacting specified roles) than with "expressive socialization" (the development of beliefs and various forms of sensibility).[5] At stake is the process of education as Durkheim viewed it: "a methodical socialization of the younger generation . . . the action exercised by adult generations on those who are not yet ripe for social life . . . [the aim of which is] to create and develop in the child a certain number of physical, intellectual, and moral states which both political society as a whole and the special milieu for which he is particularly destined demand of him."[6] This discussion, then, will examine the implications for self-development, values, and racial attitudes under local community control and parental participation, and the implications of the community school concept for a democratic polity and social system.

The Sociological Concept of the Community

Sociologists have traditionally viewed the community as one of the basic forms of the human group. Its unique status stems from its anchored position in space, typically connoting an autonomous, inclusive, self-sustaining social system—a society. While there is considerable variation in the precise definition of the concept among sociologists, studies of the community have generally emphasized one of two basic approaches. In the first, the community has been viewed as essentially an ecological order, a matter of functional relationships among human groups and institutions that evolve from sharing a common living space. The second approach considers the community as a social order: "the smallest territorial system which encompasses the major features of society, that is, a society

[5] See Charles E. Bidwell, "Students and Schools: Some Observations on the Client Role in a Socializing Organization" (paper delivered at "Organizations and Clients," A Symposium at the University of Rhode Island, June 27, 1968).

[6] Emile Durkheim, *Education et Sociologie* (Paris: Alcan, 1906), p. 49.

in miniature."[7] Whereas the former emphasizes primarily unself-conscious developments, the product of the collective solution to the problem of sustenance by a population residing in a limited territory, the latter stresses the self-conscious and willed social action and organization of persons, individuals with status in a social system. The essential connotations of community are thus clear: social organization and collective action of a relatively permanent resident population. In addition, the members of a human community not only reside and act together, they feel and think together. There is also, therefore, a social-psychological dimension, expressed in terms of a common identity or "we-feeling"—a consensus.

The basic difficulty in the concept of community, both functionally and in research, has been in the articulation of these two approaches. This is reflected in the distinction that is made between the natural, ecological community, whose boundaries are determined by the functional interdependencies of the daily collective life, and the administrative, political community, whose boundaries are fixed by self-conscious legal and historical considerations. In other words, while every society is something of a community, every community is not necessarily a functioning society; the world situation and that of the metropolitan situation exemplify the problems involved.

Organism, artifact, or both, beyond the generic concept of community there are many varieties: the small, traditionally rural or suburban, and relatively autonomous, local community; the large, dense, heterogeneous urban aggregation that is "the city"; the extensive, functionally integrated congeries of central cities and satellite suburbs called "the metropolitan community."[8] It is especially important to consider the use of the community concept in reference to local enclaves within the city based on ethnic, racial, and cultural homogeneities.

[7] Albert J. Reiss, Jr., "The Sociological Study of Communities," *Rural Sociology*, Vol. 24 (June 1959), p. 125. For an attempt to accommodate these perspectives, see Norton E. Long, "The Local Community as an Ecology of Games," *American Journal of Sociology*, Vol. 64 (November 1958), pp. 251–61.

[8] The newest development is the megalopolis or so-called strip-city. For a discussion of this, see Robert W. Weller, "An Empirical Examination of Megalopolitan Structure," *Demography*, Vol. 4 (1967), pp. 734–43.

The analytic distinction between the natural, ecological community and the administrative, political community is best illustrated by the tendency for changes in the latter to lag dangerously behind changes in the former. Administrative arrangements that grew out of and were attuned to the small, autonomous local community continue to be the models for the new metropolitan mode. The pressure to substitute administration for politics aggravates the dysfunctional implications of this lag. This is particularly apparent in the field of education where the concept of the school district has become the symbolic, but not the functional, equivalent of the community.

The School District Concept and the Community

Professional educators have increasingly viewed the school district, once identical with the local community, as primarily an administrative device. Alford, for example, defined a school district simply as "The term . . . to designate a political or geographical division of territory within a state, created for the purpose of maintaining and administering a system of public education."[9] Most of the studies of the districting process have focused on the economic and administrative rather than the educational properties and functions of the school district. Thus, Briscoe's analysis was oriented to determining "the relation between the size of the unit of administration for public schools and the economical administration and supervision of the schools."[10]

The implications of this perspective are clearly reflected in the role that districting plays in the organization and functioning of big-city school systems and by the completely noncommunal character of the districts that are typically defined. For example, until recently the New York City system was divided into 30 districts, each with an average of 36,000 pupils and 30 schools, headed by a field assistant superintendent appointed by the central administration. One of the resultant districts

[9] Harold D. Alford, *Procedures for School District Reorganization*, Contributions to Education 852 (Columbia University, Teachers College, 1942), p. 3.

[10] Alonzo Otis Briscoe, *The Size of the Local Unit for Administration and Supervision of Public Schools*, Contributions to Education 649 (Columbia University, Teachers College, 1935), p. 1.

. . . ran up Manhattan's East Side from 10th Street to 106th Street. . . . It included the northern four blocks of the old immigrant Lower East Side; the enormous middle-class and upper-middle class white housing projects Stuyvesant Town and Peter Cooper Village north of 14th Street; the elegance of Gramercy Park; the fanciest part of the city's business district; the U.N. area; the most expensive housing in America, on Park Avenue and Fifth Avenue in the 60's, 70's, and 80's; the second-generation and first-generation German-Polish-Czech-Hungarian immigrant communities in Yorkville (east of the rich housing in the 60's through the low 90's)—and, north of 96th Street, which is a kind of invisible Chinese Wall, the teeming slum of East Harlem.[11]

The thrust of the Bundy Report is directed precisely at this central administrative tradition.[12] The most immediate device to secure for the city's schools "the advantages of community proximity and participation common to smaller cities and suburbs" is the proposal to create between 30 and 60 new districts, containing from 12,000 to 40,000 pupils.[13] To be sure, the report discusses the need to develop boundaries that are "both educationally and socially sound"; it even mentions "sense of community" as one of the determinants of the number and shape of the proposed districts. But the proposed size does not include consideration of the natural communities of the city. Most of the other criteria mentioned for defining district boundaries—efficient utilization of school buildings, school feeder patterns, number of pupils who would have to transfer from the schools they presently attend—are oriented more to administrative than educational considerations.[14] Moreover, a suburb with a pupil population of 12,000 cannot be com-

[11] Martin Mayer, "What's Wrong with Our Big-City Schools," *Saturday Evening Post*, Vol. 240 (Sept. 9, 1967), p. 23.

[12] Mayor's Advisory Panel on Decentralization of the New York City Schools, *Reconnection for Learning: A Community School System for New York City* (1967). Referred to as either the Bundy Report or the Mayor's Advisory Panel.

[13] *Ibid.*, pp. 16 and 17. See also A. Harry Passow, *Toward Better Schools: A Summary of the Findings and Recommendations of a Study of the Schools of Washington, D.C.* (D.C. Citizens for Better Public Education, undated). Referred to as the Passow Report. The complete report was originally published by Columbia University, Teachers College, 1967.

[14] In contrast, the seventy-five local communities that have been delineated for the city of Chicago range in school-age population from approximately 900 to 35,000 pupils. The chief considerations for the limits of the area boundaries were the history of the area; local identification with the area; the extent of the business area; membership of local institutions; and the natural and artificial physical barriers. See Philip M. Hauser and Evelyn M. Kitagawa (eds.), *Local Community Fact Book for Chicago, 1950* (Chicago Community Inventory, 1953), p. xi.

pared to an urban local community of the same size, while the public school system of Providence, Rhode Island, with its 27,000 students faces the same problems as New York City, with its more than one million pupils.[15]

In the final analysis, strictly administrative solutions cannot solve the basic problems of race and quality education. Certainly, the suggestion to hand over the task of redistricting to the cooperative efforts of New York's City Planning Commission and Board of Education indicates the failure to understand the real issues. Despite the Mayor's Advisory Panel's disclaimer, its recommendations are more concerned with power than education. To be sure, "the necessary study of district boundaries will be complex and time-consuming," but the more basic issue is the extent to which the black community will be a community.[16] If the panel naïvely places its faith in traditional administrative devices to bring about changes without disturbing the status quo, black advocates of the community school are inclined to speak romantically of the Harlem community and of "our neighborhood" with little appreciation of their situation and its implications for quality education.[17]

The Local Black Community

Although his analysis is almost a quarter of a century old, Gunnar Myrdal still provides a revealing perspective on the black community and its culture. He observed that as a result of caste pressures, of the history of discrimination and prejudice, and of the consequent isolation from and the traditional accommodation to the dominant whites, the Negro community developed into a pathological form of the white community: "In practically all of its divergencies, American Negro culture is not something independent of general American culture. It is a distorted development, or a pathological condi-

[15] See Harold W. Pfautz, "Providence, R.I.: The Politics of Desegregation," *Urban Review*, forthcoming.

[16] Mayor's Advisory Panel, *Reconnection for Learning*, p. 17.

[17] As Greer observes: "The general belief is that urban neighborhoods are declining to the point of triviality as social systems. Certainly the major functions of economic production and political control seem to be not just metropolis-wide but nation-wide in their jurisdiction and relevances." Scott Greer, "Neighborhood," *International Encyclopedia of the Social Sciences* (Macmillan and Free Press, 1968), Vol. 11, p. 124.

tion of American culture."[18] Indeed, as a sociologist I have always maintained that to understand many significant aspects of American social reality, it is productive to study not white but black Americans, for here crucial dimensions of American society and culture become apparent. This is especially true today insofar as the traditional structure of race relations has broken down and the black community is involved in a process of becoming.

The race problem has shown that many American cities are essentially pseudocommunities. Common residence no longer acts as a significant social integrator; the technologies of transportation and communication have increasingly separated place of work and place of residence and have led to high rates of physical mobility. But, more importantly, these technological changes, along with demographic trends, particularly among Negroes and young people, have led to pools of collective experience that have taken on the proportions of subcultures, and often these are in opposition to the larger culture.[19] Yet social and political forms to deal with these new circumstances, the creation of a new set of social relationships that these underlying shifts portend and demand, have not been developed.[20]

But if the white or dominant community is only a pseudocommunity, examination reveals that the local black ghetto is even less of a community. Like the dominant community, the black community is engaged in a collective struggle to develop functioning social forms. The cries of anguish may on occasion be more shrill, the techniques of organization less sophisticated, and often the conflicts more open and brutal, but the process is the same: the struggle of men acting together to attain self-realization and achieve a viable and democratic common life.

To be sure, the isolation of blacks from the mainstream of Ameri-

[18] Gunnar Myrdal, *An American Dilemma* (Harper, 1944), p. 928.

[19] Joseph D. Lohman, "On Law Enforcement and the Police: A Commentary" (paper delivered at the 17th International Course in Criminology, Montreal, Canada, Aug. 19–Sept. 3, 1967; processed), p. 18.

[20] Where the nature of the problem has been recognized (such as the need for school district consolidation because of the development of the metropolitan community), there still are no new political strategies to overcome the powerful resistances typically encountered. See, for example, Basil G. Zimmer and Amos H. Hawley, *Metropolitan Area Schools: Resistance to District Reorganization* (Sage Publications, 1968).

can community life has resulted in the development of a variety of indigenous community institutions as well as a subculture of various dimensions. Examples of the former are the church in the Negro community, with its multifunctional role, and the Negro newspaper. On the informal level, numerous coping devices have emerged—matriarchy, the rent party, "playing-the-dozens." On a more formal level, there are the myriad of social clubs and commercial establishments providing segregated personal services, ranging from barbering to undertaking. Yet, a number of significant facts make clear the essentially underdeveloped status of the local black community as a functioning social group.

One of the most basic and pervasive defects of the big-city black community is the high rate of physical mobility. The recently completed study of family mobility in New York City, conducted by Hay and Wantman, found that 72 percent of Puerto Rican families and 60 percent of Negro families (in contrast to only 41 percent of white families) had moved at least once during the five-year period from 1960 to 1965.[21] Moreover, the rates were highest for larger, low-income families with young children, precisely the target population of the ghetto community school.

The implications of these demographic facts for the functioning of the schools, whether the administration is centralized or decentralized, are obvious: correlative high rates of student mobility between schools. Thus, Mayer observed in the New York City school district in which he served as chairman of the local advisory board that "In most of the schools with a majority of Negro and Puerto Rican students, more than half the children in the classrooms in September would move elsewhere before June, either to another address within the district or out of it entirely."[22] In the Brownsville area of the city, according to another observer, "In one public school, from September to January of last year, there was a 100 per cent turnover of school population, 1,500 on register and 1,500 on transfers."[23] Finally, an evaluation study of the Open Enroll-

[21] Donald G. Hay and M. J. Wantman, *Mobility of Families, New York City, 1960 to 1965* (City University of New York, 1968).

[22] Mayer, "What's Wrong with Our Big-City Schools," p. 23. Mayer also stated that "In several schools in the slum area, moreover, a third or more of the *teachers* left every year."

[23] Joseph B. Judge, "Brownsville: A Neighborhood in Trouble," *Dissent*, Vol. 13 (September–October 1966), p. 505.

Another fundamental problem for the local black community is the lack of economic resources. Negro business, despite recent efforts of both blacks and whites, is still essentially a myth in terms of its scale and functions. The inability to mobilize adequate economic resources continues to stand in the way of many community developments.

As a polity, the local black community has established some specifically political organizations. Moreover, there is no doubt that the emerging political groups have increasing political strength. But their power, especially in relation to the dominant community, has been essentially a veto rather than an initiating power. They set the conditions under which the "white army of occupation" (especially government agents administering money from state and federal programs) can operate. On the whole, Wilson's analysis of the political situation in the ghetto community in 1960 remains valid: There is little effective Negro leadership; there is little organization as a community to seek communal ends; the great majority of organizations are essentially social with purposes other than Negro protest or improvement; and, although there is political activity, there are few results.[26]

In fact, in many of its most important functional aspects the ghetto remains a community that is governed largely from the outside—by the white policeman, the white social worker, and the white educator.

Viewing the black community as a social structure, it is not just as Frazier has suggested—that the "black bourgeoisie" is a fraud because it has "status without substance."[27] Rather, even its status is sociologically suspect. The very concept of a Negro class structure is unreal, for the status of middle-class blacks is validated by neither the Negro nor the white communities. In the former, the element of mutual respect, however grudging, that is the basis of any viable community status system is lacking. Lower-class Negroes are not only jealous of their middle-class fellows but suspicious of their motives; lower-class blacks know, or at least sense, that despite his "success," the middle-class Negro does not really have it made. In

[26] James Q. Wilson, *Negro Politics: The Search for Leadership* (Free Press, 1960), pp. 3–17.
[27] Franklin E. Frazier, *The Black Bourgeoisie* (Free Press, 1957), p. 195.

ment program instituted in New York City during 196
gests the pervasiveness of pupil transiency in ghetto el
schools. According to the data in Table 1, 58.2 percent of
(sending) schools had pupil mobility rates of 50 percent
while this was true of only 7.7 percent of the predominan
(receiving) schools. Conversely, 74.6 percent of the predo
white, nonghetto schools but only 26.4 percent of the ghet
had pupil mobility rates of less than 40 percent.

TABLE I

Pupil Mobility in Open Enrollment Public Elementary Sch
New York City, 1961

Percent of pupils moving during the school year[a]	Sending schools (ghetto)		Receiving sch (nonghetto
	Number	Percent	Number
75 and over	7	6.4	0
50–74	57	51.8	11
40–49	17	15.4	25
Under 40	29	26.4	106

Source: Eleanor Bernert Sheldon, James R. Hudson, and Raymond A. Glazier, "Open Enr
York City," in Albert J. Reiss, Jr. (ed.), *Schools in a Changing Society* (Free Press, 1965), p. 1
a. Excluding first-graders and graduating classes entering or leaving school, during school yea

This situation not only creates serious difficulties in the
tration and educational functioning of schools in the lo
community but it also cripples efforts to carry out and eva
form programs. Mayer, for example, cited a principal who
he could not introduce a new reading program because "
dren move in and out too fast—of the 1,100 in the schoo
tember, fewer than 500 will still be there in June. New arr
have taken the place of the other 600."[24] And Lauter rec
ported that the turnover of children in the Adams-Morg
munity school project in Washington, D.C., exceeded 40
during the year.[25]

[24] Martin Mayer, "Frustration Is the Word for Ocean Hill," *New York T*
zine, May 19, 1968, p. 66.

[25] Paul Lauter, "The Short, Happy Life of the Adams-Morgan Commu
Project," *Harvard Educational Review*, Vol. 38 (Spring 1968), p. 248.

the dominant community the inner social barriers of the color line remain essentially unbreached. For most white Americans, the successful, educated, middle-class black is still a Negro and outside the status system of "their community." And, the ubiquity of the concept *so-called* (for example, so-called leaders) in the lexicon of Negro social and political discourse is mute testimony to the cogency of this thesis.

The most recent data containing black views on racial issues—in regard to separatism in general and public education in particular—are most revealing. According to the Kerner Report, of the twelve deeply held specific grievances of ghetto residents, inadequate education only ranked fourth on "the second level of intensity."[28] And in a more recent survey conducted in fifteen major American cities the data showed that while Negroes were, understandably, less satisfied than whites with the neighborhood services (quality of public schools, parks and playgrounds for children, sports and recreation centers for teenagers, police protection, and garbage collection) that the city was supposed to provide, "The service which evoked the least difference in the evaluations of Negro and white respondents was the public schools . . . [and] the quality of the public schools is one of the least frequently complained-about services."[29]

Even more significant are the findings that only small proportions of Negro Americans living in fifteen major cities preferred to live in all-Negro neighborhoods (8 percent); preferred their children to go to predominately Negro schools (6 percent); and believed that a school with primarily Negro children should have a Negro principal (14 percent) and mostly Negro teachers (10 percent). Furthermore, the explanations given by the majority that favored mixed schools were based on either a nonracist perspective—race did not matter (36 percent)—or the positive educational benefits of integrated education situations—better facilities (24 percent) and learning to

[28] *Report of the National Advisory Commission on Civil Disorders* (Government Printing Office, 1968), p. 4. *Summary* (reproduced by the Legislative Reference Service, Library of Congress, 1968), p. 18.

[29] Angus Campbell and Howard Schuman, "Racial Attitudes in Fifteen American Cities," *Supplemental Studies for the National Advisory Commission on Civil Disorders* (Government Printing Office, 1968), p. 39.

get along with others (30 percent).[30] The authors concluded

> . . . that in early 1968 the major commitment of the great majority of the Negro population in these 15 cities was not to racial exclusiveness insofar as this meant personal rejection of whites or an emphasis on racial considerations in running community institutions. Negroes hold strongly, *perhaps more strongly than any other element in the American population*, to a belief in nondiscrimination and racial harmony.[31]

The Community School and the Black Power Movement

All of this does not mean that there have been no changes in the ghetto or that no move has been made toward community development. Since World War II, the most dramatic change has been in the basis, function, and style of Negro leadership and, correspondingly, in the increasing capacity of black Americans to protest collectively outside the status quo. Here, Wilson's 1960 analysis, which traced the transition from accepted leaders based on personal prestige and achievement, through omnicompetent volunteers with a mass following who were oriented to reformistic welfare goals (such as safe, adequate housing), to the professional, middle-class, and civic agency leaders, with no mass following who were militantly oriented to revolutionary status goals (such as integrated housing), is patently dated. On the local level as well as on the national level, the ideological shifts in the Negro protest movement from "we shall overcome" in the 1950s, through "freedom now" of the early 1960s, to "black power" in the late 1960s has been paralleled and catalyzed by the rise of militant activists.

There is clear-cut evidence of a growing solidarity in both behavior and attitudes among black Americans in urban ghettos. Thus, in the supplemental study to the Kerner Report, a majority (53 percent) of Negroes interviewed regarded some form of protest (in contrast to the use of laws and persuasion) as the best way for Negroes to gain their rights: 38 percent opted for nonviolent pro-

[30] *Ibid.*, Table II-a, p. 15; Table II-b, p. 16; Table II-c, p. 16. The highest percentage reported—18 percent—was for the belief that stores in a Negro neighborhood should be owned and run by Negroes; only 6 percent agreed that "there should be a separate black nation here" (p. 16).

[31] *Ibid.*, p. 17. (Italics added.)

test and 15 percent opted for violence.[32] It is essential, however, to understand the bases and nature of this solidarity in order to estimate its functional significance for the development and maintenance of community schools.

Historically, the growing solidarity stems from a shift from the tradition of accommodation and dissimulation to confrontation and conflict on the part of black Americans with respect to white Americans. This shift has been produced by the vast scale and pace of demographic, economic, and educational changes that have taken place in the Negro population since World War II together with the rise of a new leadership that is no longer beholden to the dominant white community for its status. These leaders go beyond the conventional channels to achieve immediate ends that have legal sanction as a result of civil rights legislation.[33] Consequently, the solidarity that has developed to date is a function of conflict, making it primarily negative in content and occasional in appearance.

While Wirth is probably correct in his observation that "Apparently there is no limit to the extent to which pressure from the outside is able to solidify a group," it is important to recognize that black power is a movement and not an organization.[34] To be sure, social movements are typically incipient organizations, and for that reason they are attempts by large numbers of people to act together in the absence of a consensus and a fully developed social structure. Leadership in a social movement differs from that involved in nations, communities, or business corporations because it has no clear lines of communication or legitimate lines of authority. Social movement leadership is characteristically tenuous, shifting, and, most important, it involves a minimum of control.

Furthermore, movement ideologies—the primary bases for the integration of a tenuous and shifting membership—especially in their early stages, are distinguished more by their sound than by their content. Expository statements by movement leaders are aimed at tapping a common sentiment rather than producing a

[32] *Ibid.*, Table V-j, p. 52.

[33] See Harold W. Pfautz, "The New 'New Negro': Emerging American," *Phylon* (Fourth Quarter 1963), p. 366. Between 1940 and 1960, in less than a generation, American Negroes were transformed from an essentially regional, rural, and agricultural population to a national, urban, and industrial one.

[34] Louis Wirth, *The Ghetto* (University of Chicago Press, 1928), p. 273.

rational discussion of alternative tactics and strategies. Precisely in its developmental stage, the function of a movement's ideology is more psychological than political. In the case of black power, it is not, as Lasch would have it, that the "loud exclamations of militancy . . . conceal an essential flabbiness of purpose" but rather they suggest the basic nature and function of the ideology: it is a call more than a program; it is more expressive than instrumental; and it stems more from a basic rage than from either political or philosophical motives.[35]

The salience of the community school concept stems from its relationship to the American dilemma and, in the context of the conflict over the larger issue, it has become part of the ideology and tactics of a movement of protest. This relationship is underscored, on the one hand, by the increasing tendency to base black separatism on the political rather than the economic or educational "benefits" of residential segregation and, on the other hand, by the central role of power in the concept of the community school. Thus, the issue of who controls the schools has been more important than the quality of education. This is illustrated by the histories of extant experiments such as the Adams-Morgan community school in Washington, D.C., and Intermediate School (I.S.) 201, Two Bridges, and Ocean Hill-Brownsville in New York City.[36]

While the politics and administration of community schools have little to do with guaranteeing quality curricula and quality teaching, the lack of community in the black urban ghettos and the transient nature of the solidarity that arises from the Negro protest movement indicate that viable and educationally productive community schools will be difficult to achieve. The black power movement has romanticized the ghetto's qualities, but objective observers are in agreement as to its defects. An analysis of the I.S. 201 experiment noted that the extreme divisiveness of East Harlem has made it ex-

[35] Christopher Lasch, "The Trouble With Black Power," *New York Review of Books*, Vol. 10 (Feb. 29, 1968), p. 10.

[36] See for example, Lauter, "The Short, Happy Life of the Adams-Morgan Community School Project"; Jason Epstein, "The Politics of School Decentralization," *New York Review of Books*, Vol. 10 (June 6, 1968), pp. 26–32; Arthur Tobier, "Decentralization," *Center Forum*, Vol. 2 (Jan. 26, 1968), pp. 1–7; and Mayer, "Frustration Is the Word for Ocean Hill."

tremely difficult for the community to go after whatever it feels it wants.[37] Featherstone expressed this problem in his critique of the Bundy Report:

> There is the problem that at the outset there is no real community. In a small school this means that a circle of insiders starts the school and then gradually and with much distress has to link the school into the lives of other people, who are often apathetic or suspicious. On a larger scale . . . there is the same problem magnified. Elections are opened to a district that is not organized, that is not a community in any of the many senses of the word. Any given area, including any given black area of a city like New York, is seething with suspicion and mistrust. Groups that are already organized . . . are ready to act, and their expertise often creates tremendous suspicion among groups that are slower to organize.[38]

And Brownsville is described as "a microcosm of all the city's social ills. It is a community of unrelieved poverty, dirt, decay, drunkenness, and despair. . . ." The desire to escape "continues to be the obsession of the average Brownsville resident."[39]

Thus, at this time it is doubtful that real possibilities exist for the development of a public rather than a private political ethos among the residents of the urban ghettos. There is no natural inclination to view and plan for the community as a whole; the residents lack a sense of personal effectiveness and have not acquired an appropriate time perspective; they do not have a general familiarity with or confidence in citywide institutions.[40]

Individuals with a private political ethos are least likely to develop organizations for carrying out long-range civic tasks, but when they do organize for collective action, it is primarily in response to threats. Wilson concluded:

> Because of the private-regarding nature of their attachment to the community, they are likely to collaborate when each person can see a danger to him or to his family in some proposed change; collective action is a way, not of defining and implementing some broad program for the

[37] Tobier, "Decentralization," p. 6.

[38] Joseph Featherstone, "Community Control of Our Schools," *New Republic*, Vol. 158 (Jan. 13, 1968), p. 19.

[39] Judge, "Brownsville," p. 505.

[40] James Q. Wilson, "Planning and Politics: Citizen Participation in Urban Renewal," in Roland L. Warren (ed.), *Perspectives on the American Community* (Rand McNally, 1966), p. 480.

benefit of all, but of giving force to individual objections by adding them together in a collective protest.[41]

According to this analysis, then, the community cannot successfully develop and maintain educationally effective community schools if the position of the Negro protest movement in general and black power as a specific expression of the movement—where the community school is a political rather than an educational instrument—is adopted.

The Community School and the Socialization Process

Whereas the community status of the black ghetto reflects upon the ability of urban Negroes to organize and maintain their own system of public education, the community school and the socialization process raise questions concerning the educational output of such a system. The theoretical link between the community school concept and the educational process is that if the ghetto schools were made more accountable to their clients, they would do a better educational job.[42] This view is based on two assumptions: first, that accountability should be achieved through direct parental participation in the control and daily functioning of the schools; and second, that the schools should be predominantly, if not totally, black. Any estimate of the educational output of such community schools, whether instrumentally defined (in terms of the teaching of cognitive skills) or expressively defined (in terms of the teaching of norms, values, and personal competence) must take these assumptions into account.

[41] *Ibid.*, p. 482. As Kornhauser has observed in his study of the opponents of fluoridation, who were found to be generally the unattached and alienated segments of the community: "Usually the lack of attachment to community groups leads to apathy, but under critical conditions it may lead to extremist responses . . . people who do not participate in any way in the community are much less likely to understand what is going on, and this lack has particularly serious consequences. For when a crisis does appear and these people become involved in community controversy, their actions and opinions are not tempered by an understanding of the true nature of the situation. Thus you get highly irrational and extremist interpretations of events. . . ." William Kornhauser, "Power and Participation in the Local Community," in Warren (ed.), *Perspectives on the American Community*, p. 494.

[42] See, for example, the discussion by Mario D. Fantini, "Implementing Equal Educational Opportunity," *Harvard Educational Review*, Vol. 38 (Winter 1968), pp. 160–75. See also Mayor's Advisory Panel, *Reconnection for Learning*, and Epstein, "The Politics of School Decentralization," pp. 26–32.

Apart from the questions of the politics of funding[43] or the availability of tested methodologies for teaching large numbers of unmotivated and poorly prepared children,[44] parental control and particularly direct parental participation in the schooling process offer little guarantee that big-city segregated schools will become more educationally efficient. The theoretical and empirical evidence available, as well as historical experience, point in the opposite direction.

In the broadest sense, the socialization process refers to the abiding social transactions that take place between an individual and others and that are responsible for the achievement and maintenance of selfhood and society. Its most general product is what Sullivan has referred to as "interpersonal competence,"[45] while its aim is to prepare its youth to fulfill the social responsibilities given to them by society.[46] Education, then, is simply a part of the more general socialization process, especially when information and cognitive skills are basic to developing interpersonal competence.[47]

The contexts of socialization extend from family interaction between parents and children and among siblings, through the transactions between pupils and their teachers, among peers, and between children and civic authority figures inside and outside of school, to the interpersonal experiences on a job and in the community. Indeed, the complex causal linkages that operate in Duncan's

[43] See David K. Cohen, "Policy for the Public Schools: Compensation and Integration," *Harvard Educational Review*, Vol. 38 (Winter 1968), pp. 114–37.

[44] In fact, there is a consensus in the current literature that there is little known about either learning or children. See, for example, Joseph Featherstone, "A New Kind of Schooling," *New Republic*, Vol. 158 (March 2, 1968), p. 30. Jerome S. Bruner, in "Culture, Politics, and Pedagogy," *Saturday Review*, Vol. 51 (May 18, 1968), p. 69, observed that there is no well-defined or widely accepted theory of education. And Henry S. Dyer, in "School Factors and Equal Educational Opportunity," *Harvard Educational Review*, Vol. 38 (Winter 1968), p. 54, made the point that researchers have, for the most part, failed to observe in any systematic way how teachers actually organize instruction and how pupils learn under various conditions.

[45] Harry Stack Sullivan, *The Interpersonal Theory of Psychiatry* (Norton, 1953).

[46] See Alex Inkeles, "Social Structure and the Socialization of Competence," *Harvard Educational Review*, Vol. 36 (Summer 1966), p. 279.

[47] Cognitive development in general and sociolinguistics in particular are receiving increasing attention from both theoreticians and researchers in connection with the social determinants of educability. See, for example, L. S. Vygotsky, *Thought and Language* (Wiley, 1962), pp. 144–68, and Basil Bernstein, "A Socio-linguistic Approach to Social Learning," in Julius Gould (ed.), *Penguin Survey of the Social Sciences, 1965* (Penguin, 1965), pp. 144–68.

"socioeconomic life cycle," are just beginning to be appreciated. Here, schooling is but one of a number of interrelated variables that operate between individual family background and ultimate self-satisfaction and morale.[48] Brim, who has crystallized the view of socialization as a continuous process rather than one confined to the early years of life, has attempted to clarify the changes in the content of socialization at different stages of the life cycle:

> . . . the emphasis in socialization moves from motivation to ability and knowledge, and from a concern with values to a concern with behavior. . . . Early-life socialization thus emphasizes the control of primary drives, while socialization in later stages deals with secondary or learned motives generated by the expectations of significant others.[49]

Finally, Inkeles, in a compact social-psychological statement, has indicated the specific criteria needed to participate effectively in modern industrial and urban society:

> . . . certain levels of skill in the manipulation of language and other symbol systems, such as arithmetic and time; the ability to comprehend and complete forms; information as to when and where to go for what; skills in interpersonal relations which permit negotiation, insure protection of one's interests, and provide maintenance of stable and satisfying relations with intimates, peers, and authorities; motives to achieve, to master, to persevere; defenses to control and channel acceptably the impulses to aggression, to sexual expression, to extreme dependency; a cognitive style which permits thinking in concrete terms while still permitting reasonable handling of abstractions and general concepts; a mind which does not insist on excessively premature closure, is tolerant of diversity, and has some components of flexibility; a conative style which facilitates reasonably regular, steady, and persistent effort, relieved by rest and relaxation but not requiring long periods of total withdrawal or depressive psychic slump; and a style of expressing affect which encourages stable and enduring relationships without excessive narcissistic dependence or explosive aggression in the face of petty frustration.[50]

With varying degrees of self-consciousness, public schools have been concerned with character building and the molding of good

[48] See Duncan and others, *Socioeconomic Background and Occupational Achievement*, and Otis Dudley Duncan, "Discrimination against Negroes," *Annals of the American Academy of Political and Social Science*, Vol. 371 (May 1967), p. 87.

[49] Orville G. Brim, Jr., and Stanton Wheeler, *Socialization After Childhood* (Wiley, 1966), p. 26.

[50] Inkeles, "Social Structure and the Socialization of Competence," pp. 280–81.

citizens. The formal curriculum, with its emphasis on civics, and other aspects of the school situation directed to the formation of patriotic attitudes (such as the presence and saluting of the flag), exemplify this broad goal of schooling. Moreover, there is a de facto community school status of our public educational system that is revealed by the extracurricular life: it is a sort of mirror image of "the world," with its emphasis on competition for status, the possession of material goods, and so forth.[51] However, the purpose here is not to analyze all the dimensions of the socialization process but rather to focus on those aspects that are at stake in the schooling process: the socialization implications of the classroom[52] and, more specifically, of the segregated community school classroom.

Assuming that the school functions as the link between the private realm of the family and the larger public domain, Dreeben has attempted to clarify "what is learned in school" on the basis of certain fundamental differences in the character of the family and the classroom as socialization settings, with emphasis on the normative rather than the symbolic outcomes of schooling.[53] His cogent thesis is that the unique structural characteristics of the classroom provide pupils with experiences that teach norms crucial to participation in the public sphere—on a job and in political life. Learning, according to Dreeben, means acquiring knowledge as to what the norms are, accepting these norms as legitimate, and behaving in accordance with such norms.

The classroom makes demands on children that are different from those encountered in the family because of basic structural differences: (1) the boundaries and physical size of the social domains; (2) the duration of social relationships; (3) the relative numbers of children compared to adults; (4) the composition of adult and nonadult populations with respect to age-spread, class, religion, ethnicity, race, sex, and so forth; and (5) the visibility of the child among his peers. More specifically, successful coping in the classroom leads to the learning of the norms of independence, achievement, uni-

[51] See James S. Coleman, *The Adolescent Society; the Social Life of the Teenager and Its Impact on Education* (Free Press, 1961).

[52] See, for example, Talcott Parsons, "The School Class as a Social System: Some of Its Functions in American Society," *Harvard Educational Review*, Vol. 29 (Fall 1959), pp. 297–318.

[53] Robert Dreeben, *On What Is Learned in School* (Addison-Wesley, 1968).

versalism, and specificity. Dreeben sums it up in the following manner:

> . . . they [the children] accept the obligations to (1) act by themselves (unless collaborative effort is called for), and accept personal responsibility for their conduct and accountability for its consequences; (2) perform tasks actively and master the environment according to certain standards of excellence; and (3) acknowledge the rights of others to treat them as members of categories on the basis of a few discrete characteristics rather than on the full constellation of them that represent the whole person.[54]

Dreeben explicitly notes that there is no guarantee that pupils will learn these norms, and that while these norms support the existing social system, there is no reason why other norms, supporting other social systems and growing out of different classroom situations, might not be developed. Nevertheless, he also observes:

> . . . the same norms seem to contribute also to a sense of tolerance, fairness, considerations, and trustfulness, and to the expectation among members of the populace that they possess a legitimate claim to participate in all areas of public life and that none shall be entitled to special treatment of whatever kind—expectations whose prevalence today underlie some of the more radical social changes that have taken place in American history.[55]

If there is any merit in this analysis, then the second-order effects of direct parental participation in the classroom deserve careful consideration. Parental participation might threaten the ability of schools to teach and pupils to learn basic societal norms. Indeed, some hint of the difficulties involved is indirectly provided by a remark of one young Negro pupil attending an integrated community school that recruited college students to serve as interns: "I ain't got a teacher, I got a white boy."[56] In the Adams-Morgan community school project, Lauter reported two problems connected with the work of the community interns (area residents who participated in the classroom). One problem was the interns' attitudes toward the children, which reflected "the rather authoritarian perspective of the community," while the other was the suspicions of people in the community concerning "the idea of that woman teach-

[54] *Ibid.*, pp. 63–64.

[55] *Ibid.*, p. 148.

[56] Lauter, "The Short, Happy Life of the Adams-Morgan Community School Project," p. 249.

ing my children."[57] Perhaps the suspicions of the parents were well founded: direct parental intervention in the classroom is dysfunctional for the socialization process.

Even more damaging to the socialization process, however, are the implications of racially segregated community schools. There is no reason to believe that black teachers will prove more adept than white teachers in overcoming the motivationally debilitating effects of inadequate family background and low socioeconomic status. Rather, if the aim of the socialization process is the production of competent people, there is at least some evidence for the positive impact of integrated schooling; there is none for segregated education, even if accompanied by compensatory measures.[58] Moreover, there is evidence that schooling in segregated contexts has negative outcomes for both academic achievement and the broader aims of socialization. For example, Coleman and his associates found

> . . . that a pupil's achievement is strongly related to the educational backgrounds and aspirations of the other students in the school . . . that the principal way in which the school environments of Negroes and whites differ is in the composition of their student bodies, and it turns out that the composition of the student bodies has a strong relationship to the achievement of Negro and other minority pupils. . . . [That] a pupil attitude factor, which appears to have a stronger relationship to achievement than do all the "school" factors together, is the extent to which an individual feels that he has some control over his own destiny. . . . Furthermore, while this characteristic shows little relationship to most school factors, it is related, for Negroes, to the proportion of whites in the schools. Those Negroes in schools with a higher proportion of whites have a greater sense of control.[59]

More relevant to the socialization process is the data supporting the proposition that experiences in integrated schools (as well as in other institutional settings) lead to improved racial attitudes and preferences.[60]

[57] *Ibid.*, p. 245.

[58] See David K. Cohen, "Teachers Want What Children Need . . . Or Do They?" *Urban Review*, Vol. 2 (June 1968), pp. 25–29.

[59] James S. Coleman and others, *Equality of Educational Opportunity: Summary Report* (U.S. Department of Health, Education, and Welfare, 1966), p. 22.

[60] See Thomas F. Pettigrew, "Race and Equal Educational Opportunity," *Harvard Educational Review*, Vol. 38 (Winter 1968), pp. 66–76, and U.S. Commission on Civil Rights, *Racial Isolation in the Public Schools*, Vol. 1 (1967), pp. 109–11.

Of course, the data are only suggestive, and school integration has productive educational and socialization outcomes only when it involves "social-class desegregation . . . , interracial acceptance, classroom desegregation, and minimal tension. . . ."[61] At the same time, the negative outputs of segregated schooling seem fairly clear. Low academic achievement is well documented, but, in addition, gross and misleading stereotypes are generated and perpetuated, and without the benefit of direct, interracial experiences, are exaggerated. More particularly, what Negro children tune in on is their rejection by the dominant polity and status system. It is the registration of this categoric rejection and devaluation in the competent psyches of black youths that is the basis for dropping out and other essentially adaptive responses. As Lohman has observed:

> The human animal, of course, attempts to find answers to problems. The subcultures are, in short, the problem-solving answers to their situations of stress and trial; correspondingly, the subculture, which many of us see only as the evidence of a set of negative attributes and only to be deplored, is to many individuals a solution to their life's problems. It is their means of making life tolerable under the conditions of their deprivation. . . . Failure is their experience, for we do not give them rewards that are contingent upon their own natural learnings and adjustments to the world of deprivation from which they come. Their material and psychological deprivation has generated problem-solving responses. The residual piling-up of the problem-solving responses has produced the subcultures of the deprived groups. In this background lies the significance of the behavior of the Negro child who comes from a black ghetto. If he is combative or inattentive, it is almost a certainty that a significant cultural pattern is there. His defiant attitude has in his milieu a survival value and his hostility is a partial answer to the situation in which he finds himself.[62]

Thus, the segregated community school will be a monument to this debilitating isolation and exclusion.

Conclusions

Our urban public education systems are in need of drastic reforms, if not revolution. Sensitive and critical participating observers such as Kohl and Kozol have documented the boredom and terror that

[61] Cohen, "Policy for the Public Schools," p. 130.
[62] Lohman, "On Law Enforcement and the Police," p. 21.

unnecessarily and all too often permeate the atmosphere of big-city classrooms.[63] In addition, there is mounting evidence of an attitude of ambiguity at best and racist self-fulfilling prophecies at worst on the part of many ghetto teachers concerning the learning and behavioral potentials of their students. For example, a recent survey of teacher attitudes in fifteen cities concluded that while education in the ghetto was not viewed as "a blackboard jungle," it was seen

> . . . as a hard task of motivating students of poor preparation and inadequate community backing in achieving up to their potentials. Theirs [the teachers'] is a view of the problems of education . . . which relies heavily on the "cultural deprivation" theory. They saw their schools as adequate, their own preparation as good, but their success as teachers hampered by the material they have to work with.[64]

Even in an experimental, integrated community school, the central assumption of many teachers that their students were inferior and incapable of learning was clearly evident.[65]

It is not necessary to agree with the global critics of American education such as Paul Goodman (who would simply dismantle the whole system) to appreciate the urgent need for significant and massive educational changes.[66] The consequences of having mindlessly allowed the latent functions of education (economic and social mobility) to be substituted for the manifest function (the achievement of competence) are in need of critical reappraisal. Unfortunately, it has always been easier to diagnose than to prescribe cures for our social problems.

In my view, however, it is a cruel deception of both black and white Americans to suggest that the segregated community school will successfully solve the problems that have precipitated its proposal: the failure of the public education systems in urban centers to

[63] Herbert Kohl, *Thirty-Six Children* (New American Library, 1967), and Jonathan Kozol, *Death at an Early Age* (Houghton Mifflin, 1967).

[64] David Boesel in Peter H. Rossi and others, "Between White and Black: The Faces of American Institutions in the Ghetto," in *Supplemental Studies for the National Advisory Commission on Civil Disorders*, p. 138.

[65] Lauter, "The Short, Happy Life of the Adams-Morgan Community School Project," p. 254.

[66] Paul Goodman, "Freedom and Learning: The Need for Choice," *Saturday Review*, Vol. 51 (May 18, 1968), pp. 73–75.

serve black students and to provide the educational and socializing experiences for their self-development and participation in a common life. In a racially heterogeneous nation dedicated to the idea of a democratic polity, integration as one of the major ingredients of quality education must be our goal. And the most obvious prerequisites for the achievement of this aim are the acceptance of the metropolitan organization of modern social life and the commitment to develop the social and political forms that match this life. Certainly, in a society whose essential character and viability are anchored in advanced technologies of communication and transportation, there is little reason for schooling to be tied to the myths of another era: neighborhood and locality.[67]

Black Americans must participate in the polity and social system of the nation and the local community, and their quest for power is a proper and productive one. But power does not reside in the neighborhood, especially the power to provide the level of funds that quality education necessitates and which our big-city public education systems have to date been denied. However visible and vulnerable, the neighborhood school is not the most effective target if the ultimate concern is the institutional racism that afflicts the nation. Indeed, most big-city school systems probably suffer from too little rather than too much centralized power; in the vacuum, the tradition of principal autonomy and the development of powerful teachers' unions have been the major factors in thwarting efforts for needed changes in both the system and the classroom.

No amount of rhetoric can change the lesson of the ghetto that is "despair, which as it deepens, paralyzes the mind and will."[68] The ghetto community is the least likely to organize and maintain a system of quality education because, in the last analysis, it is inherently a small world and as Epstein notes

> . . . in its struggles with white prejudice the racial underclass in America has produced not an assured and functioning alternative to the dominant culture but a depleted and anguished version of it whose corrosive effects on the parents are often pathetically reflected in the confused and alienated children.[69]

[67] For a discussion of the concept of a "league of metropolitan schools," see Noel A. Day, "Implementing Equal Educational Opportunity," *Harvard Educational Review*, Vol. 38 (Winter 1968), pp. 139–40.

[68] Epstein, "The Politics of School Decentralization," p. 30.

[69] *Ibid.*, p. 30.

Similarly, it is indisputable that the past as well as the future of black Americans is inextricably tied to their status as Americans. Moreover, none of the characteristics of a sociologically viable and functionally autonomous separatism—religion, language, culture—are present to any significant degree.

In addition to the sociological faults of the ghetto and the ideology of separatism, the defects of the segregated community school far outweigh its qualities. To be sure, urban blacks, at least in the near future, will continue to be taught largely by other blacks in defacto segregated schools. But if a democratic polity is to be upheld, neither national nor local community institutions (least of all the schools) can be permitted to espouse a policy of segregation, nor can a minority collectively waive its right to free and equal participation in the common life.

The antonym of society is isolation, not conflict, and the racial isolation that has been part of our society and culture in the past is all too evident. As Louis Wirth pointed out long ago:

> It is not altogether obvious, however, that the contacts between cultural groups inevitably produce harmony as well as friction, and that the one cannot be promoted nor the other prevented by any ready-made administrative devices. Interaction is life, and life is a growth which defies attempts at direction and control by methods, however rational they may be, that do not take account of this dynamic process. In the struggle to obtain status, personality comes into being.[70]

In America, there is no status in the ghetto. Adult egos may benefit temporarily from the joys of conflict with the Establishment (a conflict that is inherently socializing); and the advocates of black power may use the schools as political instruments. But for the children, who are our focus and hope, segregated education cannot provide the socialization that is the basis of society and individual self-realization in a racially heterogeneous society; rather, it can only promise future conflicts, continued and cumulative inferiority, and ultimate national disaster.

[70] Wirth, *The Ghetto*, pp. 280–81

MARIO D. FANTINI

Community Control and Quality Education in Urban School Systems

Since it coincided with the black power movement, the demand for community control of the public schools is usually viewed in political terms—as a clash of forces, each vying for dominance of the other, or at least for weakening of the other. But the politics of community control is a means. More significant—and usually drowned out or deliberately ignored in the clamor over the beginnings of community control—is the educational reform toward which community control is aimed; that is, the direct effects of control on education. This chapter seeks to suggest the connections between control and the quality, shape, and goals of education.

Long before widespread racial rioting and the *Report of the National Advisory Commission on Civil Disorders*, national awareness of a crisis in urban education had developed. The country was not blind to the failure of the schools to improve the economic and social mobility of millions of Negro children. It was an isolated or calloused educational leader who did not acknowledge ten years ago what the Kerner Report said in 1968: "Particularly for the children of the racial ghetto, the schools have failed to provide the educational experience which could help overcome the effects of discrimination and deprivation."[1]

[1] *Report of the National Advisory Commission on Civil Disorders* (Government Printing Office, 1968), p. 236. Referred to as the Kerner Report.

Of course, the problem had long existed, but it was kept in the background as the country dealt with what were regarded as the chief postwar educational crises: the deficit in facilities and personnel and the Sputnik-induced clamor over inadequacy of training in science and mathematics. The failure of education to reach a major segment of the population might still have been ignored if a growing civil rights movement had not turned national attention to the full, grim scene of deprivation and injustice. Because the problem has been so widely acknowledged in professional circles—to say nothing of growing public attention—an enormous amount of effort has been spent in attempts to intervene and break the spiral of educational decline and failure.

Intervention Alternatives

The better-known approaches of intervention have failed to reform the outmoded education system.

Compensatory education. The most widely employed alternative—compensatory education, which attempts to overcome shortcomings in the learner—only deals with symptoms. It is built on a theory that fixes the locus of the problem of school failure primarily with the learner—in his physical, economic, cultural, or environmental deficits. It prescribes additives to the standard educational process. Title I of the Elementary and Secondary Education Act of 1965 is the major thrust of the compensatory movement with its fund of more than a billion dollars applied to remedial efforts for the poor. While succeeding in focusing attention on the problem, Title I has not paid off as anticipated.

Compensatory measures, having little significant effect on the achievement of disadvantaged children, are viewed with increasing distrust by the parents of academic failures, who are rejecting the premise that the fault lies in their children. Rather, they are saying that the system is failing, that it is in need of fundamental rehabilitation. Ghetto parents feel that the school's obligation is to know the child and respond to him—to diagnose the learner's needs, concerns, and cognitive and affective learning style, and adjust its program accordingly.

Integration. On the assumption that Negro pupils' achievement is enhanced in an "integrated" school environment, desegregation efforts also constitute a form of intervention in the quest for quality education for disadvantaged Negro pupils. In most urban settings, however, desegregation or integration (the forms are wrongly used synonymously) has proved elusive, if not impossible, for demographic or political reasons. Moreover, there is a growing shift of emphasis by minority group members away from integration at the option of the white majority. While integration is desirable as a long-range goal, they feel it cannot be achieved as a short-term objective. Rather, true integration can be attained only through success in an intermediate phase in which blacks control their community institutions, of which the school is most central. At present, many of them perceive that such desegregation is condescending because it perpetuates the dependent status of the Negro. It implies that the only way to help the black child is to seat him alongside white children. While the growing demand for greater control by Negroes over predominantly Negro schools defers integration as a primary short-term goal, it does not imply acceptance of a separate but equal doctrine. Some black power advocates reason that when Negroes achieve quality education by their own efforts—through control over their institutions, leading to a sense of potency and racial solidarity—then they will be prepared for the stage of connection (integration) with the white society on a foundation of parity instead of deficiency.

Model subsystems. Another approach to educational reform is the use of experimental units within the public schools. Here, educators hope to develop improved training, retraining, and curriculum and methodology patterns that may be demonstrated and disseminated throughout entire school systems. Such model subsystems, consisting of a single school or a cluster of schools, represent substantial progress toward a realization that more-of-the-same approaches have failed. Nonetheless, they have not been successful in altering the form and structure of the total school system. One reason is that they are dependent on the larger system. They are new organs that the larger body tends to reject. A subsystem is not likely to affect a whole system that is governed by an adept and hierarchy-hardened bureaucracy conditioned by fixed patterns of behavior. Moreover, most subsystems tend to deal with fragments, such as team teaching, new careers for the poor, role playing, or reading, rather than with the whole system. Recently, the concept of developing new comprehensive subsystems has received increasing attention. Stimulated by Model Cities legislation, educational planners are focusing on conceptualizing completely new educational systems such as Fort Lincoln New Town in Washington, D.C.

Parallel systems. Another approach to quality education consists of offering the poor an escape from public education into a parallel system—for example, privately managed schools in the ghetto, or Project Head Start schools that are not subject to the stultifying rules and habits of the public schools. Parallel school systems have achieved impressive results with disadvantaged children, but it is unlikely that they can handle significant numbers. This would require public support, establishing, in effect, a private system of publicly supported schools. The scheme faces strong political, if not constitutional, battles. However, the drive for alternate systems has only recently been tackled. For example, in the spring of 1967, the Massachusetts legislature passed an act that in essence sanctions the support of parallel experimental public school systems for the state. The first experimental school system is presently being planned in the Roxbury section of Boston by the Committee for Community Educational Development—a nonprofit community-based corporation. In New York City, Harlem CORE has proposed an independent Harlem school district that would have the same status as a Scarsdale or Yonkers. While defeated in an earlier state legislative hearing, the plan is expected to be reintroduced during future legislative sessions.

System-wide reform. Some attempts are being made at total system reform. Unlike the subsystem approach, this approach is not constrained by the inertia of the status quo. In Philadelphia, for example, a reform-minded school board is seeking to provide new leadership for the whole system. Another type of system-wide reform is the proposed merger of the school systems of two or more political jurisdictions—for example, the city of Louisville and Jefferson County—into a metropolitan system that would consist of a number of subdistricts, each with considerable autonomy yet federated into a single system to preserve the best of both bigness and smallness.

By far the most advanced stage of total system reform is the New York City movement for decentralization of its public schools. The movement, which calls for increasing the voice of the community in determining educational policy, has been accelerated in the past several years by such efforts as the Bundy Report[2] and the creation of three experimental decentralization districts: Intermediate School (I.S.) 201 and its feeder schools in East Harlem; Ocean Hill-Brownsville in Brooklyn; and Two Bridges on the Lower East Side.

Thus far, this movement has been attended by bitter controversy, but the trend seems unmistakable: the schools of New York City will be decentralized and they will be governed with a community voice to a degree without precedent in the modern history of American education.

Other intervention efforts have led some educators, such as Fantini and Weinstein[3] to render the verdict that the problem is with the school as an institution. It is outdated and, therefore, lacks the capability to respond to the growing demands that are being placed upon it. Most efforts to improve the institutions have resulted in improving an outdated system. What is needed is a new institution —a new system—based on fundamental reform that generates a new model for education instead of perpetuating the old one. This is the same verdict that proponents of community control are rendering—proponents whose base is with the black movement and its quest for self-determination.

Out of these intervention attempts has also arisen the need to establish a strategy for obtaining control of the decision-making mechanism of the present system. The strategy selected depends in large part on the stage of deterioration that the urban school system is in and on the level of frustration that the community has reached. Some communities will accept a form of decentralization that attempts to redistribute school system power equally among the major parties that make up the urban schools—parents and community leaders, teachers, administrators, and the central board of educa-

[2] Mayor's Advisory Panel on Decentralization of the New York City Schools, *Reconnection for Learning: A Community School System for New York City* (1967). Referred to as either the Bundy Report or the Mayor's Advisory Panel.

[3] See Mario D. Fantini and Gerald Weinstein, *The Disadvantaged: Challenge to Education* (Harper & Row, 1968), and Fantini and Weinstein, *Making Urban Schools Work* (Holt, Rinehart & Winston, 1968).

tion. This is a strategy of shared decision making. Others extend the concept of decentralization to community control, in which the bulk of the power is transferred to the community. Under this strategy, the community "reclaims" the schools and establishes its "right" to set policy for those schools under its jurisdiction. This approach inevitably leads to a struggle with the existing institutional agents who presently have power,[4] for example, the central board of education and teachers' organizations. Still others extend the concept of community control to establishing a separate school system, in which a certain community actually proposes to secede from the larger school system to become a district responsible to the state, such as the independent Harlem school district noted earlier.

Fundamental reform. Fundamental reform leading to new and more relevant educational institutions cannot really happen unless three major pillars of the present educational system are changed. They are (1) governance—a shift from professional dominance to a meaningful parental and community role in the education process; (2) goals—an evolution to a humanistically oriented curriculum, modifying the skill-performance standard by which educational quality is primarily measured; and (3) personnel—opening the educational system to a far broader base of talent than the conventionally prepared career educator and training teachers through the reality of community needs and expression. Such changes are beginning, in various stages, in New York City, Washington, D.C., and elsewhere.

The distinguishing features of both the traditional school system and a system reformed through parent-community participation are shown in Table 2.

School reform under community participation should—and evidence is beginning to accumulate that it does—take three main paths. First, it will add new hands and minds to the task, from the parents and the community-at-large. The new participants will come to know the educational enterprise from their own experience rather than simply accepting its established goals and procedures as virtues as pronounced by its professional managers. Second, it will encourage innovation and flexibility on the part of profes-

[4] For a fuller account of the professional domination of urban school systems, see Marilyn Gittell's *Participants and Participation* (Praeger, 1967).

TABLE 2

Characteristics of Traditional and Reformed School Systems

Distinguishing feature	Traditional system	Reformed system
Center of control	Professional monopoly	The public (the community)
Role of parents' organizations	To interpret the school to the community, for public relations	To participate as active agents in matters substantive to the educational process
Bureaucracy	Centralized authority, limiting flexibility and initiative to the professional at the individual school level	Decentralized decision making allowing for maximum local lay and professional initiative and flexibility, with central authority concentrating on technical assistance, long-range planning, and system-wide coordination
Educational objectives	Emphasis on grade-level performance, basic skills, cognitive achievement	Emphasis on both cognitive and affective development; humanistically oriented objectives; for example, identity, connectedness, powerlessness
Test of professional efficiency and promotion	Emphasis on credentials and systematized advancement through the system	Emphasis on performance with students and with parent-community participants
Institutional philosophy	Negative self-fulfilling prophecy, student failure blamed on learner and his background	Positive self-fulfilling prophecy —no student failures, only program failures; accountable to learner and community
Basic learning unit	Classroom, credentialized teacher, school building	The community, various agents as teachers, including other students and paraprofessionals

sionals and will expand the base of professional recruitment. Finally, it will promote the development of a more humanistically oriented curriculum.

Governance and Educational Change

In our society, it is the public that decides on the kind of schools it wants, delegates to the professionals the function of implementation, and reserves for itself the function of accountant. Consequently, when the schools are not performing in terms that are acceptable to the community, the community has the right to an accounting. For example, the professionals explain the lack of scholastic achievement on the part of black and other minority children as a function of "cultural deprivation." The community may reject this rationale and say that it has the right—since these are its schools—to establish new policies if the professionals, whose job is to implement the community's objectives, cannot.

Thus, it is the public that must demand a new educational system, and this is exactly what is taking place today in the quest for community control. The community has rendered the verdict that the present educational system and those who run it are inadequate to the needs and aspirations of black people. Black communities are, therefore, demanding a more relevant educational system. In the continual absence of fundamental reform, the community has resorted to its right to supervise the reform of its schools, that is, to make sure it really happens. Moreover, in demanding a relevant educational system, the community provides a legitimate opportunity for educational reformers to join the community in modernizing urban education.

In essence, the demand to govern schools in their own community has opened the door to change of the other basic pillars of education: curriculum and personnel. But in doing so, the community has established new ground rules in the belief that all children can and will learn.

Governance and Participation

While the movement toward community control has its immediate impetus from ghetto frustration at the failure of public education, it is the latest stage of a developing concept with roots deep in the American educational tradition.

The tradition is twofold: education as a governmental responsibility and public education as essentially a community-governed enterprise. Thus in essentially homogeneous and small communities, the public school was a community school since the school board could adequately be said to represent the community. In large modern cities, however, the school board is more likely to consist of middle- and upper-class members. They are not likely to be close to the racial ghettos that provide the majority of the total public school enrollment. Moreover, the sheer size of urban school systems widens the distance from the policy makers to the community. And finally, with the growth of professionalism and unionism—however necessary the origin of these movements—control over the education process has moved even further from the community.

Along with the increasing concern about educational disadvantage, in addition to such general problems as delinquency, poverty, and urban decay, a new community school concept has arisen. Epitomized by schools in New Haven, Connecticut, and Flint, Michigan, the school serves the community as a center for a variety of educational, cultural, recreational, and local social development activity for both youngsters and adults. The initial motivation for such schools was at least as much economic as social—the desire to make more efficient use of the school plant. The community school, therefore, is supposed to remain open day and night. It is supposed to provide a center to which adults can come for advice on a variety of problems and for training ranging from literacy to skills development. Such a community school continues to be governed by professionals, still mainly educators but now augmented by specialists in employment, homemaking, and other fields. The role of the community remains that of a client. A later stage of the community school embraces all the elements of the New Haven and Flint models but includes a more active role for the community—the use of parents as teacher aides, the use of skilled residents as resources in instruction, and perhaps the strengthening of parents' associations or other groups in advisory or consultative capacities.

Finally, the most advanced concept of the community school includes all the foregoing elements but features a fundamental change in the role of the community. The community participates not only as a client, not only in an advisory role but also as a decision maker. It joins with professionals in planning and operating the school. The clients no longer take it on faith that the school exists to serve the community; they take an active role in determining the nature of the services and in insuring that it is continually responsive to their needs as they see them.

The depths from which the new style of community school springs was expressed by the parents who founded the Adams-Morgan community school in Washington, D.C.:

> People want the kind of school where they and their children are treated with respect and allowed to carry themselves with dignity.
>
> People want the kind of school that welcomes them and their children as they are and does not insult them by indicating that there is something wrong with the way they look, speak, or dress. They believe that the school staff and school board should be responsible to them and their needs and should not dictate to them what someone else has decided is "good for them."
>
> The school should take its character from the nature of the people living in the community and from the children utilizing the school rather than rigidly defining itself as an institution accepting only those people who already fit into a set definition.[5]

The roots of the Adams-Morgan community school lay in such new neighborhood institutions as a walk-in science center, a storefront art center, an alley library, a community preschool center, and a neighborhood house. The community school plan was drawn up by neighborhood parents with the assistance of Antioch College. But the predominant role of the community became clear when the parents insisted that the school open a year before their university advisors felt it really was "ready," and the community's wishes prevailed.

The community school concept, previously cherished and unquestioned, has now become highly controversial, for it seeks basic structural reform of the system in order to attain quality education, and its hallmark is meaningful community participation. Beginning in New York City, the movement is overshadowing in intensity the somewhat analogous struggle that has raged around client participation in decision making in the antipoverty programs. In addition, it may be foreshadowing similar movements in other governmental services—for example, law enforcement and welfare programs.

THE NATURE OF PARTICIPATION

Parental and community participation in the education process declined as professionalization of teaching advanced. Two other

[5] Morgan Community School, "Annual Report to the Community, School Term 1967–68" (processed; Washington, D.C., 1968), pp. 9–10.

forces also tended to keep parents from participating in the education process. One, common in the days of large-scale European immigration and still persisting in the urban ghetto, has been the low level of the parents' own education relative to the teachers' education. Regardless of their desire for education for their children, most ghetto parents were not apt to challenge the assigned authority represented by a better-educated teacher.

The other factor is the growing size and impersonality of the public school systems in large cities. Even well-educated, middle-class parents who seek to engage in meaningful school decisions are deterred by either the inertial mass of the system or the aura of professional exclusivity. The atmosphere in school buildings discourages parental presence (parent visiting days two or three times a year are prime evidence) and most parents visit the school mainly in response to trouble. Also, the schools have carefully drawn boundaries as to how far parents (singly or in parent-teachers' associations [PTA]) may go, even in asking questions of professionals. A sophisticated PTA member may nag at a school board that does not offer French in elementary school, but she will rarely ask for research results (or for research to be initiated) on the effectiveness of the school's language instruction. She is even less apt to ask for such information concerning the school system's criteria for teacher selection or for evidence of its aggressiveness and imagination in recruiting teachers. Even when probing questions are asked, information is often safeguarded as being in the professionals' domain alone. Only now are some school systems beginning to accumulate and release performance data on a school-by-school basis.

Educators have not been totally oblivious to the concept of participation, but they define it in one-sided terms. Elaborate structures and devices have been fashioned—parent-teachers' associations, visiting days, American Education Week, parent education programs, dissemination of information—all ostensibly to "inform" the parent. The administrator who seeks a "happy" school (or "tight ship," as the case may be) will see that his parents are paid some attention and even a degree of deference. He will be patient in explaining homework policies. Schools of education include community relations in their curricula; and in many systems, advancement through the administrative ranks requires a certain number of credits in community relations. The professional feels his role is to interpret the school to the community.

The chief motivation of most professionals in such a concept of community relations is to make their system work more smoothly. From the parents' point of view their concept has a basic flaw: when a school system is dysfunctional, the community is acting against its own interests and those of its children in maintaining the system, in failing to criticize it. In short, the existing concept of parent and community participation in education is basically misdirected toward supporting the schools' status quo.

The new movement for involvement demands "meaningful" participation. At present, meaningful participation stands somewhere between professionally circumscribed participation on the one hand and total community control on the other. It calls for a parental and community role in such substantive matters as budgeting, personnel, and curriculum. The vehicles of participation may be structures at the individual school level or elected bodies on a neighborhood basis. In either case, one of the chief criteria is proximity of educational decision makers to the affected schools. The major political criterion is accountability of the professional and the school system to the community.

In the present stage of decentralization in New York City, the existing demonstration districts have attained a high degree of meaningful participation, including the crucial matter of the choice of the district's chief educational administrator. Demands for total control are still being made, however, and they are likely to grow if meaningful participation is thwarted or obstructed. The distinction between true *participation* and *control* is important. The former envisions reform of the total school system through participation. The latter despairs of reform of the system and seeks to achieve quality through a totally *separate* structure over which the community exercises essentially *autonomous* control. One of the chief difficulties in a separately controlled system, especially in low-income areas, would be the ability to finance itself. Even if separate community-controlled systems within large cities were given taxing powers, the economic base would be insufficient to sustain the schools. The alternative is a system directly dependent on state aid, and attempts to create such a structure through state legislation are only now being contemplated and will undoubtedly face stiff political battles.

THE GOALS OF PARTICIPATION

To participate with others in virtually any enterprise has intrinsic values. It fulfills the human need for contact with fellow men. It also relieves the isolation to which, in some degree, everyone is subject, and isolation if carried to the extreme grows into alienation. In addition, participation is likely to enhance self-esteem; the very act of involvement with others is some proof to the participant that he is accepted. Even if his role is minor, he feels that he is not totally without worth. Participation can also provide some measure of intellectual stimulus through exposure to the viewpoints of others. It is educational if only because it is a form of experience. In interpersonal terms, participation teaches—at least at the subconscious level—the skills of give-and-take, of power relationships, and of planning and working toward goals.

Yet no matter how valuable the rewards of participation are to the individual nonstudent participant, the final measure of the value of public participation is the quality of education pupils receive.

The partisans of participation, their opponents, and the skeptics all focus on this test. The advocates believe that participation will not only improve education but that quality education without participation is a contradiction in terms. The opponents say that even if participation contributes to quality education it is just one of several components and, moreover, participation can endanger quality education if it is carried too far—for example, to the point where it impinges on the primacy of the professional educator. The skeptics call for evidence.

Educational Objectives

DEFINING QUALITY EDUCATION

Basic to an examination of the relation between participation and quality education is an understanding—in fact a redefinition—of quality education.

First, quality is relative. The performance, or level of learning, of an individual child can be measured against that of fellow pupils in an individual class, or against that of others in the school or an entire community. In highly developed countries with rapid communications, the effective benchmark is the total society into which pupils pass and in which they must live and earn a living. Thus, the all-A pupil in a Negro high school in the South can hardly compete for college admission with a C student from a middle-class surburban high school in the North. The double standard of education (and grading) has been a notorious scandal in American education, not only between regions but often from school to school in the same city. Standardized national tests of achievement at various grade levels have served some useful purposes: they have helped to expose vast discrepancies in "standards" of quality education. They also serve the purposes of such specialized users as college admissions officers and recruiters for business and the armed forces. (For the moment the defects of standardized tests, including the cultural bias that places a premiun on verbal ability and favors middle-class students, will be ignored.) But the individual student who is receiving passing or even superior grades in an inferior school is still suffering a deception and is due for a rude shock when he enters the competitive world outside.

In addition, quality has a time dimension. What passed for a first-rate science course twenty years ago would hardly suffice for an advanced course in today's better high schools. Vocational education suffers not only from a social status stigma but also, in most instances, from obsolescence. Its content is overladen with crafts and skills that are either outmoded by the time the student enters the business world or are relevant only to dead-end jobs. No matter how well an obsolete or irrelevant course is designed and taught, it falls outside the definition of quality education. This applies not only to vocational relevance but to personal relevance, as will be shown later. Quality education must include content that revolves around a reality that the learner knows.

THE COGNITIVE DENOMINATOR

The most crucial element in the definition of quality education is the meaning of education. Despite the rhetoric among educators and philosophers, the heart of the prevailing definition of quality education in the American school is grade-level performance on standardized tests. For all major school subjects, standardized tests currently exist that are administered across the country. In studies of educational quality of disadvantaged learners and of students from poverty areas, reading is the subject on which most interest centers.

Despite disclaimers, the overwhelming emphasis of the American school curriculum is on cognitive learning and the development of academic skills. In the high schools and, increasingly, as early as elementary schools, the academic subjects hold sway. How a student performs on standardized tests of cognitive learning and academic skills determines what academic course he will be placed in and which college he will enter, or whether he will enter at all.

The acceptance of grade-level performance as the measure of quality education is nearly universal. It is the standard by which both the middle-class surburban parent and the ghetto parent measure how well their children are doing in school. Indeed, the most potent ammunition that ghetto parents have used in their attack on the inadequacy of the public schools in recent years are the achievement scores in reading and arithmetic. That knowledge of the scores would be damaging was evident in the resistance to their disclosure by some school systems; they were guarded like state secrets. The revelation, under pressure, of reading scores for the New York City public schools was a decisive chapter in the movement for community participation in the education process.

ROOTS OF A NEW DEFINITION

It is interesting to contrast the outcry of a decade ago against school dropouts with the current ferment over the failure of ghetto education. In essence both charges were directed against the same object—the failure of urban education. But the former, directed mainly by national agencies, was motivated by a concern for the aggregate costs to the nation—the shortage of skilled manpower and the costs in welfare and rehabilitation of a sizeable undereducated population. The latter, finding its most poignant expression in the cries of ghetto parents, is concerned with the individual human tragedy created by undereducation. Thus the failure of education becomes a matter of "the life and death of children" and "educational genocide."

These cries no longer refer only to the fact that ghetto children are being shortchanged in reading skills and the other aspects of quality education defined as grade-level achievement. Ten years ago the desires of Negro parents might have been satisfied with equality of performance. But today deprivation has acquired other dimensions, and in the process the definition of quality education is taking a new shape.

The dominant theme in the new definition lies in the *affective* domain—the development of human beings with a sense of self-worth and an ability to function affirmatively and humanely with their fellow men. To the planners and policy makers of the post-Sputnik era such goals represented the "soft side" of education. They carried unpleasant overtones of the progressive school of education and were regarded as irrelevant, if not downright inimical, to cognitive learning, the mastery of skills, the stockpiling of knowledge—in short, to quality education as it was then defined.

But the events of a decade are bringing the affective aspect of education out of exile. For one thing, as noted earlier, the vast compensatory programs designed to redress the educational imbalance between the rich and the poor—programs aimed squarely at raising the grade-level achievement of the children of the poor—have failed. Some educators continue to maintain that compensatory education has not had a fair chance. They believe that with more funds for more programs quality education could be brought to the disadvantaged. Again, it must be pointed out that ghetto parents (and indeed a growing number of educators) no longer subscribe to this argument. They have seen educational budgets and educators' salaries increase and class sizes shrink without comparable improvement in their children's achievement. They are unwilling to continue writing blank checks for programs founded solely on rehabilitating the casualties to fit the educational system. They are calling for change in the system itself.

The emergent redefinition of quality education is also a product of the new voices and new avenues of expression that thwarted minorities found in the accelerating civil rights movement. At one pole, ghetto anger—black rage as two Negro psychiatrists have put it[6]—and justified impatience found expression in civil disorder.

[6] William H. Grier and Price M. Cobbs, *Black Rage* (Basic Books, 1968).

At another, a generation of skilled leaders began to emerge, creating new dialectics and calling the whole prevailing society into question. It is unwise, and dangerous, to rationalize either riots or ultramilitant black power separatism as the behavior of a small minority of the Negro population. They are the visible spokesmen for a large, nonvocal group and should serve as a warning that danger, frustration, and questioning of the dominant order are widespread.

The new sense of worth has found expression in a rich variety of activity and behavior, ranging from the adoption of African dress in some Negro circles to the formation of black student groups on Ivy League campuses. But the core of this expression was stated simply by a small group of Negro demonstrators at the 1968 Republican convention. A thirteen-year-old Mississippi boy led them in a chant:

> "I may be black," he shouted.
> "But I am somebody," the demonstrators responded.
> "I may be poor,"
> "But I am somebody."
> "I may be hungry,"
> "But I am somebody."

Thus, the climate for changing business-as-usual in the schools was developing strength from a widespread challenge, if not revolt, to the conventional order in all aspects of American life as it affected racial minorities. As racial pride began to grow, fetters of centuries of self-hatred and imposed inferiority began to loosen. Parents could no longer accept the dominant reasons given by the educators for educational failure; that is, the parents' own inadequacy, their children's defects, or the deadening environment of their homes. Negro parents looked beyond their own alleged inadequacies to the system itself. There they found massive attitudinal defects. They found that all aspects of the school—the staff, the curriculum, the goals—derived from a culture and socioeconomic viewpoint other than their own. They found that the prevailing mood was an expectation of failure by black children.

In deciding to control its own urban schools the community seeks to reverse the system's negative, self-fulfilling prophecy toward their children, that is, their children were not expected to learn, and therefore they did not. Professionals are beginning to introduce evidence that supports this practice of negative self-fulfilling prophecy in the existing system.[7] Decision makers who are to represent the concerns and aspirations of the children and community must develop a climate in which a positive self-fulfilling prophecy is practiced. In establishing the theme of accountability, therefore, the community will expect children to learn and will expect achievement results. If they do not get these results, they will continue to make changes until they do. The community would hold their representatives (usually elected) accountable for results. Carried over to the recruitment and hiring of administrators and teachers, this positive expectation theme should produce a new breed of personnel.

Ghetto parents also found that the professionals, from the classroom teacher to the high-level administrators, as well as the policy-making boards of education were either unconscious of, or hostile to, the need to stimulate the pride and self-worth of disadvantaged children. While the professionals' attitudes and behavior perpetuating a sense of inferiority among their pupils might have been functioning at the subconscious level, the net effect was the same as an overtly racist system. In fact, it might have been more pernicious since it operated under cover of forms and rhetoric that proclaimed equality and denied the existence of discrimination.

Consequently, the ghetto's demands for educational reform now embrace both a concern for the psychological health and racial integrity of the children as well as their grade-level achievement. The former, known to educators and psychologists as the affective domain, is not external to education as commonly defined. It is not optional or soft but is intrinsic to quality education, and demands a wholesale reorientation of educational goals, practices, and personnel.

REFORMERS OLD AND NEW

Ghetto parents are not alone in shaping the new definition of quality education. Their demand is often more implicit than explicit. But a group of articulate critics of the prevailing educational order have been quite explicit. Moreover, they have leaped over the traditional professional channels to spread their ideology to the

[7] Robert Rosenthal and Lenore Jacobson, *Pygmalion in the Classroom: Teacher Expectation and Pupils' Intellectual Development* (Holt, Rinehart & Winston, 1968).

public. They include John Holt, Jonathan Kozol, Herbert Kohl, Abraham Maslow, Carl Rogers, and Robert Coles. Most recently, *Look*'s senior editor George Leonard depicted tomorrow's education as affective in *Education and Ecstasy* (Dial, 1968).

A glance at American educational history quickly discloses that a humanistic, personality-centered view of education is not new. John Dewey and George Counts, to cite two of the leading philosophers of humanistic education, believed that quality education must include conscious efforts to foster a sense of individual identity and a consciousness of the social order. The Progressive Education Association instituted its Eight-Year Study in 1933. This study showed that graduates of progressive schools performed better in college than did graduates of standard schools.

Some of these ideas were put into practice throughout American schools. Yet they were implemented at a level removed from the students. Students were taught about personal concerns, identity, and social responsibility, but the curriculum did not provide for students actually living such situations and learning through their own real experiences. The schools acted as though talking about empathy and give-and-take constituted learning them. The values were never firmly embraced so as to be legitimate educational goals accorded equal status with traditional subject matter. In short, the humanistic curriculum was not organically applied. Such a system was effectively applied and still continues only in such isolated instances as the New Trier, Illinois, public schools, the Pennsylvania Advanced School in Philadelphia, and private schools like the Dalton School in New York City. But for the most part, not only was it imperfectly attempted but it never had sufficient popular understanding and support to withstand the assault that eventually fell on it. This attack branded progressive education in simplistic terms, as a frill, as soft-headed, as inimical to "hard," subject-centered learning.

The new reform movement, on the other hand, is evolving from an intense process of self-development. It is intrinsically organic because it has arisen from personal concerns—in the ghetto, the need for survival; outside the ghetto, the need for purpose in life.

DEPRIVATION AMONG THE HAVES

Pressure for new educational objectives is being exerted not only by parents of children who are failing but also by some of those who have made it in the prevailing terms of quality education. The college student rebels from Berkeley to Columbia have by and large been high academic achievers. Their revolt has several roots, ranging from the Vietnam war to the impersonality of mass education. One of their discontents is the limitation—some call it aridity—of curricula that are purely cognitive, that bear little relation to their own concerns. Discounting the genuine anarchists among the dissenting students, many seek a more humanistic academic climate in which the traditional pursuit of knowledge for its own sake, or for the sake of a political or technological order, is leavened with the pursuit of individual fulfillment. They, too, are fed up with paternalistic educational hierarchies, with credential-based authority that discourages true inquiry by the uncredentialized (particularly the young), and with cynical adherence to the tradition-bound rules of the game. As the Cox Commission report on the disturbances at Columbia University noted:

> In the case of many seemingly irrelevant scholastic requirements there may be something to the charge (that schools and colleges exert too much pressure upon students). . . . Many students are not being given responsibilities which sufficiently challenge their capabilities. The formal structure of most universities is authoritarian and paternalistic in relation to students, and it often excludes even the faculty from important aspects of university policy. . . . Bringing students closer into a community of all the parts of a university, including the process of decision-making, would promote that intimate exchange of ideas and experiences which is vital to maturity. It would also aid them in learning how to control rapidly changing technological, social, and cultural conditions.[8]

Some part of the student movement may be seeking participation for its own sake. But the strategy of the others recognizes that only the power structure can legitimize an institution's objectives. Therefore, to legitimize new objectives in higher education, they seek access to power—not to do away with authority but to become a part of that authority. Their programs for restructuring higher education may be largely inchoate for the moment, but the demand common to all the student protests is that the students have a meaningful role in the decisions that affect their lives, in the institutions

[8] *Crisis at Columbia*, Report of the Fact-Finding Commission Appointed To Investigate the Disturbances at Columbia University in April and May 1968 (Vintage Books, 1968), pp. 6–7.

that ostensibly exist to serve them. Thus, as in the schools, the political struggle for a share in governance is a means toward educational ends.

Middle-class questioning of the traditional terms of quality education begins earlier than campus revolt. It is close to the surface right in the most "successful" schools, those outside the ghettos, in well-to-do suburbs and middle-class urban neighborhoods. These are the schools that produce not only tomorrow's college rebels but also the young men and women whose disaffection with society takes the form of extreme alienation and retreat into drugs, hippiedom, and other forms of deviant behavior. Their schooling alone is not responsible for such behavior, but it has contributed. At the very least, their education has failed to respond to their deep personal concerns. The price of playing the academic game is paid in the most successful schools. Students who know that they must feed back what most teachers want, that they must accumulate high grades at any cost (including cheating or droning memorization) are storing up resentment. For some, the bubble bursts some time after they enter college. Others may contain the resentment but mature as selfish, incomplete human beings, feeling either superior to those who have not achieved or fearful of the have-nots. They may turn out to be the social and political reactionaries whose apathy or active resistance impedes progress toward justice and equality.[9]

Slavish devotion to the traditional definition of quality education is perhaps most evident in the secondary schools, where emphasis on subject matter is heavier than in the early grades. But the consequences of the limited goals begin even before schooling starts. For example, a child below the official age for entering school may be deemed "unready" for formal schooling, not only because of an arbitrary age barrier but also because he allegedly lacks the intellectual or physiological capacity to handle first-grade work. That the same child may be socially "ready," endowed with sensitivity beyond his years, and is an empathetic human being, is not considered in the determination of when he may start his formal academic training.

[9] For a fuller account of the disadvantaged middle class, see Fantini and Weinstein, *The Disadvantaged.*

PRESSURE FROM THE MARKETPLACE

In such unexpected quarters as the business world, the prevailing definition of quality education is also under scrutiny. The commercial and industrial world depends on the educational system to provide trained, skilled manpower. At one time, training and skills were largely synonymous with knowledge of the processes of the office and factory. But two strong trends in the commercial world are broadening the definition of skilled and trained manpower.

Automation, the first trend, has eliminated many repetitive human tasks that require constant attention to machinery, precision in measurement, and voluminous processing of forms and data. It has also advanced standardization, so that basic differences among products and services are growing smaller. Increasingly, the decisive distinctions in manpower lie in human factors, such as courtesy, flexibility, or reputation for reliability. Furthermore, automation has combined with increased communication to expand the size of commercial and industrial units. The seat of highest power once occupied exclusively by financial or sales experts is now shared by "pure managers," whose prime talent is the ability to manipulate and motivate other people. At lower levels, too, interpersonal skill is an increasingly sought characteristic. Since machinery and systems have been engineered nearly to infallibility, the greatest potential for inefficiency, failure, or error lies in the human factor.

Another significant trend is the vast growth of the service sector in which the "product" is the attention and responsiveness of the seller to the buyer. This is true both in the service and product sectors. The importance of morale, clarity in communication, responsibility, and motivation has soared. Yet all along the line, management finds that its personnel, highly trained in technical and professional skills, is grossly inadequate in the skills of human interaction. This is especially true at the junior executive and middle-management levels, but it also appears at the executive level, where men are found wanting in awareness of the psychology and dynamics of individual and group behavior. They are also unaware of the bases of their own strengths, inadequacies, and drives. The need for such skills is further accentuated by the growth of international business, coinciding with the rise of nationalism in former colonial countries as well as in the West. Sensitivity to other cultures and races is no longer an interesting oddity but a practical necessity for effective functioning of business abroad.

To overcome these deficiencies, a new field has arisen in the business world—sensitivity training. In rudimentary form, sensitivity training may be conducted on the job, through manuals or lectures, supplemented by retreats away from the office where personnel can concentrate in individual study and group-dynamics exercises on problems of communications and employee-supervisor relations. At a more sophisticated level, management sends its staffs and executives to sensitivity-training schools, of which the best known is National Training Laboratories at Bethel, Maine.

In short, what many educators consider idealistic, soft, and unnecessary or disruptive to the "proper" curriculum, the commercial marketplace now regards as a most practical, indeed vital, component of quality education. Thus, the debate over whether education should have a vocational bias takes a new and interesting turn, for humanistic matter is now valuable in the business world as well as for individual growth and fulfillment. Resistance to or disparagement of a humanistically (affectively) inclusive curriculum and school climate becomes less defensible than ever. If professional resistance continues, educators may be the last to define quality education in its new terms.

Business has long-standing complaints against the failure of education to produce immediately productive workers, both at the blue-collar and white-collar levels. Extensive training and retraining programs exist in major companies for new workers, and the training schools of some large industrial firms rival colleges in size. Business and industry will fill the gap in the area of human relations training, too, if the schools and higher education ignore it. But society should question the wisdom of leaving such training primarily to business and industry. Profit, their chief motive, is not always compatible with democratic ideals or the integrity of the individual personality. One does not have to be distrustful of business to prefer that such matters be left to institutions, like schools and colleges, which are dedicated to broad social purposes.

GOVERNANCE AND THE NEW OBJECTIVES

To sum up, outmoded educational systems are now under simultaneous pressure from four sources: internal reformers, parents and other members of the surrounding community, business and industry, and students.

The internal reformers, such as Abraham Maslow, Carl Rogers, Theodore Brameld, have kept alive the basic doctrines of Dewey and his intellectual ancestors. But without support they will not be any more successful in fundamentally reforming education toward humanistic objectives. Experience has shown that educational objectives grafted onto the educational structure by professional reformers alone are extremely vulnerable to misunderstanding and ridicule. In order for educational objectives to take firm root, to be legitimized, there must, first of all, be a demand for them by the public. This demand, as noted earlier, is rising in the ghetto communities from a confluence of two currents: first, a questioning of the effect on black children of the prevailing white middle-class culture as embodied in the staff and the tone of the schools and, second, the quickening sense of racial pride and an intense search for racial and personal identity. These are fast assuming a place of equal importance with the attainment of marketable skills and conventional academic mastery. Yet they are not regarded as mutually exclusive; in fact, they can intimately reinforce one another. Running concurrently with this demand is the politics of gaining a voice in the education process. Politics, then, despite the controversy it arouses, is essential to legitimizing new objectives for profound educational reform and to constructive outlets for deep-seated cultural and psychological movements.

The New Quality Education

Under community control, educational objectives are likely to depart radically from the exclusive standard of grade-level performance in skills. Skill training and academic mastery will not be abandoned; rather they will be totally meshed in a curriculum, a mode of operation, and a total school staff that are vastly more relevant and adaptable to the learner than traditional systems.

The school's curriculum and social reality will be intrinsically connected. For example, the desire for instruction in Swahili in some predominately Negro schools has been ridiculed by opponents of community control of education. Yet the pursuit of this language is a legitimate means of self-discovery and cultural and historical perspective for large numbers of black Americans, both adults and children. (It is worth noting, incidentally, that postwar linguistic theory attaches value to the learning of any language as a means of acquiring a sense of linguistic structure and dynamics, which is applicable to virtually all languages.) A school system that respects cultural diversity—as American urban school systems have long said they do—should not only tolerate such elements in the curriculum but should affirmatively make use of them. At the Adams-Morgan community school in Washington, D.C., there are three teachers from Africa. One is teaching Swahili as a part of African history while another is teaching Arabic.

The traditional urban school is bent on assimilating or acculturating children to an arbitrary norm. It either fails to capitalize on diversity or, worse, penalizes pupils who do not surrender their culture; Mexican-American pupils in some southwestern schools, for example, are punished for speaking Spanish on school grounds. Bilingual instruction in communities with large numbers of Spanish-speaking pupils is an educational acknowledgment of both social reality and cultural diversity and was one of the first programs established in the experimental Ocean Hill-Brownsville school district in New York. The district's schools are also trying to capitalize on the students' strengths by offering courses in African history, art, music, and sociology, and Spanish and Puerto Rican history. In mathematics classes, they include African methods of counting by using a game in which seeds are transferred from one bowl to another.

In a relevant curriculum, children will learn the skills and behavior needed to deal with social realities—principally, their quest for identity, their feelings of power or powerlessness, and their desire for personal connection with the other individuals and the external forces and institutions that will affect their lives. For example, through interaction with different groups of people, the curriculum will be continuously dealing with children's concerns. The aim of such a curriculum will be to equip children with a richer repertoire of responses to handle their problems.

As the black community (and other minorities, such as Spanish-speaking people) begins to legitimize affective objectives, it is also likely that objectives related to social action will be introduced. The emergence of direct action is a legitimate expression of participatory democracy, especially as an instrument necessary to achieve social change. The old system taught blacks to accept and adjust to an unjust social system and a negative environment—slums, poverty, racism—that stunt or distort human growth and development. The new objective will attempt to introduce those behaviors in the learner that will lead to active reconstruction of these negative environments so that, in turn, the environment can affect human development in a more positive way.

In order for these objectives to be realized, the communities will begin to expand the conception of the classroom to include the entire community. Thus the talents of a social worker, assemblyman, merchant, industrialist will be utilized, not as speakers in the schools but as clinical teachers in the actual setting in the community. Recently, Fantini and Young conceptualized an advanced educational system for Fort Lincoln New Town in Washington, D.C., in which the entire community will be the classroom.[10]

Many urban teachers who are charged only with the traditional objectives of academic skills and subject-matter content are understandably annoyed with consultants who feed them sociopsychological descriptions and analyses of their pupils and communities and ask that they be embodied into their teaching. The teachers' habit and mandate is to teach the subject. But only when such objectives as meeting the children's sociopsychological needs and concerns, dealing with social reality, and giving full scope to individual and group identity are given equal status as objectives with cognitive goals—in short, are legitimized as school policy—can an effective humanistic curriculum be constructed.

In order for a school to meet these objectives, it must assume the following three tiers of responsibility:[11]

1. *Skills and knowledge development.* This consists of objectives related to the mastery of the basic skills of learning and the major con-

[10] Mario D. Fantini, Milton A. Young, and Frieda Douglas, *A Design for a New and Relevant System of Education for Fort Lincoln New Town* (Washington, D.C., School District, 1968).

[11] For a fuller account of the tiered school, see Fantini and Weinstein's *Making Urban Schools Work.*

cepts of disciplines that are essential building blocks for the cognitive development of the child (including reading, computation, writing and speaking skills, and basic information in science and the social sciences).

2. *Personal talent and interest-identification and development.* This involves drawing forth talents or abilities from the pupil and developing them in him. The range would be broad—from learning a musical instrument to mastering a subject that is not a part of tier 1. It includes talents usually associated with that part of education oriented to work careers but is limited to vocational education students.

3. *Social action and exploration of self and others.* This comprises the school's main responsibility for the affective aspects of education—power, identity, and connectedness. In this area the school must not simply allude to social realities but must skillfully employ them to make intimate contact with the learner. This not only exposes pupils to the concept of personal power and power in relation to other people but also provides clinical situations for actions related to pupils' concerns, both inside and outside the classroom. It is here that cognitive knowledge must be married to pupils' concerns and feelings as they affect behavior. For knowing something cognitively does not always result in behavior based on that knowledge. For example, millions of Americans have knowledge of injustice and poverty but do not act on them—or, in fact, resent or oppose such action by others. Knowledge can be a basis for feeling, but only feeling generates behavior. If the goal of education is to produce better people and a more humane society, then knowledge (education) should relate to feeling, for otherwise it is not likely to affect behavior. That democratic principles and ideals have been poorly taught by the nation's public schools (if taught at all) is evident in the discrepancy between them and the behavior of individuals in society—as indicated in the Kerner Report.

The three-tiered model opens up possibilities for greater student participation and self-awareness, through teaching younger pupils; for greater responsibility as a citizen, through understanding of social interaction and cultural diversity, as well as social-action opportunities built into the curriculum; and for the student's future role as a parent, since he will be more aware of himself and others.

Staffing Community-Controlled Schools

Public demand will legitimize the new educational objectives and the political struggle for a part in governance of a restructured system will break down the barriers to the new objectives. But it is too much to expect the guardians and controllers of the old system to translate them into action, into the breath and habit of the schools—in other words, to be the agents to reform their own system. For such a change, new energies are required. The agents, on one hand, must include a new breed of professionals. But even more important, they must include the prime agents in the socialization of children, a process that begins long before the child enters school and continues to exert a major influence on his growth and development afterward. These agents, of course, are the children's peers, parents, and community. They are "teachers" in the curriculum of the home and the streets. One of the roots of educational failure in ghetto areas is the divergence of the several curricula of the home, the streets, and the schools, as studies under Basil Bernstein of the University of London's Sociological Research Unit have illustrated.[12] At present, the agents in the child socialization process are passing from the stage of detached discontinuity. They are beginning actively to oppose one another, creating havoc. The conflict in New York City between teachers and administrators on the one hand and the parents and the community on the other is the most sharply drawn case to date. Therefore, the process of parents and community seeking meaningful roles in the governance of their schools is also a process of reconnecting the various agents that influence child development—of restoring continuity in the socialization process of the children.

OPEN-ENDED STAFFING

Greater proximity to children's needs and to the community pulse should free community school systems of staffing rigidities that are almost inevitable in huge centralized systems whose rules must satisfy a citywide denominator and cover a range of contingencies,

[12] Basil Bernstein, "A Socio-linguistic Approach to Social Learning," in Julius Gould (ed.), *Penguin Survey of the Social Sciences, 1965* (Penguin, 1965).

any one of which may be altogether unsuitable or undesirable in a given community.

The staffs of community-controlled schools can vary along a wide horizontal spectrum from the professional to the lay, the latter including parents, community residents, and even the students. It can vary vertically as well, to include not only professional educators but specialists from other disciplines and professions. For example, the chief education officer in the I.S. 201 experimental district in New York City is, foremost, a public administrator, although he has professional education credentials. The experimental districts have made wide use of lawyers, engineers, and others outside professional education. The recruiting pattern of regular teachers has broken with tradition, too, by fanning out beyond the city limits for personnel. Furthermore, new teachers in the Ocean Hill-Brownsville district have a high proportion of graduates from top-ranking liberal arts colleges.[13]

A participatory school system changes the role of the professional but it does not subordinate it. Since the professional is now accountable not only to professional superiors but to the community, his job would appear to be more difficult because he is under closer scrutiny. But this is a superficial appraisal of his role. More significant, he is now supported by the energies of parents and community agents in the education process, as well as by an entire system that is more open and flexible. Such a system is likely to draw into the teaching process a variety of resources—teacher aides, university and business teams, specialists from professional fields and from the community, and a greater diversity of teaching materials and learning sites. Thus, the role of many professionals will consist in greater part of coordinating a rich range of inputs. This applies even more forcefully at the higher professional levels, and administrators will be judged more on their ability to coordinate than on their effectiveness in keeping things under control, which is now too often the chief criterion.

Fears that staffing would be racially slanted have not materialized in the few instances of community-controlled schools to date. For example, 70 percent of the new teachers in the embattled Ocean

[13] See "Teachers Who Give a Damn," *Time*, Education Section, Oct. 4, 1968, p. 50.

Hill-Brownsville demonstration district are white. And despite the fact that the district's pupils are predominantly Negro and Puerto Rican, two of six principal vacancies were filled by white administrators and one by a Chinese-American. Of the three other principals, two are Negroes and one is Puerto Rican—the first Puerto Rican principal in New York City.

The administrator of Ocean Hill-Brownsville is also experimenting with the deployment of teachers to meet individual learning problems. Some teachers are grouped according to their strength in teaching basic skills. One group that is particularly strong in personality development is assigned the task of organizing the various human resource elements in the schools—ranging from professional teachers to parent aides and community and professional resource personnel. Put another way, the staff is organized to capitalize on the strengths of the learners and, if necessary, to regroup if it fails to meet the learners' needs. As the unit administrator of the Ocean Hill-Brownsville experimental district put it recently, he "custom-fitted teacher strengths to children's needs."[14]

In general, the community-controlled schools give evidence of individualization in instruction to a degree realized in few conventional schools. In addition to an ungraded organization, as in the Adams-Morgan community school, several community-controlled units have plans not only for tailoring the teaching staff to pupils' abilities and learning styles but also to employ computer-assisted instruction, tutorials, and inventories of each child. Matching teacher style to learning style is a significant pedagogical advance. It begins to move away from the "wall-to wall" teacher and matches teacher competence to individual educational objectives. The community-controlled experiments make wide use of paraprofessionals as tutors to teach talented students music, art, drama, and the like. Moreover, use of the technique of cross-age teaching, having students teach each other, is quite common.

With natural ties to the community, and with freedom from centralized regulations that must be conservative in order to cover city-wide contingencies, the community school can use a variety of sites for learning, not merely as field trips but on a continuous basis. For

[14] *New York Times*, Oct. 9, 1968.

example, the Parkway School in Philadelphia has, in effect, broken out of its four walls and become a complex comprising the art museum, the Franklin Institute, the Fels Planetarium, and several business offices, industrial plants, and laboratories.

The implication for teacher training in such systems is clear: the school itself—and in a larger sense the community—will teach the teacher. Even in the past, teacher-training institutions had difficulty in simulating real situations for the preparation of teachers, especially for those who would be teaching in a milieu different from their own. In the true community school, it will be even more important that formal training institutions examine and use the actual school processes, which influence teacher behavior far more than the campus. Leaders in the community could be used as resource personnel in the training of teachers, and student-parent-community teams could help teacher-training institutions in the identification and reduction of negative racial attitudes among prospective teachers. By developing openness and awareness through such techniques as basic-encounter groups, sensitivity training, and group-dynamics systems, negative attitudes may be overcome.

The basis for expanded recruitment of teachers is that community-based schools are an accurate reflection of social ferment and striving for social justice, equal opportunity, and ethnic pride, and have a climate in which innovation and feeling have replaced outmoded traditions and Establishment mentality. These characteristics are strong attractions for young college graduates, black and white, with deep personal and social commitment, whose dissatisfaction with society's shortcomings finds expression in constructive activity rather than in alienation or escape. Prototypes for this kind of young teacher are Peace Corpsmen, Teacher Corpsmen, VISTA volunteers, and civil rights workers. The New York City experimental school districts have already attracted a number of such men and women. Two of the projects are also the scene of a teacher-initiated program (Teachers, Inc.) for orienting and training new teachers including those from both the Peace Corps and VISTA, regular new recruits to the New York City school system, and civil rights and antipoverty workers who are volunteering for ghetto teaching. The program includes intensive training and practice in the use of instructional methods and materials specially designed for local needs, close ties to the community through involvement in projects outside the schools, and, where needed, formal courses to satisfy Board of Education requirements. During the summer session, participants found living quarters in the neighborhoods where they planned to teach.

Teachers in both the Ocean Hill and I.S. 201 experimental districts have been singled out for representing a new breed that "give a damn."[15] One reporter, quoting a family worker who has worked in one of the Ocean Hill schools for three years, noted:

> You get a really positive feeling when you go into the school. The children give those teachers a tremendous amount of respect. There have always been discipline problems, but now there aren't as many as before.
>
> These teachers really care. They didn't come with their minds made up that the children can't learn. They came with open minds. The children can tell the difference.
>
> I even find more parents coming in—maybe twice as many as before. And after they bring their children to class, they stop and talk to the principals. Others come in and talk to the teachers during their lunch breaks.

Another teacher in I.S. 201 described what it means to teach in a community-controlled school:

> Being a teacher at I.S. 201 is a way of life. It makes teaching more than a job. Teaching is a career at 201. If you ever come to visit 201, and just about everyone does eventually, in the principal's office there is a slogan that sums up the goals and ambitions of the professional staff: "parent power+teacher power=powerful children."[16]

While it is too early to produce charts indicating grade-level achievement gains, it is interesting to note that the Adams-Morgan community school was one of six schools in the Washington, D.C., public school system that showed a gain in reading achievement after only one year as a community-controlled school.

In addition to the four experimental community-controlled schools (three in New York City and one in Washington, D.C.), others are beginning to emerge. The most notable proposal—made in response to President Lyndon B. Johnson's request to develop a

[15] Bill Kovack, "Teachers Working on J.H.S. 271 Staff Feel a 'Vibrance,' " *New York Times*, Oct. 21, 1968.

[16] SCOPE (School and Community Organized for Partnership in Education), Bulletin (New York, 1969).

model of excellence in urban education—is the Anacostia Community School Project[17] in southeast Washington, D.C., planned for ten schools with a strong community participation component. Other projects are beginning in San Francisco (Hunters Point), Newark, Philadelphia, and Boston.

NONPROFESSIONAL PARTICIPATION

Both the schools and the parent and community participants benefit from active involvement in the education process. The very act of participation—a sense of greater control over a decisive institution that influences the fate of their children—contributes to the parents' sense of potency and self-worth: "If I have a voice, if what I say counts for something, I am somebody." Armed with experiential potency and a heightened sense of self-worth they become better equipped as models for their children and as teachers of that part of the curriculum that is exclusively theirs—rearing in the home.

That the parent and community agents undergo growth and development in the difficult process of participating in the education process is inherent in the process. Moreover, since the inflow of parents into participatory roles will be continuous, the danger of institutional rigidity will be averted (the schools serve as open rather than closed institutions). The participants' own growth and development helps assure that the reformed system will be readily inclined to adjustment and change. It will contrast sharply to the professionally dominated, bureaucratized school systems which are rigid in their functions and habits and highly resistant to change. Unlike the professionally controlled, limited participation mode presently prevailing, the parent and community participants will learn their roles in the process of real participation.

Participatory democracy in education should also give parents and the community a tangible respect for the intricacy and complexity of the problems in urban education. Participation has a positive effect on the participants as well as on the system. For example, as parents in East Harlem became more engaged in the education

[17] Community Planning Council, "The Anacostia Community School Project," a proposal submitted to the U.S. Office of Education (processed; Washington, D.C.: Community Planning Council, August 1968).

process, "quality education" and "give a damn" replaced "black power" as the slogan. Responsibility comes with the power of effective voice. After responsibility, judgment, stability, and dedication to constructive purpose are likely to follow. The classic pattern of the revolutionary is that once he has taken power, he shifts from destroying institutions to building order and new institutions (of his own kind, to be sure). It is not likely that parents who have gained admission as true partners in the process will oversimplify and lay the blame for educational failures solely on the professionals. As things stand now, low-income communities outside the system understandably place the blame squarely on the assigned professionals: "You are paid to teach, to deliver a certain product. When overwhelming numbers of our children fail to learn you are not delivering. You are not meeting your professional obligation." The syllogism is simplistic: it ignores the fact that professional talent can be thwarted by a system, and it does not take into account extra-school factors in teaching and learning. But it is an altogether natural response from parents to whom the system provides no access and offers but two alternatives: total resignation and apathy; or anger, protest, and, sooner or later, some form of retaliation.

Skeptics who concede the right of parents to participate in the education process nevertheless question their technical qualifications to engage in educational decisions, particularly (though not exclusively) the low-income, poorly educated parents. But the question should be not what parents know now but what they can come to know about the technicalities of education. That they want to know is suggested by the few instances in which they have become equal partners in the process. Their concerns soon broaden; they begin to ask, for example, who are the most talented reading specialists in the country, because we want them to help us. In qualifying for school board membership, too, they seek training for themselves—something rare among would-be school board members even in wealthier communities.

Indeed, the processes of training, and participation of, parents and community residents fulfills one of the tenets of American democracy: the existence of an informed electorate. Participation affords direct knowledge and facilitates understanding and insights far more effectively than attempts to learn abstractly. Experience is the great teacher. One of the surest guarantees that parents and community will govern responsibly is that they will be able to know the education process from the inside, through personal involvement. They will thereby know what is best in their own interests. Moreover, they are less likely to be susceptible to propaganda, personal charisma, and other diversionary political devices that are common in elections in which the electorate's knowledge of the issues is distant and rarely touched by personal exposure.

In brief, the process of participation and involvement in the substantive affairs of urban education will make the citizens aware of the differences between what is and what could be, between keeping an outdated educational system or moving toward an updated model. Until the citizens are informed concerning the irrelevances of our conventional system, they will not demand change.

Moreover, a decision to move toward a community school offers unusual opportunities to create community education and orientation vehicles, that is, create training mechanisms that increase community capability for assuming its new educational role.

Schools that are to be intimately attuned to the identity needs and concerns of the children and to the community climate and aspirations must be staffed by professionals with highly developed sensitivity and skill. Given the current teaching personnel market, this will entail retraining many of the present staff as well as recruitment of new teachers from both traditional and untraditional sources. The new cadre of teachers—both trained and newly recruited—will be more accountable for their performance, especially in the cognitive and affective areas.

CONFLICT OR COLLABORATION?

Where the professionals resist the movement toward parent-community participation, conflict is inevitable. The stand of the teachers' union in Washington, D.C., and the position of the new president of the National Education Association, both of whom support urban school decentralization and community participation, contrast sharply with the stance of the New York teachers' union. This union demonstrated its opposition long before the Ocean Hill-Brownsville controversy by actively (and successfully) lobbying in the state legislature against a strong bill for decentralization and community participation.

Where the professionals cooperate with the movement, possibilities of productive collaboration open up. Teachers have organized labor unions, among other reasons, to overcome their low status in the social system of the public schools, where administrative sanctions are powerful. In such tightly regulated systems, teachers protect whatever operational gains they have achieved within the ongoing system, and, in so doing, often become guardians of the status quo without realizing it. A community school system can replace essentially authoritarian domination by one of the parties with shared authority and responsibility. The process is two-edged since overweening parent-community domination would itself constitute authoritarian rule. The dangers of this occurring are, of course, heightened in a repressive society. But grounds for optimism exist because of two factors. One is the assumption that the parents' prime interest is the well-being of their children and their recognition that good teaching is not likely to emanate from teachers who are intimidated, fearful, and hindered in their own freedom and capacity to innovate. Second is the growing demand for a humanistically based curriculum. The objectives of such a curriculum are inconsistent with authoritarianism: they demand a professional staff in which empathy and sensitivity are required professional qualifications. A parent-community governing board that maintains an authoritarian atmosphere will not be able to assemble such a staff. Professionals—especially teachers—have an unusual opportunity to practice leadership by collaboration with the community in the movement for urban school reform and new quality education.

LEONARD J. FEIN

Community Schools and Social Theory: The Limits of Universalism

Writing in the late 1950s, Myron Lieberman put quite plainly what was, until recently, the dominant view of liberal critics of the public school system: "The public interest is almost invariably better served by leaving professional questions to the professionals.[1] . . . local control results in the same kind of intellectual protectionism that characterizes schools in totalitarian countries."[2] At the time that Lieberman was writing, critics of public education were particularly concerned with issues of censorship, growing out of the McCarthy period, and with problems of desegregation, growing out of the 1954 Supreme Court decision.[3] In both cases, it seemed to the critics that the barrier to reform was persistence of local control.

As intellectuals were concerning themselves with structural reforms that would temper the parochializing power of local communities, those communities were becoming increasingly alarmed at the prospect of a decrease in their autonomy. These were the post-Sputnik years, and talk of national standards and federal involve-

[1] Myron Lieberman, *The Future of Public Education* (University of Chicago Press, 1960), p. 60.

[2] *Ibid.*, p. 38.

[3] *Brown* v. *Board of Education of Topeka*, 347 U.S. 483 (1954).

ment was widespread. Against such pressures, communities asserted their own historic jurisdiction and were, in the main, successful—largely by virtue of their movement toward the necessary reforms within the prevailing structures.

A good deal has happened in the past decade, and now we find the liberal critics badly split. Many continue to stress the virtues of a secular system, as against the threatened parochialization that neighborhood control suggests; at the same time, large numbers appear to endorse a more elaborate degree of neighborhood control over the schools than was ever seriously contemplated by the traditional exponents of local autonomy.

This shift has been sudden, and it is, to say the least, most curious. Even if important public policy issues were not involved, this shift should elicit our attention as an interesting footnote to intellectual history. Since it does, in fact, embrace pressing matters of public policy careful attention to the change in perspective is all the more important. Moreover, as we shall see, analysis of the split within the liberal community takes us a long way toward understanding the central issues of the current debate.

It must be evident at the outset that the debate is based, in large measure, on a general disagreement over both the meaning and the legitimacy of community in American society. This problem is at the heart of our present perplexity, and much of what follows here is an effort to thread through its mysteries and clarify its ambiguities. But we must recognize that the concept of community is not the only source of confusion, and, therefore, we shall turn first to a set of related problems that require clarification.

One major theme in the recent literature on the subject couches the demand for community control in terms of historical precedent. It calls for a return to an earlier and more manageable arrangement. "Once upon a time, the people created public schools, and the schools belonged to them."[4] But as the cities have grown, the school system has become a hyperbolic enterprise, too large to be effectively influenced, let alone controlled, by the community. Thus, the schools "have taken on the shape of massive corporate enterprises," and now, at last, "the public is seeking to repossess its schools."[5]

[4] Mario D. Fantini in his Foreword to Marilyn Gittell, *Participants and Participation: A Study of School Policy in New York City* (Praeger, 1967), p. vii.

[5] *Ibid.*

This position does not depend critically on a negative assessment of the present performance of public schools. From a logical standpoint, it could as easily be tied to normative theories of democracy, insisting on more popular participation in school management as an end in itself. But the fact is, of course, that those liberal intellectuals who call for a return are induced to do so largely because they believe that the schools have failed.[6] For this reason, their expression of nostalgia should not be mistaken for the instinctive response to nationalizing trends that is so common to local school people. Furthermore, most of them know that there never was a time in industrial America when schools were definitively controlled by the local community, much less the neighborhood. The tension between professional judgment and community values has been part of the story of public education in the United States at least since educators began to view themselves (and, occasionally, to be viewed by others) as professionals. And, in general, intellectuals have sided with the professionals in the continuing debate, for they have seen community control as essentially repressive rather than liberating.

Hence, talk of return or repossession is misleading. It proposes a return to a time that never was, and to a commitment that intellectuals rarely shared.[7] From what, then, does the current interest derive?

[6] Whether the extraordinary interest in participatory democracy to which we are now witness would have occurred had our institutions not faced a crisis of effectiveness is a moot question. It is, however, reasonable to suppose that the popular (as distinguished from intellectual) enthusiasm for the idea that is now developing, especially in the Negro community, would have been substantially reduced.

[7] Indeed, there was a time when communities had more to say about how their children would be educated. This was not so much because schools were subject to more community authority then but rather because extraschool educational inputs were more systematic and more manageable. In preurban, preliberal, and, especially, pretelevision America, parents could and did feel more confident that the established institutions were effectively transmitting their own values to the young. But tasks once assumed by the family and the church have now passed, by and large, to the mass media, and parents have no control over the stimuli to which their children are exposed. This situation has become so acute that genuine community efforts to retain (or to reassert) control over the schools may be regarded as a last attempt to gain some control over the education of the young—an effort directed at the schools not because they are the traditional transmission belts of community values but because they are the only educative institution that remains, to some degree, vulnerable to direct political pressure.

But this perspective, once again, is not what intellectuals are talking about. For in-

In the epidemiology of American ideological currents, we often find that the experiences of New York City are the infecting bacillus. For better or for worse, what happens in New York is then writ small around the country. In New York City, there have been reports calling for one form of decentralization or another in the public schools in 1933, 1940, 1942, 1949, 1962, 1965, 1967, and again in 1968.[8] Yet decentralization in New York has yet to take place.[9] Since New York is at the same time the largest public school system in the nation and, evidently, the most rigid, the conclusion seems warranted that reform can take place only through radical change in the very structure of the system. In other words, although it might be true that moderate parceling out of the central system's powers would be sufficient to introduce the required flexibility, we must recognize that heavily centralized systems are unlikely to permit any real reduction in their power. It follows that the only alternative is a radical structural transformation, in which the power to allocate power among the participants in the system is taken away from the central agency.

Moreover, and apart from New York, there is a severe crisis in the observed effectiveness of the schools, and a significant frustration with attempted reforms. The crisis in effectiveness is both general and specific. The general, and continuing, crisis is a result of the growing disagreement about what the schools ought to be teaching. Neither in traditional societies, where the task of the schools was the transmission of a consensual culture, nor in societies that required large numbers of competent and autonomous mechanics, such as our own until quite recently, were questions regarding the substantive orientation of public education particularly critical. But it has now become evident that no person can become the intellectual master of his environment, for the environment is far too complex, far too technical, to permit universal mastery. It is not even clear that the schools, staffed in the main by people at the periphery of the tech-

tellectuals, far from lamenting the erosion of parochial influence on the schools, have remained firm in their commitment to secular education, and hence to the increasing nationalization of the curriculum content of the schools.

[8] Cited by Jason Epstein in "The Politics of School Decentralization," *New York Review of Books*, Vol. 10 (June 6, 1968), p. 26.

[9] At least as of this writing. And it can safely and sadly be predicted that if the situation has since changed, it will have been with great stress and bitter dispute.

nical environment, have anything particularly useful to say about it. Nor, finally, have the schools been able to bridge the gaps gracefully between our several competing ideologies of education, some stressing the virtues of personal autonomy, some the importance of ethical guidelines, still others the current requirements of the collectivity for teamwork.

It is not surprising, then, that the schools are in trouble, nor that they tend to cling to external indexes, such as college admission rates, or to tradition as measures of their success.[10] And this general crisis is likely to endure for some time, at least until we have come to terms with the new relationship of man to things, and to other men, implied by the developing technology.

At the same time, a more specific and more urgent crisis affects the public schools. This is the special crisis of their effectiveness with respect to low-income people and, in particular, to black people. There is general agreement that no matter what the schools are supposed to be teaching they are not teaching it very well to the poor and the black. In an era when it was commonly believed that blacks could not learn what others could, the inequity in product was of little public moment. But in our present egalitarian mood, the continuing inequity is a source of very sharp unrest.

Thus a reformist spirit developed, determined, more or less, to redeem the schools. If we take just the last decade or so as our time span, we can readily identify the leading doctrines of the reformers. The first was the professional-technical approach: Our teachers are not qualified and our classrooms are crowded. Raise salaries, reform teachers' education, build schools, and all will be better, if not well. We then realized that teachers, who were predominantly recruited from the lower-middle class, had special problems and anxieties in communicating with lower-class children. Several solutions were pursued. Teachers' salaries were raised, in order to make them less status-anxious; they were offered courses designed to evoke empathy with their students; the students were told repeatedly that if only they would shape up, middle-class success would be theirs. And most teachers continued in the reliable defense pattern, which was

[10] See the works of Edgar Z. Friedenberg for an astonishingly elegant statement of the problem, especially *Coming of Age in America* (Random House, 1965) and *The Vanishing Adolescent* (Beacon, 1959).

(and is) to believe that their students were not, and would not be, successful, as society defines success.

Since these were either unacceptable or ineffective solutions, reformers turned in new directions. Attention was directed away from professional-technical characteristics and toward the psychological phenomenon of educational deprivation. The most urgent reforms, it was concluded, were enrichment programs for the culturally deprived to compensate for the inadequacy of their home-neighborhood environment. If low-income children suffered because they had less educational resources than their more affluent peers—less space to study, fewer books, a limited vocabulary—the solution was to offer them compensatory programs.

It did not take long to realize that more of the same might not be an adequate remedy. The issue was not simply the lack of specifically educational resources but also victimization by an environment that distorted self-image, made a mockery of hope, and challenged the relevance of the school, even when it had elaborate compensatory programs. Eventually, a more macroscopic sociological stance began to replace the individualized approach of educational psychology, and emphasis shifted to a comprehensive poverty program, with a heavy educational input.[11]

None of the attempted reforms has revolutionized the condition of education for the poor and the black. The hasty conclusion that each reform was inadequate has led to a renewed search for more effective remedies.[12] In that search, two tendencies predominate. One view considers the chief reason for the failure of the attempted reforms to be the inertia of the school bureaucracies. That is, the reforms themselves are not at issue but our failure to give them sufficient support. According to the second view, it is the reforms that are inadequate because they have missed the point. Even if they had been fully implemented—and those who hold this view agree with the others that they have not been—they would have

[11] See John Seeley's Introduction to Morris Gross, *Learning Readiness in Two Jewish Groups* (New York: Center for Urban Education, 1967), for a brief, useful, and somewhat different summary of recent educational policy.

[12] Hasty, of course, in the typical American way. We promise too much for each proposed reform, invest too little in it, and then profess disappointment with the results. In this regard, see Aaron Wildavsky, "The Empty-head Blues: Black Rebellion and White Reaction," *Public Interest*, No. 11 (Spring 1968), pp. 3–16.

been insufficient, for, in important ways, they would have exacerbated the very conditions they were designed to relieve.

In particular, we are now witness to a specific rejection of what had been generally regarded, and is still regarded by many, as a most enlightened view of educational deprivation. That view, emphasizing environmental disadvantage, argues that the culture of poverty, passed on from parent to child, is educationally disabling, and that the children who are its victims cannot, therefore, be expected to thrive in school. It simultaneously acknowledges inequities in capacity and relieves the incapacitated of any moral blame.

The theory is enlightened insofar as it does not depend on genetic inferiority; on the contrary, it depends upon a relatively sophisticated social psychology. Unfortunately, however, it can also be used to relieve the schools of any fundamental responsibility for inequitable educational results. The argument based on this theory would reason as follows: "We understand how difficult it is and how unfair, therefore, it is to expect low-income (more commonly, disadvantaged) children to do as well as the more affluent. We can, and we shall, try to repair the inequities. But we are only one agency among many, and unless there is basic change in the culture of poverty itself, there are limits to the likelihood of our success." Schools are used to dealing with individuals. The less we blame the individual for his failings, the more we hold the environment responsible; the more we hold the environment responsible, the less we can expect of the school.

There are, however, more serious problems with the now conventional concept of educational disadvantage. Some of these have to do with the validity of the theory, an issue that has already evoked a substantial literature. But even beyond the question of validity we now discover that its application is problematic. This is so not only because it provides a too convenient excuse for the failure of the schools, but because to an even greater extent it has come to be recognized as an untoward self-fulfilling hypothesis. By holding that the poor cannot be held to the same level of academic performance as the affluent, the theory, by its enlightened, even empathic, lowering of expectation has produced a continuing inadequacy in performance.[13] Hence, though the cause of poor performance is now seen as benign, at least so far as the children are concerned (it is now the society at large that is held culpable), it is not necessarily seen as more malleable. Compensation helps, but compensation coupled to reduced expectation reinforces the conviction of both teacher and child that the poor are problem cases.

Out of frustration and impatience with recent approaches at reform, critics have turned in several directions. In the view of some, especially when dealing with New York City, any change is seen as beneficent: ". . . a change—almost any change—would stir the city's schools in useful ways."[14] Here, evidently, the chief problem is seen as systemic rigidity. Others believe that school officials, especially when threatened, cannot—or will not—be relied upon to care enough; thus, "Parents can be trusted to care more than anyone else for the quality of the education their children get."[15] But regardless of the specific remedy proposed, more and more observers agree with the general indictment: ". . . it appears that the present system of organization and functioning of urban public schools is a chief blockage in the mobility of the masses of Negro and other lower-status minority group children."[16]

Thus the search for a villain comes to focus on the organization of the system itself. There is increasing agreement that reorganization of the educational system is, at the very least, a necessary condition (some would also say sufficient) for educational reform. It is important to recognize that, having identified the system as a leading culprit, we are not inevitably led to endorsement of community control, or even of the more innocuous decentralization. Instead, the importance of greater independence, or more expertise, or improved professional standards might have been stressed. It is

[13] A point intriguingly demonstrated in recent experiments, discussed in Robert Rosenthal and Lenore Jacobson, *Pygmalion in the Classroom: Teacher Expectation and Pupils' Intellectual Development* (Holt, Rinehart & Winston, 1968).

[14] Theodore R. Sizer, "Report Analysis," *Harvard Educational Review*, Vol. 38 (Winter 1968), p. 180.

[15] Mayor's Advisory Panel on Decentralization of the New York City Schools, *Reconnection for Learning: A Community School System for New York City* (1967), p. 68.

[16] Kenneth B. Clark, "Alternative Public School Systems," *Harvard Educational Review*, Vol. 38 (Winter 1968), p. 109.

a mark of the unusual level of dissatisfaction that such avenues have, in the main, been rejected in favor of the more radical call for major institutional reorganization.

We should not conclude, however, that the call, widespread though it is, is consensual. The outward appearance of a concerted effort, focused on increasing community participation and control, is, in fact, the least consensual of recent proposals for educational reform. This is true not only because it is a threatening doctrine to many participants in the system, but because even its adherents come to it for diverse reasons and mean by it conflicting things. The earlier alliance of educational reformers has come apart; the appearance of an alliance is a function of the ambiguities of the concepts, the issue to which we now turn.

Those who believe that the schools have been inept in instituting the various reforms of recent years generally blame that ineptitude on conventional bureaucratic resistance to innovation and on a cumbersome bureaucracy. While it is not obvious that decentralization of the bureaucracy is the way to induce innovation, some causal relationship between the two is assumed. Thus, in a recent interview, William Haddad, a member of the New York City Board of Education, argued that "decentralization could aid reform because local election of local school boards could help parents get power that could be 'translated into modernization of the system.' Up to now . . . the New York City system has been plagued by 'heavy bureaucracy that stifles creativeness.' "[17]

In its simplest version, the thrust toward decentralization is based on insights derived from administrative theory. It is a traditional argument with immediate appeal only in large school systems, and it is not necessarily linked to the call for greater community control. It is logically possible, for example, to seek at the same time both greater decentralization and greater insulation from politics—hence continuing insulation from public control.

The movement toward community control, as distinct from decentralization, derives not so much from the general crisis of effec-

[17] As reported in the *New York Times*, Sept. 8, 1968, p. 51. Note also that Haddad is speaking of a specific form of decentralization, one in which parents would have some power over local school officials.

tiveness of the schools, but rather from the specific failure of the schools in dealing with the poor, and, more particularly, with black children. Indeed, it is unthinkable that we would now witness so dramatic a turn of interest to community control were it not for the civil rights movement and the crisis in black and white relations in America. Although the crystallization of support grows out of diverse experiences—in some cases the recognition that integration is demographically improbable, in others the conviction that white school boards will never provide the necessary resources to black schools and will be sluggish about integration, and in still others a more direct response to the general doctrine of participatory democracy—it is an aspect of the civil rights struggle rather than of educational reform per se. It draws from a different and much more recent tradition, and it carries with it, therefore, substantially different implications. It is not, for the most part, that the administrative reformers, seeking decentralization, and the political reformers, seeking community control, have converged upon a common stance. The appearance of commonality is, as noted, a function, first, of ambiguity, and second, of an occasional similarity in views between some of the variations on the broader themes.

Thus, among the administrative reformers, there are those who believe that community control is the only tactic that has a chance of achieving the goal of decentralization. And, among black supporters of community control, there is a significant number whose advocacy is less political than educational in origin. Their view, briefly, is that black children have special educational needs, and that preeminent among those is exposure to positive role models and knowledge of their own past. These specific needs have little validity in and of themselves but must be met in order to unblock the impediments to general learning. Variants of this approach stress the inevitable racism of white teachers, or the inequity in the distribution of educational investments by school boards oriented to white middle-class children.

But the powerful thrust toward community control goes far beyond the simple allegation of ineffectiveness. Together with black reformers interested particularly in educational reform, the advocates of community control view the present system as grossly ineffective, but they go on to insist that ineffectiveness is a necessary corollary of the prevailing educational structure. Community control is no longer seen as merely one way to revitalize a rigid system but as the only way in which the school system can be made legitimate. In the extreme version of this perspective, the present school system, as managed by whites, would be no more acceptable even if the various indexes of performance were suddenly transformed. This is so because the overriding crisis of the schools is one of goals, not performance.

We may describe these several positions in somewhat different language. One widely shared perspective holds that the essential problem of the schools, insofar as they fail black children, is related to differential inputs; either there is systematic discrimination in favor of white schools or there is insufficient sensitivity to the extra needs of black children, occasioned by their impoverished environment. These discriminatory inputs are identified as the chief reason for the inequitable outputs of the educational system. But the contrasting view questions whether equitable outputs—where equitable means standard—are desirable. It is this second view that links up logically rather than merely tactically with the concept of community control,[18] and is at the heart of the present debate between white liberals and black militants. So long as the issue is administrative reform, or educational reform, or even the need to recognize differential content as a way of achieving uniform results, there is little disagreement, for the discussion falls within the tradition of educational debate. But it is when the issue is political-ideological reform that the debate sharpens, for there appears to be no precedent for such a debate.

It is too easy to dismiss the opposition to community control as either a masked form of bigotry or a case of conservative bureaucratic response to threatened change. Such opposition tends to be noisy and serves, therefore, to obscure the deep bias against community control of many liberal intellectuals who have traditionally supported both educational reform and civil rights. Yet it is the

[18] I am aware that some would argue that racism is so powerfully institutionalized in America that inequities in input can only be remedied by permitting blacks greater autonomy over the institutions that serve them. Even if this view is accepted—and I find it exaggerated—it is not at all clear how it solves the problem of inequitable investment.

ideological opposition of intellectual liberals that may be the more important block to achieving community control, for their opposition, if it continues, puts an end to an alliance that has, in recent years, enjoyed astounding political success. When school boards whose power would be undone, or teachers' organizations concerned with tenure, or bigots who oppose anything Negroes favor, oppose community control, that is to be expected. But when liberals part company with the civil rights movement over the issue of community control, some explanation must be sought, for the reasons are not obvious.

At the beginning of this chapter, it was suggested that many liberals had shifted from an enthusiastic espousal of professional control to a more community-oriented position. Further elaboration is now necessary. While some have moved toward positions favoring administrative and educational reforms, which do not emphasize professionalism nearly as much as leading doctrines did a decade ago but which fall short of endorsing community control, others—far fewer—have, indeed, moved to support political reform, or community control per se. But many have not moved at all and are, as noted, deeply troubled by the current thrust of their former allies. Their trouble derives from their recognition that what black militants now seek violates the basis of the liberal tradition in fundamental ways.

The liberal commitment, in education as in other spheres, is to universalism. We approach liberal salvation as we move from the sacred to the secular, from *Gemeinschaft* to *Gesellschaft*, from folk society to urban society, from tradition through charisma to rational bureaucracy. The liberation of man, which is the aim of secular wisdom, proceeds on diverse fronts: liberation from nature, achieved through science; liberation from bondage, achieved through law; liberation from self, achieved through psychoanalysis; liberation from myth, achieved through education; liberation from the past, achieved through commitment to progress; liberation from the confines of time and space, achieved through intellectual and physical mobility, through the good offices of the mass media. At the very least, scholars have generally seen the process of secularization as inevitable: "Secularization . . . and its concomitant rationalization may be good, or it may be bad, but it is our destiny. . . . To him who cannot manfully bear this destiny . . . the doors of the old churches stand forgivingly open . . . if he will but make 'the sacrifice of the intellect.' "[19]

The descriptive proposition that modern, industrial society requires a transformation of folk culture requires no elaboration. It is a central precept of virtually all the social sciences, and especially of students of modernization, as the following two quotations illustrate:

> Relationships among individuals [in small groups] . . . are mainly *ascribed* (fixed by birth or other involuntary membership), *diffuse* (covering a wide and open-ended range of rights and duties), and *particularistic* (based on particular relations to particular persons or statuses, not on generalized, impersonal rules). In modern complex societies, the four basic structures [kinship, territorial community, social stratification, and ethnic grouping] are interlaced and overlaid by economic and political systems that are organized in considerable part on radically different principles—the principles of achieved, competitive placement rather than ascription by birth, of impersonal universalistic norms, and of highly specific, narrowly defined relations among persons. Also, in our society [the United States], the major religious traditions all stress universalism in the ethical domain.[20]

> . . . the passage from "traditional" to "modern" society . . . involves a complex set of changes in the organization of the society and in man's perspective on his society. There is a movement from identification with primary groups to identification with secondary groups, from social norms in which status is derived from inherited place in the order (ascription) to the function that one performs in society and how well one performs it (achievement). It is a movement toward more complex, highly differentiated and specialized social institutions and social roles. Life becomes less viewed as a whole, less diffuse, within the setting of the village and traditional agriculture. . . . Modern society [similarly] requires a different sort of political order, one serviceable to a much expanded notion of the relevant community, as the scope of social life changes from the order of the village to the order of the nation.[21]

But more than simple description is generally implied in such characterizations of the process of modernization. For liberal intellectuals have cast their own lot with the forces of modernization, and

[19] Max Weber, "Wissenschaft als Beruf" ("Science as a Vocation"), in *Gesammelte Aufsätze zur Wissenschaftslehre*, translated and cited in Howard Becker and Harry Elmer Barnes, *Social Thought From Lore to Science* (Dover, 1961), p. 770.

[20] Robin M. Williams, Jr., *Strangers Next Door: Ethnic Relations in American Communities* (Prentice-Hall, 1964), p. 356.

[21] Charles W. Anderson, Fred R. von der Mehden, and Crawford Young, *Issues of Political Development* (Prentice-Hall, 1967), pp. 4–5.

hence with secularism, rationality, and universalism, and against tradition, ritual, and—community. As Robert Nisbet has pointed out, "To regard all evil as a persistence or revival of the past has been a favorite conceit of liberals nourished by the idea of Progress. . . . Present evils could safely be regarded as regrettable evidences of incomplete emancipation from the past—from tribalism, from agrarianism, religion, localism, and the like. In one form or another, the theory of cultural lag has been the secular approach to the problem of evil."[22] Or, "The demands of freedom appeared to be in the direction of the release of large numbers of individuals from the statuses and identities that had been forged in them by the dead hand of the past. A free society would be one in which individuals were morally and socially as well as politically free, free from groups and classes. . . . Freedom would arise from the individual's release from all the inherited personal interdependencies of traditional community, and from his existence in an impersonal, natural, economic order."[23]

It might seem that decades of experience with the recalcitrance of parochial loyalties would have subverted the liberal commitment. Indeed, there are a number of scholars who grapple seriously with the recurring evidence of the urge to community and an even greater literature that expresses skepticism about man's capacity to cope with the new freedom.[24] Some manage to retain their optimism in the face of the evidence:

> Human beings throughout the world are fundamentally alike. They share a common anatomical structure; they all have the ability to engage in reflective thought; and they share a pool of common sentiments. Hence, whenever social distance is reduced, individuals recognize their resemblances. The basic differences between ethnic groups are cultural, and conventional norms serve as masks to cover the similarities. Whenever men interact informally, the common human nature comes through. It would appear, then, that it is only a matter of time before a more en-

[22] Robert A. Nisbet, *Community and Power* (Oxford University Press, 1962), p. 214.

[23] *Ibid.*, p. 22.

[24] The examples are numerous, but see especially Nisbet, *Community and Power*; Gabriel A. Almond and Sidney Verba, *The Civic Culture: Political Attitudes and Democracy in Five Nations, An Analytic Study* (Little, Brown, 1965); Scott Greer, *The Emerging City: Myth and Reality* (Free Press, 1962); Nathan Glazer and Daniel P. Moynihan, *Beyond the Melting Pot* (MIT Press, 1963).

lightened citizenry will realize this. Then, there will be a realignment of group loyalties, and ethnic identity will become a thing of the past.[25]

Most, even when sensitive to man's reluctance to assume the burdens of freedom, take the evidence to mean that we still have a long way to go, not that we may be going in the wrong direction.

Liberal commitment to the secular city is supported by the American myth of the melting pot. The commitment is not total; some instances of the survival of folk culture are still viewed as quaint rather than threatening. Nevertheless, the traditional liberal perspective maintains its utopian commitment to a world of universal brotherhood, a world in which the private community would be obsolete.

Insofar as the educational system promotes the secular ideal, it conforms to the liberal perspective. For this reason the public school has always emphasized liberty and equality over fraternity, except when fraternity has been understood to encompass all mankind. Relying heavily on the storied experience of New York City during the days of its heavy in-migration, liberals have seen the public schools as society's best hope for achieving comprehensive integration.

From this broad perspective, a number of specific theorems derive: The schools should embrace heterogeneous populations; schools are to be ethically neutral, except for their endorsement of the scientific ethic; the curriculum is to be secular, and is to emphasize the shared culture; school personnel should be selected and advanced according to their merits, the best approximation being the civil service laws; children fail for idiosyncratic (individual) reasons, or because of insufficient funds or wisdom, not because they occupy a special stratum in society.

These several beliefs are directly at odds with the theses now propounded by defenders of community schools. In fact, they conform quite closely to the views of the present educational establishment in most cities. The reason for this is that most establishment managers, no matter how conservative in their administrative behavior, are liberals in their social ideology. Moreover, nothing in these views logically requires a commitment to intense centralization of author-

[25] Tamotsu Shibutani and Kian M. Kwan, *Ethnic Stratification: A Comparative Approach* (Macmillan, 1965), p. 589.

ity. Therefore, the decentralizers, too, can share the social theory, even though they dispute the administrative arrangement. And that is why the difference between school authorities and administrative reformers, however obstinate, is not logically fundamental.

It is evident that Negroes have always been a special case in the history of integration in America. But traditional liberal ideology has had no difficulty in embracing the question of race. Over the years, the central tenet of liberals, when dealing with race, has been to assert its irrelevance. The argument has been that color is an accidental characteristic, which, in the truly rational, liberated, social order, ceases to have any empirical correlates. Acknowledging the gap between reality and norm, liberals actively oppose reality. The main thrust of the civil rights movement has been, therefore, in the direction of persuading white America to become color-blind. The corollary of the liberal ethic that white people ought not pay attention to the blackness of Negroes was the proposition that Negroes ought not pay attention to their own blackness.

It is arguable whether such an approach might have worked. In the event, of course, it did not, for continuing white reluctance to ignore blackness made it impossible for blacks to ignore it. Hence, the movement toward black consciousness and black pride, toward black community.

But the emergence of community consciousness among blacks flagrantly violates the traditional liberal ethic of universalism. It parochializes society instead of secularizing it; it evokes a mystical bond instead of a rational contract.

Liberal guilt over white failings permits many white liberals to accept the new direction of the black community, at least in part, albeit always with the hope that society will move fast enough to "outgrow" the need for community soon. But liberal commitments to the secular city prevent an even larger number of liberals from any empathy with present directions of the civil rights movement.[26] Hence, we are witness to an increasingly problematic relationship among historic allies.

The linkage of these general issues, here so briefly touched upon,

[26] One mark of the historic success of liberals is the persistent acceptance of secularism as utopia by the masses of Afro-Americans.

to the question of community control is quite specific, and more basic even than rejection, by liberals, of so explicit an assertion of community—though that is a major aspect. The liberal axiom that society is an aggregate of independent individuals, rather than an organic compact of groups, necessarily points to a polity in which all legitimate authority is vested in the state.[27] Assertion that a sacred entity[28] should be viewed as a legitimate partner to the secular authority threatens not only the institutions of liberal society but its assumptions as well; the movement toward community control is a profound rejection of the core of liberal ideology.

If Negroes were not involved, but some other ethnic community, the battle would be far more intense, for liberals would doubtless recognize the threat and act with vigor to reduce it. It takes only memory, not imagination, to visualize the intensity of liberal rejection of parochial management of the schools, whether the parochialism is expressed by Southerners opposed to integration, Rotarians opposed to the *New Republic*, or Catholics committed to prayer in the schools. Lieberman has expressed the dominant liberal mood of the 1950s: " . . . national survival now requires educational policies and programs which are not subject to local veto. . . . It is becoming increasingly clear that local control cannot in practice be reconciled with the ideals of a democratic society. . . . Local control is a major cause of the dull parochialism and attenuated totalitarianism that characterizes public education in operation."[29] As it is, the reaction of white liberals to black people is so mixed with guilt, with patronization, and with anxiety that the force of liberal opposition to the parochial threat is blunted.

In short, insofar as liberals have countenanced the concept of community at all, they have sought what Scott Greer calls "the community of limited liability," a community based on either shared taste, shared neighborhood, or shared specific interest.[30] This is quite different from the diffuse organic community, based as

[27] This point is elaborated by Nisbet, *Community and Power*, passim.

[28] "Sacred" as Becker uses the term, to distinguish nonrational ties from the secular rational. See Howard Becker, *Through Values to Social Interpretation; Essays on Social Contexts, Actions, Types, and Prospects* (Duke University Press, 1950).

[29] Lieberman, *The Future of Public Education*, p. 34.

[30] *The Emerging City*, Chap. 4, pp. 107–37.

much on mystique as on reason, acting as a primary group to its members and speaking a private tongue.[31] Black people, in increasing numbers, having despaired of their acceptance under the terms of liberal writ, have begun to emphasize the organic community. What debate there is among black militants on this issue is over the question of whether building community is a temporary tactic (the community will be used as a springboard into the secular society) or an end goal (black separatism).

Once the underlying logic of community is understood, we can also move toward an understanding of the position of the political reformers. Their position does not depend, as so many white radicals think, on a romantic belief in the inherent wisdom of "the people." Their insight is not that black parents are more likely to provide effective educational programs for black children than white professionals are but rather that black parents (or their agents) are the legitimate managers of such schools; whites are not and cannot be. The schools, in short, are to be community schools in a sense that differs dramatically from previous usage in American educational history. They are to belong to a community that is defined organically rather than contractually, and their ownership by the community will in turn help to establish the point that the community does exist as a legitimate social entity.

They are political reformers precisely because their insistence on the legitimacy of community is inevitably associated with an equal insistence on the need for a redistribution of power within the society. The issue of power—less relevant, perhaps, to other ethnic groups, which were neither so systematically excluded from power nor so dependent on politics as a source of power—is not a specific aspect of educational theory, nor even simply a way of guaranteeing sufficient attention to black children. It is rather a corollary of a social theory requiring that communities within the whole be made viable. Acceptance of the concept of organic community necessarily points to decentralization; acceptance of the desirability of educational reform does not.

[31] Recognizing implicitly the legitimacy of a private language, some educators have proposed that black children be taught middle-class English as a second language, rather than as the correct replacement of the natural language.

In this view, therefore, the question of whether the schools, if managed by blacks, could do a better job than they are now doing, or even a better job than they might do if various proposed administrative and educational reforms were instituted, becomes meaningless. For the word "better" can only be taken to mean better according to some secular standards, and it is precisely those standards that are now rejected. The purpose of teaching black children African languages is not solely to develop in them the kind of confidence and pride that will then permit them to do better work in the conventional curriculum; it is ideological rather than tactical. The theory is highly specific; there is no intimation that the schools ought to be controlled by their neighborhoods, a view held by some white liberals. Instead, the theory holds that organic communities of interest—which may, coincidentally, be neighborhood based—be considered legitimate. The schools are not, then, ineffective simply because they are badly organized or ignorantly operated but because they lack legitimacy. And they lack legitimacy because they are incapable of taking into account the special requirements of diverse groups. This incapacity is most serious for blacks, for other groups that feel they have special needs can often bend the system to their needs *sotto voce*, without appearing to disturb the secular norms of the system.

In brief, blacks are treated particularistically and ascriptively, but are held to universalist standards of achievement. The administrative and educational reformers seek to change the treatment; the political reformers, despairing of change in the treatment, seek to change the standards. They thereby endorse a theory of social structure that is directly at odds with the prevailing liberal theory.

I have deliberately cast the views of the political reformers in starker relief than the reformers most often see them. I have done so not only because the implications of diverse views require clarification but because a continued rupture in black-white relations will doubtless lead increasing numbers to explicit articulation of extreme positions.

There are those who take comfort from an alleged cyclicality in political tides, which permits them to assume that any stage of the moment will pass in due course. While it is likely that if the schools had been more effective in dealing with the needs of black students, the crisis of legitimacy would be less marked, it would be a mistake to view the new political demands as part of a cyclical reordering of social emphases. The increasingly explicit rejection of a social theory that is deeply embedded in the nation's consciousness is new, and quite possibly irreversible.[32] That is why the emergence of this new doctrine is greeted with so much discomfort by the liberal community. Even when the argument is not explicit, there is an almost instinctive hostility to so marked a departure from the American past and the American belief.

There are a limited number of ways in which the conflict among the several doctrines of reform might be resolved or, at least, reduced. The most obvious is to make the schools more effective—that is, to operate on the theory that a surplus of effectiveness would obscure the question of legitimacy. This is a respectable social strategy, based on the premise that people with full stomachs are unlikely revolutionaries. According to the evidence of the polls, most Negroes remain persuaded of the viability of traditional integrative theory, and there is no question that a sudden and dramatic improvement in the performance of the traditional system vis-à-vis the Negro community would undermine the appeal of the new parochialism.

Such a development seems unlikely, however, especially in the area of education, which is probably the least tractable in which society now seeks to improve conditions for black people. If I am correct in assuming that no dramatic improvement in the effectiveness of the schools is forthcoming, what possibilities exist for a change in the traditional view of legitimacy? In other words, to what extent is it reasonable to anticipate that the doctrine of the political reformers will gain adherents among white liberals?

[32] At least it is irreversible without dramatic, and quite unlikely, change in the performance of the system. It is the failure of the schools and, more broadly, the failure of universalist theory when applied to Negroes that gave rise to the new departure, but that departure will, in time, become divorced from its origins, achieving a self-sustaining status. The departure is new enough, and fragile enough, not to be able to stand on its own yet; but it gains currency daily, and thus loses its dependence on its origins.

The present tempest in America has led to some shifts in the conventional liberal perspective. In particular, the notion that the nation is best governed by a highly centralized bureaucracy has begun to lose respectability, and it is possible that the commitment to a secular bureaucracy will, similarly, weaken. Some liberals do argue for suspension of the civil service regulations in specific instances, although this deviation from tradition is countered by the continuing commitment to national standards on key policy issues. It is, however, folly to predict a major ideological transformation, since the sources of such transformations remain so mysterious.

There is some logical relationship between the doctrine of participatory democracy and a parochialization of social theory. Obviously, the more power that is provided to people to make their own political rules, the more likely those rules are to be particularistic rather than universal. At this stage in the movement toward participatory democracy, however, it seems no more warranted to predict its eventual victory than to suggest that its limits will be set by its threat to the secular tendencies of the system.

There is, then, one mode of reconciliation left, admittedly, a rather academic mode, worth more as solace than as program. It is to accept that the social system has never been as secular in its operation as the norm of universalism implies or as many American liberals generally suppose. The evidence for this view is somewhat speculative, but three different arguments lend it weight.

First, there is the persistence of ethnic identities, not only as a psychological phenomenon but also as reflected in the economy. Different groups have established themselves in different sectors, and their persistence as identifiable groups, in the face of a social ideology that is chilly toward them, suggests that they cannot be dismissed lightly as an aberrant anachronism. As Glazer asserts, "The ethnic group in American society [has become] not a survival from the age of mass immigration but a new social form."[33] Whether this new form is benighted, as the ideology suggests and scholars often assert, or is socially functional, is beside the point; it exists, and belies the inevitability of secularization.

[33] Glazer and Moynihan, *Beyond the Melting Pot*, p. 16.

Second, it can be argued that the political system itself has not been as secular as is assumed. Such an argument has genuine validity in the case of black Americans, who have obviously not been encompassed by the doctrine of universalism. The current challenges to American political institutions, and especially to universities, suggests that this argument may be valid in other spheres as well. Those challenges may be interpreted as a rejection of elaborate institutions which profess their neutrality but which, in fact, operate to the advantage of particular groups within the society. Moreover, institutions play favorites independently of the good will of those who manage them, since the rules of the game and institutional inertia conspire to overwhelm modest efforts at reform. What is obvious with respect to Negroes is no less true, if less obvious: the structure of the system, which is to say, of our institutions, and the rules according to which they are managed, preserve a reality of particularism and of ascription, elaborately disguised by a mythology of universalism and achievement-orientation.

Third, despite the prevailing myth that education is a secular institution, the history of the schools can, and should, be read as an example of creative tension between the particular and the universal. The standard compromise has been to create largely parochial structures while emphasizing fundamentally universal content. On the face of it, this seems an implausible development, since conventional sociology informs us that there is necessarily an identity between structure and content. But if the two tendencies are viewed, after Parsons and Shils,[34] as representing a continuing dilemma, it becomes clear how they might have been played off against one another. Unable or unwilling to commit itself wholly to the one choice or the other, society has managed, however improbably, to sustain both together.

The operational implication of this failure to choose, if it is to be continued, is, first, that the best of two worlds may be available, or, at least, the worst of both may be avoided. There is, after all, a cyclicality to these affairs, and the balance, most recently heavily

[34] Talcott Parsons and Edward A. Shils (eds.), *Toward a General Theory of Action* (Harvard University Press, 1954), esp. Parsons and Shils, "Values, Motives, and Systems of Action," pp. 45–275.

weighted toward the universalist norm, now needs to be adjusted to favor the particularistic. This implies a greater openness to community control as long as certain universalist criteria are maintained.

In other words, the fear of balkanizing the society through endorsement of community schools would be warranted only if many other institutions, and particularly the mass media of communication, were not on the side of nationalizing, hence secularizing, education. If all the secular educational inputs are added together, a school system based on more parochial claims may seem less threatening to the traditional ideology and more a way of preserving some balance between consensus and diversity.

Further, we must emphasize the degree to which universalist doctrine is fundamentally normative rather than descriptive. Liberals who insist on applying universal norms are unable to make exceptions for black people without undermining their fundamental ideological commitments. They therefore either reject current Negro demands or rise to defend community control of the schools as if it were a helpful doctrine everywhere, a position few of them seriously entertain. The obvious resolution of this problem is to recognize the exceptional position of the black community—exceptional because of history, exceptional because of current needs, and exceptional particularly by virtue of the growing degree of community consciousness. It is difficult, of course, for liberals to accommodate such exceptions, to recognize that what may be good, or appropriate, or legitimate for one group need not be a secular standard for all groups. But such recognition is bound to be less tortured than the continued rejection of the demands, on the one hand, or the fatuous endorsement of the demands as a new and comprehensive norm for the entire educational system, on the other.

Yet, on the whole, there is little reason to be sanguine about the ability of the system to sustain the historic compromise between the universal and the particular. It was easier to sustain when it was not so explicit as it now threatens to become. Once choices are clearly outlined and seen as alternatives, it becomes difficult to avoid choosing. The social change we now witness, unless we successfully—and improbably—opt again for compromise, will lead in sinister directions. Scott Greer suggests, wisely and sadly, that as contemporary social change

> . . . leads to efforts at predictability by the actors in one organization, these efforts tend to result in merger, accommodation, the rationalizing of the organizational environment. Thus, the networks of interdependence in the society continually expand, and from interdependence evolves an increasingly large organizational system. The more complex and mutually contingent the resulting social structure, the fewer its alternative courses of development. The way back to a simpler, smaller-scale society, is barred in the near future at least by the commitments necessary to insure the survival of the one that exists: only catastrophe can radically transform the evolution.[35]

To be sure, one man's catastrophe is another man's romp, but the trouble with catastrophe is that one can never be sure whether what follows the flood is the dove or a swamp. It is most curious that the warning of social science that the mass, undifferentiated, atomized society—that is, the secular society—is psychologically disabling, socially chaotic, and politically unstable has not led to a more critical questioning of the validity and utility of liberal ideology. It is, to say the least, cynical to undermine the ideological foundations of community and then to express disgust with the results. We need not agree with Goethe that "the thrill of holy dread is the best trait of mankind" in order to accept Tocqueville: "A highly civilized community spurns the attempts of a local independence, is disgusted at its numerous blunders, and is apt to despair of success before the experiment is completed. . . . Nevertheless local assemblies of citizens constitute the strength of free nations."[36]

[35] Greer, *The Emerging City*, pp. 206–07.

[36] Alexis de Tocqueville, *Democracy in America* (Schocken Books, 1961), pp. 54–55.

ROBERT C. MAYNARD

Black Nationalism and Community Schools

The search for methods by which black people can control those institutions and areas that affect them is not new. It has only burst upon the consciousness of this generation of Americans as a surprise for two reasons: first, the preoccupation since the end of World War II with the ethic of assimilation, an ethic that often has lacked the substance of any real attainment, and, second, the failure of the commonly taught version of American history to explain what David Walker and Denmark Vesey were all about.[1] Had history been properly taught, the roles of Walker and others in the Abolition Movement of the middle 1800s would have been well known. These men worked diligently to wrest control of that movement from those who wanted blacks to accept less than full equality within the movement for their own liberation. It is curious that abolitionist history is taught through the eyes and mouths of Wendell Phillips and William Lloyd Garrison and not David Walker or Frederick Douglass.[2] When blacks today say they want to control the manner in which their history is taught, they are saying that their heroes are hidden by history and that the tradition of black resistance to oppression has been all but blotted out.

The framework for discussion about the current drive for libera-

[1] For an account of this history, see Lerone Bennett, Jr., *Before the Mayflower: A History of the Negro in America, 1619–1964* (Penguin, 1966).

[2] A discussion of this other viewpoint is contained in Lerone Bennett, Jr., *Pioneers in Protest* (Johnson, 1968), and Benjamin Quarles, *Frederick Douglass* (Prentice-Hall, 1968).

tion is simply this: From the dawn of slavery to the last black student uprising, black Americans have been resisting attempts to qualify their humanhood with dual definitions of what is a man.

Slightly less than fifty years ago, a black nationalist named Marcus Garvey led a movement—Universal Negro Improvement Association—with the goal of uniting black people the world over into a single unified movement with a homeland in Africa.[3] By the 1930s his movement was dead and nationalism as a serious political force among black Americans was not to rise again until the 1950s.

By the time Malcolm X and the Lost Found Nation of Islam (commonly known as Black Muslims) parted company in 1964, one thing was clear: Together they had ridden and helped create a wave of new militancy and nationalism in the nation's black urban centers. While Malcolm X preached the commonality of destiny of blacks and colored peoples, his principal mission was the unification of black Americans into a potent political force.[4] His own voice in that drive was silenced by death in 1965; nonetheless, the movement has become the basis for contemporary black ideological activism.

While Malcom's drive was to unify a nation of blacks, the nationalistic voices that emerged from the movement spoke of the nation in terms of units. Men such as James Boggs and Albert Cleage of Detroit evolved the concept of control of the city.[5] Boggs outlined his doctrine in "The City Is the Black Man's Land," which appeared in *Monthly Review* in April 1966. No less a nationalist than Malcolm, Bogg's formulation was one way of defining territoriality: since blacks predominated in the cities, the land of the city should be theirs.

The common thread that binds Garvey to Malcolm and Malcolm to Boggs is that all have sought to exact from the existing political system a living space controlled by blacks. There is no black Israel, which is basically what Garvey was promulgating twenty-five years before it existed for the Jews; there is no separate state, as Malcolm would have wished, but Boggs' concept of city control is being approached, although it is not yet achieved.

[3] See E. David Cronon, *Black Moses* (University of Wisconsin Press, 1955).

[4] Malcolm's position emerges clearly in *The Autobiography of Malcolm X*, with the assistance of Alex Haley (Grove Press, 1965).

[5] For a discussion of this concept, see Robert Maynard, "Integration: A Nearly Forgotten Goal," Pt. 2 of "The Black Revolution," *Washington Post*, Sept. 25, 1967, p. 1.

What each of these men has defined is the expression of the search by black people in America for a community of their own. Blacks, having found no appreciable success with larger units of space, have turned today to the community, intended here to mean a spatial unit smaller than a city. Yet even within that relatively small scope, specific entities are sought, almost as though a people in search of a mountain are scouring the plains for pebbles; as shall be seen later, they seek enough pebbles to build a mountain of their own. And again, as it was in the time of Garvey and since, underlying black nationalism is precisely what its name implies: to make of black people, wherever they are, a nation.

Thus, the role of black nationalism in community schools is a dual one. First, the schools are, in the cosmic sense, pebbles. Second, if there is ever to be a mountain, it will depend for its success on the zeal with which the young build it. Where is there a better place to draw them a picture of a mountain than in a schoolroom?

Black nationalism has other goals at the community level, principally concerning commerce and the police. But the schools are being focused upon as all important to the fostering of the ethic of black pride and black self-determination since a people who seek their liberation from a colonialist system must control what is being taught to their young. Because the foundation of nationalism is that blacks are a nation within a nation, it rejects the notion that integration is synonymous with equality. It argues that demanding a place for black children in a white school system is an admission of inherent black inferiority.

Rejecting the suggestion that "Negroes must be integrated into middle class white schools," Floyd B. McKissick, former national director of the Congress of Racial Equality, has said that such a suggestion is "saying mix Negroes with Negroes and you get stupidity. . . . Maybe a school committed to respect the individual, a school enjoying the confidence and support of the community, a school recognized to reflect its faith in the pupil and the parent can achieve excellence—even if that community is poor and black."[6]

Things appear to have moved backward in time from 1954 (*Brown* v. *Board of Education of Topeka*)[7] to 1895 (*Plessy* v. *Ferguson*).[8]

[6] *Ibid.* [7] 347 U.S. 483 (1954). [8] 163 U.S. 537 (1895).

The Plessy case, involving segregated street cars in New Orleans, became the basis for a wide range of segregation laws that swept the South in reaction to Reconstruction. Accompanied by a reign of white terror, these laws set the stage for the great migration from the South to northern cities, which reached its zenith between 1910 and 1920.[9] Poor blacks on the move searched in the cities for the answer to a hunger for community, for a place to be what they could not be in the South because Reconstruction had failed them. Thus, they sought a new "reconstruction" in the North. The record of their failure was written with blood in East St. Louis, Illinois, in 1917 and with fire in Watts in 1965.[10]

In the interim, there was *Brown*. The Brown case set off a chain reaction across the country that promised a new day for black Americans. Declaring the *Plessy* doctrine of "separate but equal" unconstitutional, the Supreme Court further said that separate implied unequal. The court was unequivocal. The drive for integration was on in earnest.

Martin Luther King, Jr., resuming the battle that Plessy had lost a half century before, went after the segregated buses of Montgomery, Alabama, and Jim Crow fell.[11] There were marches, sit-ins, summer projects in the South, boycotts in the North and South, bussing in the North, marches on Washington—then suddenly, the voices for integration fell silent. On a day in June 1966, a veteran of the cause raised his hand and said, "Nothun's changed. We want black power."[12]

For Stokely Carmichael and many who followed him in black nationalism—as they followed him in his pursuit of integration—the search for community within the white society had failed.[13] He,

[9] See John Hope Franklin, "The Two Worlds of Race: A Historical View," *Daedalus*, Vol. 94 (Fall 1965), pp. 908–11.

[10] For the history of these failures, see John P. Davis (ed.), *The American Negro Reference Book* (Prentice-Hall, 1966), pp. 61–64, and Robert E. Conot, *Rivers of Blood, Years of Darkness* (Morrow, 1968).

[11] An account of this struggle is contained in Martin Luther King, Jr., *Stride Toward Freedom: the Montgomery Story* (Harper & Row, 1958).

[12] For a vivid description of the meaning of black power, see Stokely Carmichael, "What We Want," *New York Review of Books*, Vol. 7 (Sept. 22, 1966).

[13] For a full discussion of this transition, see Stokely Carmichael and Charles V. Hamilton, *Black Power: The Politics of Liberation in America* (Random House, 1967).

McKissick, and many of the leaders of the Negro drive of the early 1960s turned to the concept of community control as the only answer. Carmichael now said, "Black people must control the institutions of their communities."

To be sure, not all of those who support the concept of community control of the schools are black nationalists. Many believe that by decentralization the schools will become more responsive to the needs of the children and their parents. But this belief coincides with a widely held black nationalist belief that black Americans have reached a point where they want to go it alone, having as little as possible to do with whites and confining their political activism to gaining total control of the land and institutions that surround and serve them. Up to now, these institutions—particularly the schools—have been viewed as insensitive to the needs of poor blacks and capable of damaging already fragile psyches by instilling even deeper senses of inferiority. This point has been thoroughly documented by such writers as Kenneth Clark, Jonathan Kozol, Herbert Kohl, and David P. Rogers.[14]

The period following the Brown decision ending de jure school segregation in the South was accompanied by demands in the North for an end to de facto segregation. In New York City, parents kept several Harlem schools closed with boycotts in 1959 and 1960, demanding that the school board alter its pupil assignment policies. Later, proposals to break up persistent segregated patterns, based on rigid residential segregation, touched off political storms in cities such as New York, Chicago, and Boston. Whites, regardless of the serious condition of ghetto schools, were not willing to share their schools with blacks, even on a token basis. Still, there was sufficient controversy over the benefits of such integration to raise questions in the minds of Negro parents.

But many believe that the burden for the failure of integration rested neither with the parents nor the children but with the big-

[14] Kenneth B. Clark, *Dark Ghetto* (Harper & Row, 1965); Jonathan Kozol, *Death at an Early Age: The Destruction of the Hearts and Minds of Negro Children in the Boston Public Schools* (Houghton Mifflin, 1967); Herbert R. Kohl, *36 Children* (New American Library, 1967); David Rogers, *110 Livingston Street: Politics and Bureaucracy in the New York City Schools* (Random House, 1968).

city school boards. Here is one judgment on the New York City Board of Education:

Ironically the demand for decentralization or, more properly, community control of the schools began with the failure of the central board to effectively implement integration. Board of Education administrators often said that they could not and would not "tell the principals how to run their schools." Integration failed at least partly because it was resisted by many principals, and because the system was already administratively decentralized to the point where recalcitrant principals were not forced to comply with Board policy on integration.

Integration was not abandoned by black parents but by the Board of Education. The demand for community control was a direct response by ghetto residents to the lack of access to decision-making processes that vitally affected the lives of their children.[15]

Samuel Bowles, Harvard economist, carried the point one step further:

Decision-making in the educational system is a sensitive barometer of the power relations within a society. The selection processes, the promotion probabilities, and the formulation of educational policy reflect who really counts and who really governs.

Raising Negro achievement levels confers definite benefits on those directly involved, and on many not so directly involved. But if we view the individual gains from education in relative rather than absolute terms, equality of educational opportunity is a two-way street. Some stand to benefit by it and others stand to lose. The competition for places in good colleges and the competition for good jobs must cause many white parents to regard the narrowing of racial discrepancies in educational opportunity with mixed feelings, or worse.

And Professor Bowles concludes that it may be necessary to

. . . broaden our attack and attempt to increase the degree of participation in educational decision-making and to transfer power to groups presently excluded from influence. . . .

Let us continue to ask *what* school policies should be adopted. But let us also ask *who* should decide, and *how*.[16]

Of all those working for community control of schools, the group least likely to disagree with Bowles would be the nationalists in the

[15] New York Civil Liberties Union, *The Burden of Blame: A Report on the Ocean Hill-Brownsville School Controversy*, quoted from *I.F. Stone's Weekly*, Vol. 16 (Nov. 4, 1968), p. 3.

[16] Samuel Bowles, "Towards Equality of Educational Opportunity?" *Harvard Educational Review*, Vol. 38 (Winter 1968), pp. 98–99.

black community. For their goal, in broad terms, is to effect a transfer of political power in the black community while also improving the quality of education. They believe community-controlled schools to be the solution to those quests.

James Garrett, former director of Black Studies at the Federal City College in Washington, D.C., challenges the legitimacy of the present system:

> In a situation in which there are thousands of dropouts from elementary schools and junior high schools, the questions that must be raised are not whether there is something wrong with the children or their mothers or fathers, but whether there is something wrong with the educational system.
>
> They say that black children's attention spans are short. Is that true? Has anybody tried to gear the educational system toward their needs? Why is it that white children can sit and hear high-flown rhetoric all day long and dig it? And why is it that black children can sit and listen to records all day long and dig that? Are their attention spans short? Or is it that the information they receive has nothing to do with what they're doing every day? Why is it that black children who can't even sign their own names know how to spell respect?[17]

It should be said here that there is a deep concern among black parents in this country that the urban school systems have become a relentless and unstoppable machine, grinding down the creative qualities of their children. They see, as Clark describes it, bright youngsters leave home for kindergarten only to go into the streets after the tenth grade as hopeless, drifting people with neither an adequate sense of themselves nor of the world around them.

I was having a conversation with a young man in one of Washington's black communities about how people improve their circumstances. As it happened, his particular way was by methods that flirt along the edges of legality. We talked about his alternatives and began discussing education. "That school stuff, man, that's all played out now," he said. "There's nothing for a young boy in school these days. A young boy, he gets his education on the corner." There are many parents painfully aware that today's community school is a pool hall. And as the machine grinds on, making stunted humans of their children, black parents are beginning to believe that regardless of the danger the machine must be stopped.

[17] James Garrett, "Black Power and Black Education," *25*, Vol. 1 (October 1968), pp. 33–34.

As has been said by Bowles and Garrett, the schools represent a critical link in the chain of oppression that blacks see as binding them to poverty and general inequality in the American political system as it now exists. Integration, as defined by *Brown*, has been set aside by many black activists in favor of building the black community into a solid political base. Although it is entirely too soon to be conclusive, the evidence seems to indicate that in the New York City communities where local control is being tried—the Intermediate School 201 complex and Ocean Hill-Brownsville—one of the effects has been to bring the communities closer together. An issue has been raised around which many residents can rally as never before and one in which their mutual, or community, interest is most clearly defined. Such a step is the beginning of real community, the necessary ingredient to unified political action on other issues. And it should be added here, based again on premature evidence, that the opposition of predominately white teachers' groups to the community control experiment in New York is welding the community together to a degree that would have been unlikely had the experiment been carried out with considerably less opposition from outside the community.

The crisis in the schools of New York City[18] is an excellent vehicle for examining what can best be called the myth of alliance—the notion that there are political and ethnic groups that blacks can link up with to fight for liberation. Black nationalists have become convinced that such alliances dissolve when the interests of blacks conflict with the interests of entrenched groups previously on their side. For example, labor was disposed to civil rights when it meant hamburgers in Mississippi and coffee in North Carolina. But when it meant jobs in New York City's construction unions, the conflict of interests deteriorated the alliance.[19] However, that issue was mild compared to the idea that blacks might take over and run school

[18] For a summary and description of this crisis, see Martin Mayer, "The Full and Sometimes Very Surprising Story of Ocean Hill, the Teachers' Union and the Teacher Strikes of 1968," *New York Times Magazine*, Feb. 2, 1969, pp. 18 ff.

[19] See Herbert Hill, "The Racial Practices of Organized Labor—The Age of Gompers and After," in Arthur M. Ross and Herbert Hill (eds.), *Employment, Race, and Poverty* (Harcourt, Brace & World, 1967), pp. 365–402, and Herbert Hill, "Racial Practices of Organized Labor: The Contemporary Record," in Julius Jacobson (ed.), *The Negro and the American Labor Movement* (Doubleday, 1968).

districts where organized teachers and principals have been all powerful for generations. At this point, black liberation became an intolerable burden.

As a result, the critical question becomes where will the black community schools gain the funds needed to operate their schools in a hostile political climate. I wish I had a ready-made answer for that. I can only suggest that those who feel their liberation is the most important issue have decided to press for that goal, realizing that battles over gut issues are never easy and never have simple answers.

Political action in urban centers, carried out as it is by strongly nationalistic leaders in many instances, raises the question of just how strong the nationalist movement in the cities is today. Reliable studies of nationalist strength do not exist because of the suspicion many residents feel toward answering the questions of outsiders. But the absence of political organizing in the cities by nonnationalist groups suggests a time when precedence will establish the nationalist claim to the streets as their own. Yet within the nationalist movement, as in any political movement, divisions have arisen and promise to continue to rise, particularly as successes are achieved and access to power is gained.

For certain, the time is upon the black communities that George Orwell once described, when there will be "smelly little orthodoxies . . . contending for our souls."[20] Oppression, inequality, and effective disenfranchisement of the black poor have all guaranteed that solutions based strictly on black self-reliance will force power struggles within the black community. Some are counseling that the schools be used as training grounds for revolution, linking the youth to a struggle against "white imperialism," while others would have the black community fight from a base of solid unity for concessions from the white power structure. Between these two loosely defined objectives, there is a broad spectrum of voices within the nationalist movement. But all are now focused on the small units of power—the schools, the police departments, the corner groceries, and the real estate offices. Indeed, all that is either owned or controlled by whites

[20] "Charles Dickens," in Sonia Orwell and Ian Angus (eds.), *The Collected Essays, Journalism and Letters of George Orwell*, Vol. I: *An Age Like This, 1920–40* (London: Secker & Warburg, 1968), p. 460.

are now the targets in the latest phase of the nationalist movement.

Leaving aside for a moment the possibility of black communities arriving at a consensus in favor of violent revolution, black nationalism is planning for its future potential adherents to alter basically the present power relationships of black to white. The black nationalist movement is seeking to create in Negro communities what it divines is being practiced in white communities: training youth to rule the territory in which they predominate.

If the glories of European culture and the Renaissance are being taught to white children, then the glories of African culture, of the Dahomeans and Ashantis, must be taught to black children. Beyond that, the role of education in the nationalist scheme is to interrupt the cycle of self-abnegation, the forces that cause young black children to see themselves as less than human. As Frantz Fanon—popular among nationalists—puts it:

> I am a Negro—but of course I do not know it, simply because I am one. When I am at home my mother sings me French love songs in which there is never a word about Negroes. When I disobey, when I make too much noise, I am told to "stop acting like a nigger." . . .
>
> Somewhat later I read white books and little by little I take into myself the prejudices, the myths, the folklore that have come to me from Europe. . . . Without turning to the idea of collective catharsis, it would be easy for me to show that, without thinking, the Negro selects himself as an object capable of carrying the burden of original sin. . . . To come back to psychopathology, let us say that the Negro lives an ambiguity that is extraordinarily neurotic.

The dilemma of unworthy self-images is described by Fanon: "Moral consciousness implies a kind of scission, a fracture of consciousness into a bright part and an opposing black part. In order to achieve morality, it is essential that the black, the dark, the Negro vanish from consciousness. Hence, a Negro is forever in combat with his own image."[21]

Healing the broken images of black children, then, is one of the basic goals of a black-controlled community school setting. For the nationalists, the restoration of black pride is all important to the political process. A bit of graffiti outside of a freedom school in Chicago's South Side said in bold, vivid letters: "A people that does not believe in itself won't defend itself."

[21] Frantz Fanon, *Black Skins, White Masks* (Grove Press, 1967), pp. 191–94.

Social-psychological studies of mass behavior remain greatly unexplored in terms of the questions that might be asked about the current direction of black activism, which is turned inward. It is not known and cannot be known, for example, the degree to which the current demand for community control and black autonomy within the universities is not an *autodidacticism of necessity.* Remembering that the autodidactical individual is one who is a self-teacher, who insists upon discovering that which is already known by his own curious route and his own methods, it would be exciting to explore the possible foundations for such a process as applied to communities and larger groups, such as the black masses in America.

Bearing in mind also the thrust of today's black politics, with its emphasis on total independence of the white structure around the black community, it is important to note Robert Butler:

> One might ask whether independence of mind does not describe the phenomenon referred to here as autodidacticism. Independence of mind does not go far enough, however; it does not emphasize the central focus upon the self and the teaching of the self. It is not simply that the autodidact doubts and distrusts, but that he assumes that whatever has been said, or is thought to be understood, is *incomplete.* There is something more —if only one searches further, studies more, and reflects more comprehensively. One must start from scratch, at the ground, and blaze one's own trail to the unattainable summit; not destructively per se, not only through doubt, but also through personal optimism about the possibility of a solution, always, however, cast in terms of an ultimate and personal despair because nothing can be whole or complete. *This appears to be the incisive issue, that the self is not complete; the autodidact, studying himself, finds he is not whole.* And this sense of incompleteness is a sense and fear of alienation.[22]

Attempts to understand what triggers the autodidact personality in creative individuals are still being made. But it will be some time before there is any concrete knowledge about a form of group behavior that insists upon an autodidactic motif as in politically innovative communities or among innovative college student groups of blacks.

But I call the process autodidacticism of necessity for a reason. I

[22] Robert N. Butler, "The Destiny of Creativity in Later Life: Studies of Creative People and the Creative Process," in Sidney Levin and Ralph J. Kahana (eds.), *Psychodynamic Studies on Aging: Creativity, Reminiscing, and Dying* (New York: International Universities Press, 1967), pp. 54–55. (Italics are in the original.)

claim—and this is the central point—that blacks insist today on self-teaching out of an abiding mistrust of the past processes of education with their impressive list of failures. Therefore, the self-teaching process, precarious and difficult as it is, is now being insisted upon because all the other methods have failed to satisfy the needs of black people. According to the blacks' view of the world, it has become necessary to take over the responsibility for their own education and that of their children, partly because of the hostility they divine in white systems, but also because of their new self-involvement and, thus, their rush toward self-discovery.

Clearly, any theory that seeks to ascribe to communities or nations the behavior patterns of certain individuals must be approached cautiously; all the more so because there is at the moment no literature to support it. But the intriguing possibility that a whole group within American society may be testing the educational system for a solution that is essentially autodidactic should not be allowed to go unmentioned and certainly it should not remain uninvestigated for long.

Thus, from the fields of a people's history, strewn with defeats and frustrations, the outline of a mountain of success emerges for the nationalist from the current political inferno in the streets. Flirting first with Garvey's grand scheme of Africa for all blacks, retreating from that to emerge demanding a portion of "whitey's pie," blacks now seek—certainly the nationalists do—to forge from the concrete of the streets and the buildings of the black communities a thing to call their own, many hands filled with pebbles with which to build their mountain of self-respect and self-determination, and to find, at last, a worthy way of life in the white man's land.

PART TWO

Decision Making

MARILYN GITTELL

The Balance of Power and the Community School

Changing the Balance of Power

The balance of power in urban school systems, as in all political systems, is determined by the distribution of the resources of power. Control of public policy results from control of vital resources, such as jobs, funds, social status, and expertise. Competition among groups for the resources of power generally makes for a dynamic, pluralistic system, whereas monopolies produce a static system. Over a period of time, professionals in big-city school systems have used their expertise to secure greater control over jobs and funds. By broadening their base of power, they have expanded their control to public educational policy so that other potential participants have largely been excluded from policy making.[1]

The current movement for urban school reform through expanded community control is an attempt to achieve a new balance of power by reintroducing competition into the system. Local community groups are competing with the professionals for power resources and a larger share in the decision-making process.

[1] For a more detailed discussion, see Marilyn Gittell and T. Edward Hollander, *Six Urban School Districts: A Comparative Study of Institutional Response* (Praeger, 1968), p. 196; Richard Karp, "School Decentralization in New York: A Case Study," *Interplay of European/American Affairs* (August–September 1968), pp. 9–14; Peter Schrag, "Boston: Education's Last Hurrah," *Saturday Review* (May 21, 1966), pp. 56–58.

The alignment of forces in the schools reflects the political struggle that results when new groups seek to produce effective change in the policy-making process and the participants in that process. In many ways, the school conflict is symbolic of the conflict in the larger political system of the cities. Those who have secured positions in the system and control certain of its resources are pitted against others who are directly affected by the policies but have no control over decisions. The only possible coalition for the opposition group is with people outside the system who have no interest in maintaining the status quo and may gain from alignment with a new political force.[2] At present, ethnic solidarity (particularly in the black community) and the vote[3] are the only weapons of power available to those who seek entrance into the political arena.

In an effort to broaden their base of power, community activists are trying to gain some control over the expenditure of funds and the hiring of personnel.[4] Both are essential to any active role in the exercise of power. In most school systems, these powers are tightly held by the boards of education, the professional bureaucracy, and the teachers' organizations.[5] Resolution of the conflict demands a transfer of some of this power to the communities. Because education is a state function, formal change must come through state legislation. Such legislation would be needed even if it were not formally required since a city board of education would probably not make the necessary delegation of power on its

[2] For a discussion of the role that urban forces play, see Gittell and Hollander, *Six Urban School Districts*, pp. 124–27; see also Theodore J. Lowi, *At the Pleasure of the Mayor: Patronage and Power in New York City, 1898–1958* (Free Press, 1964), p. 200.

[3] For an enumeration of the sources of power, see Terry N. Clark, "The Concept of Power: Some Overemphasized and Underrecognized Dimensions—An Examination with Special Reference to the Local Community," *Southwestern Social Science Quarterly*, Vol. 48 (December 1967), pp. 280–86; see also Robert A. Dahl, "The Analysis of Influence in Local Communities," in Charles R. Adrian and others (eds.), *Social Science and Community Action* (Institute for Community Development and Services, Michigan State University, 1960), pp. 40–42.

[4] The draft guidelines for the Ocean Hill-Brownsville, Intermediate School (I.S.) 201, and Two Bridges model school district demonstration projects were submitted by the governing boards to the superindentent of schools on March 26, 1968. Published in Maurice Berube and Marilyn Gittell (eds.), *Confrontation at Ocean Hill-Brownsville* (Praeger, 1969), pp. 19–24.

[5] Gittell and Hollander, *Six Urban School Districts*, pp. 196–97.

own initiative. In fact, it is likely that the city board would oppose state action.[6]

In New York City's legislative effort to secure decentralization in 1967–68, a coalition that included the mayor, governor, state Board of Regents, commissioner of education, local minority groups, and a select group of middle- and upper-class reformers was unable to meet the combined influence of the city's professional education forces and the teachers' union.[7] In Michigan, state legislation to create independent local districts in Detroit was opposed by the Board of Education and the upper echelons of the bureaucracy.[8] Thus, the conclusion can be drawn that the major obstacle to creating a new balance of power that includes community control is the tenacity with which a small group in the centralized city school systems endeavors to maintain its position of power.

Influence on the Balance of Power

Assuming that some political headway were possible, change might occur either by (1) a settlement that contained a large measure of community control and a consequent restructuring of the entire system, giving substantial power to the new participants, or (2) a compromise that would give the new participants a share in decision making but would preserve the largest part for the groups now in control. It should be noted that even if a formal grant of complete powers were made to local districts through state legislation, such advantages as social standing, knowledge, and technical expertise would, by their very nature, continue to reside with the school professionals.

The most immediate concern of the three demonstration districts in New York City and other communities seeking local control was the selection of a professional administrator. This administrator was

[6] See Detroit Board of Education, "A Resolution in Opposition to House Bill 3801" (processed; February 1968); Board of Education of the City of New York, "Memorandum" (processed; Dec. 7, 1968), p. 2.

[7] See the following editorials in the *New York Times*: "Decentralization Is a Must," May 11, 1968, p. 34; "Decentralization Shambles," May 28, 1968, p. 46.

[8] Detroit Board of Education, "A Resolution in Opposition."

viewed by community parents and leaders as an expert in education. But the act of delegating power will not insure educational expertise in the community; school professionals will still retain their influence in many matters.

Restructuring city school systems to provide for complete community control would require statutory abolition of all citywide education functions. All local districts would then be independent, each maintaining the same status it had as a city school district. To achieve complete independence for local districts, the union contract (where applicable) would either have to be revoked or renegotiated at the local level. Local districts within the city would receive state and city funds directly, presumably to be distributed according to some equitable formula prescribed in the legislation. The power of determining jobs and of allocating funds would revert to the local district board. (Again, the status of professionals should not be overlooked—under any circumstances they will be active participants in the policy-making process.) In New York State and Michigan, legislation that would have permitted the creation of strong local districts failed. In both cases, more modest legislation was introduced and was also defeated. In Massachusetts, general enabling legislation was passed, and creation of a state district in Boston is under consideration; the degree of community control to be exercised in the district has not yet been determined.

Under a compromise plan, more probable in most states, authority would be shared by the central board of education and the local district board. The resultant distribution of power would be significantly affected by the context of state legislation and the new procedures it may establish for changing the system. Of major concern is the means provided to carry out such a plan. If an incumbent central board is made responsible for implementation, delay and narrow interpretation may well prevent any significant change. It is worthwhile to remember the experience of school integration efforts.[9] In addition, many factors will influence the balance of power—both in how they are outlined in the legislation

[9] See David Rogers, "Obstacles to School Desegregation in New York City: A Benchmark Case," in Marilyn Gittell (ed.), *Educating an Urban Population* (Sage Publications, 1967), pp. 155–84, and Robert L. Crain, with the assistance of Morton Inger and others, *The Politics of School Desegregation: Comparative Case Studies of Community Structure and Policy-Making* (Aldine, 1968), pp. 106, 111.

and, more important, in how they are implemented: the number of districts created, the methods for setting boundaries and the location of the boundaries, the discretion of the district in budget matters, the extent of mandatory expenditures for local districts, the interrelationship among local, city, and state education agents or agencies, the allocation of control over teaching and professional staff, and the sources of standards for curriculum and personnel practices. But without appreciable local control in the areas of personnel, budget, and curriculum, it is unlikely that any significant change can be anticipated.[10]

PERSONNEL

If the local district is bound by existing personnel practices (that is, central examination and assignment of staff), obviously it will not have broadened its own power base in the vital area of control over jobs. However, meeting state certification requirements for personnel could allow for local discretion in hiring, assignment, and transfer. City requirements (particularly in urban states) are usually stricter than state requirements, especially with respect to the qualifications for selection of administrators. In most cities, the current examination procedures for principals and superintendents assure that power will be at headquarters, since that is where candidates are examined. A policy of establishing minimum state standards but allowing local selection of administrators could shift considerable power to the local district and would, in general, permit greater flexibility.

In New York City's Ocean Hill-Brownsville district, the local governing board employed seven principals with the special title "demonstration school principals," which allowed them to be state certified rather than city certified. In the various controversies that have arisen, the loyalty of these principals has been to the administrator who appointed them and to the local board. Their actions have considerably strengthened the position of the local district. A similar situation occurred in the fall of 1968: during the

[10] "Control of Schools Within the Black Community," in Preston Wilcox (ed.), "Proceedings of the Third Annual Black Power Conference" (Philadelphia, Aug. 30–Sept. 1, 1968; processed), p. 4, and Marilyn Gittell, "Problems of School Decentralization in New York City," *Urban Review*, Vol. 2 (February 1967), pp. 4, 27, 28.

United Federation of Teachers (UFT) strike[11] over 100 teachers remained loyal to the local district that had hired them.

Opponents of community control charge that hiring of personnel by local boards would produce a return to the political patronage system.[12] In reality, this protest indicates their fear that flexibility of hiring would decrease the protection afforded them by the seniority system. Strict civil service regulations and the seniority system contribute significantly to the maintenance of the status quo and to the preservation of mediocrity in the system.[13] The bureaucracy in turn uses these same procedures as a rationale for the continuation of the system.[14] It fully understands that as long as local districts are denied the prerogative of selecting administrative and teaching staffs, they will be denied a fundamental source of power.

Another constraint on local districts in several large cities would be the union contract. Under most contracts, local districts would have only limited policy-making powers in the areas of salary, fringe benefits, and utilization of staff. The restrictions contained in union contracts are unlikely to be changed under any decentralization plan, but a shift in negotiations from a central education agency to the local district would result in a substantial shift in power to the local community.[15] A system of supplementary con-

[11] See Mark R. Arnold, "A Strike About a New Kind of Gut Issue," *National Observer*, Sept. 16, 1968, p. 13. For an account of the September 1967 strike, see Karp, "School Decentralization," p. 12.

[12] Albert Shanker, "Critique of the Bundy Report," *United Action* (United Federation of Teachers, November 1967), p. 2.

[13] See David Rogers, *110 Livingston Street: Politics and Bureaucracy in the New York City Schools* (Random House, 1968), Chap. 8; Ronald R. Campbell, "Is the School Superintendent Obsolete?" *Phi Delta Kappan*, Vol. 48 (October 1966), pp. 50–58; United Parents Association of New York City, Statement by Mrs. Florence Flast, President of the United Parents Associations, before the Board of Education in Regard to Draft Proposal on Decentralization, March 7, 1967, p. 1.

[14] See Marilyn Gittell, *Participants and Participation: A Study of School Policy in New York City* (Praeger, 1967), p. 11, and Council of Supervisory Associations of the Public Schools of New York City, *Response to the Lindsay-Bundy Proposals*, Interim Report No. 2 (January 1968), pp. 5–6.

[15] During the negotiations to settle the teachers' strike in New York City, the union leadership defined pressure to bargain with local groups as a union busting tactic (*New York Times*, Sept. 16, 1968). On the other hand, Local 6 in Washington, D.C., has indicated a willingness to contract with a decentralized Anacostia district. The position of a local union may well depend upon the strength and influence it has achieved in the central structure.

tracts adopted in individual districts as part of a citywide contract could be a possible compromise.[16] It could even result in a readjustment of power in unions themselves, forcing more emphasis on local discretion of the chapter or district chairman.

DISTRICT BOUNDARIES

The only significant resource now held by the community groups is ethnic solidarity. The drawing of district boundaries could profoundly affect the basis of that power. Large local districts are less affected by solidarity than smaller ones and the established groups could more easily maintain control there. To the degree that district lines are drawn to reduce the role of minority groups, they will assure the maintenance of the status quo. Therefore, careful attention must be paid to the racial, economic, and social factors that determine the character of the district.[17] Size in itself can be debilitating and reduce the possibility of introducing genuine community control. Community participation cannot be meaningful in a district that is too large, particularly in ghetto communities. In New York City, the union and other opponents of local control have supported the larger districts because they recognize that this will help to preserve their power.[18]

BUDGET

Control over both operating and capital expenses will determine the extent of local power in all aspects of the educational program. If mandatory expenditures for teachers' salaries, established ratios for specialized personnel, and purchasing restrictions are retained, they will greatly curtail local discretion even if local district budgets are adopted.[19] Realistically, it should be recognized that certain

[16] For a detailed discussion of this problem, see the chapter in this volume by Michael H. Moskow and Kenneth McLennan.

[17] For a discussion of the characteristics of ideal school boundaries, see Mayor's Advisory Panel on Decentralization of the New York City Schools, *Reconnection for Learning: A Community School System for New York City* (1967), pp. 16–17. Referred to as either the Bundy Report or the Mayor's Advisory Panel.

[18] See Seymour Marks, "School Decentralization; An Issue Splits a City," *Long Island Press*, Sept. 22, 1968, and Shanker, "Critique of the Bundy Report."

[19] See H. Thomas James, James A. Kelly, and Walter I. Garmus, *Determinants of Educational Expenditures in Large Cities of the United States* (Stanford University, School of Education, 1966)-

items of mandated expenditure will always comprise a large share of the budget. In some cases, these items will be a commitment under the union contract. For example, building maintenance and salaries are to be anticipated as mandated costs. However, purchase of textbooks and supplies, hiring of secretarial staff, and allocation of professional personnel could be unspecified, leaving the determination of such priorities to the local districts. Experimentation with different alternatives would then be greater and perhaps would lead to increased productivity. In the area of counseling, where the professional guidance staff has been unsuccessful in many communities, greater success could be achieved through alternative approaches. For example, counseling by peer groups and community people might prove more valuable and less expensive. Districts should be free to try new methods. Unless local community boards and staff can control such policy and set a significant portion of budget priorities, their power would be insignificant.

METHOD OF SELECTION OF THE LOCAL BOARD

The method by which a local school board is selected will influence the composition of that board. Depending upon the procedure used, different segments of the population might be induced to run for office. Procedures will also influence community loyalties. The possibilities of procedures range from appointment by a central agency (making it unlikely that the board would have significant local loyalties or would include any new local power elements) to local election of all members. Local elections, if arranged at a regular community election, might reinforce the role of the existing political party structure[20] and not engage any new local interests in the process. Elections through the schools with the constituency made up either of parents of school children or of all community residents are more likely to stimulate involvement by new groups who are particularly concerned with education problems. Although established school organizations, such as parent or

[20] Louis H. Masotti, "Patterns of White and Nonwhite School Referenda Participation and Support: Cleveland, 1960–64," in Gittell (ed.), *Educating An Urban Population*, pp. 240–55.

parent-teachers' associations (PTA), will have an advantage in such elections, new groups could emerge if the community has real power.

Under a system of local control, the role of former participants in parent associations will vary in different districts. These different roles are discernible in the three demonstration districts in New York City. In two of the districts, parent association presidents were defeated in the local elections and became leaders of opposition groups. In one of the districts, several parent association presidents became militant local board members. There is, however, a general recognition of the need to change the parent association structure so that it is more oriented to general policy issues rather than to individual child or school needs.

No system of election can guarantee extensive participation unless such participation is seen as meaningful (that is, effective with regard to budget and jobs). The issue of whether local school board elections should allow all residents to vote or allow only parents to vote is a sensitive one, the dangers of which are reinforced by problems associated with placing school elections into the general political arena. Since all taxpayers share in school costs and presumably all citizens lose or gain by the character of the education offered the youth of the community, there is a sound basis to the argument for community-wide elections. A possible solution to this problem might be to have a portion of the local board elected by the community in general and the rest only by parents of school children.[21] Using the schools as a basic election unit is more likely to encourage members of the community to become active. In addition, the individual school has the potential to build meaningful mechanisms for broader participation. The usual parent association could be replaced by faculty-parent boards and committees that would concern themselves with fundamental policy issues. Budget and personnel evaluation could be dealt with in each school and then presented to the district board. Such committees could in-

[21] See Community Planning Council, "Anacostia Community School Project," a proposal submitted to the U.S. Office of Education (processed; Washington, D.C.: Community Planning Council, August 1968).

teract more fruitfully with the local district board than could the current parent associations, which are overpersonalized and limited in their scope because no powers reside in the local school or district.[22] If given a more meaningful role in a wide range of school policy questions, school groups should recruit new participants and play an expanded role in the school and the district.

It is of value to consider the experience with board membership in the three demonstration school projects in New York City. When the districts were created, it was hoped that the experiment would be a cooperative venture of teachers, administrators, and community representatives. In this way the major power holders in the school community would be reflected in governing board deliberations. All three groups were to be represented on the local governing boards.[23] Antagonisms developed during the planning period and were intensified when community people refused to support the teachers' strike in September 1967; the United Federation of Teachers retaliated by suggesting that teachers not elect their representatives to the governing board.[24] In one district during the planning period, teachers organized themselves as an opposition group in an attempt to influence the parents' representatives and oppose the community's representatives. Teachers and administrators in each district felt it was their duty to defend the system and minimize the influence of the local governing board.[25] They saw

[22] The current role of local civic and interest groups is discussed in Gittell, *Participants and Participation*, pp. 15–16; Wallace Sayre and Herbert Kaufman, *Governing New York City: Politics in the Metropolis* (Russell Sage Foundation, 1960), p. 258; Robert A. Dahl, *Who Governs? Democracy and Power in an American City* (Yale University Press, 1961), pp. 155–59.

[23] Two Bridges Model School District Planning Council of the Two Bridges Neighborhood Council, "Proposed By-Laws for Two Bridges Model School District" (processed; September 1967), p. 3; Karp, "School Decentralization," p. 10; Eugenia Kemble, *New York's Experiments in School Decentralization: A Look at Three Projects* (United Federation of Teachers, 1968).

[24] See Martin Mayer, "Frustration Is the Word for Ocean Hill," *New York Times Magazine*, May 19, 1968, pp. 28 ff., for an account of the Ocean Hill demonstration project; see also New York City Commission on Human Rights, "Report on Three Demonstration Projects in the City Schools from the New York Commission on Human Rights" (processed; February–March 1968), p. 17.

[25] Gleaned from interviews with board members of the three demonstration districts and observations of board meetings. See also Karp, "School Decentralization," p. 12.

themselves as a small representation of the interests of the teaching and administrative staff in their schools and often would not act on their own initiative. Some of the administrative representatives (principals) seemed concerned with reporting information back to headquarters or to their own professional associations. In two of the three districts, teachers and administrative staff have since resigned from the boards.[26]

Although the demonstration school districts in New York City have a special quality because they function within a larger, highly centralized system and their powers are almost nonexistent, the failure of their governing boards to function with the kind of representation originally provided is relevant. It suggests that teachers and administrators when acting as representatives of their community groups should not sit on local governing boards.[27] However, if they were elected by parents or residents in a general election, they would not be obligated to a narrow constituency but could function more in the general interest.[28] The experience in the demonstration districts also indicates that teachers and administrators largely view community control as a threat to their own status and will not be especially cooperative.[29] Concerted efforts must be made under any plan to make both groups an integral part of the new system. They should be organized locally and incorporated into the policy-making process since they represent significant power bases.

[26] Minutes of the Two Bridges Governing Board for March 28, and April 3, 1968, and the statement by professionals, dated April 3, 1968, citing conflict of interest as the reason for the resignations. Teachers interviewed at the Two Bridges schools all expressed belief in decentralization but felt that they were not consulted by community board members who wanted to exercise leadership. The teachers felt they would work better in an advisory capacity. The new bylaws being drafted by all three districts make no provision for professionals to sit on the governing boards.

[27] Interviews with teachers on governing boards of Two Bridges, Ocean Hill-Brownsville, and I.S. 201 substantiate these views. The UFT took the policy position that teachers serving on governing boards constitute a labor-management conflict.

[28] On New York City's upper West Side, an unauthorized election was held to select a local governing board. Several teachers were chosen to serve on this board.

[29] New York City Commission on Human Rights, "Report on Three Demonstration Projects," p. 17. According to this report, "Fear is expressed at two levels. Firstly, the teachers object to evaluation of their classroom performance by lay persons or outside professionals. Secondly, they oppose evaluation by the people of the ghettos." The "Anacostia Community School Project" presents the same view.

Intergovernmental Relationships

The pattern of intergovernmental relationships affecting school administration will also be a determinant in the ultimate character of any community control system. The roles of the mayor and the state education agency in this pattern will be important. Greater reliance on the state than on the city for supervision and standards will result in greater control for local districts over their own affairs. In general, city standards have been more restrictive than state standards, and immediate administrative control by city boards tends to be more extensive. The feeling prevails that with a state agency, physically removed from the local board, there will be greater local flexibility. In New York, this reaction is partly based on the lack of involvement and the general sympathy of the state Department of Education for local control. In comparing state university and city university practices, this conclusion is borne out, at least in New York State. However, if state supervision is standardized without regard for local differences, it is possible that greater inflexibility will result.

Maintaining any kind of independent city education agency, or even citywide standards, will reduce local district board control over policy. Increasing the mayor's role in a reorganization of the school system and at the same time eliminating or reducing the role of the city education agency will probably expand the power of the local district, at least initially. In fact, any reduction in the role of a citywide education bureaucracy will enhance the status of the local unit. Complete reorganization, including the abolition of the city board of education, replacement of the board by a city commissioner of education, or both, combined with a plan for local control, will provide a new set of relationships that will probably increase local district power.

Ultimately, the most appropriate method to reorganize and structure local school districts might be to follow a procedure similar to that used in city home-rule legislation: set broad requirements in the state education law and allow local school districts to determine the specific organization most appropriate to their needs and local character. General enabling legislation outlining procedures for local action would then be sufficient. Initially, however, state legislation will have to be more explicit in order to guarantee that reform of the system will take place.

Flexibility in the state legislation is essential. Detailed procedures outlined in state law might inhibit the emergence and development of new community forces and leadership, and should be avoided. The philosophical basis for community control involves commitment to a dynamic process that will allow new elements in the political system to organize and influence policy and to achieve institutional change more easily. New systems tend to produce their own constraints and protections and could establish new forces in the policy process that would suppress other potentially active groups. Any plan for urban school reform should allow for a greater breadth of participation and be sufficiently open to encourage new groups to be constantly emerging. The fluidity of involvement should be a source of constant innovation. Perhaps in the future some greater degree of centralization of structure will be desirable, and the process of adjustment to this stage should not be made difficult to achieve. The crucial test of the system will be its ability to continuously make adjustments and respond to new needs. Thus, there should be a built-in innovation factor that makes the system receptive to new ideas. This might take the form of "innovation units" or research and development centers.

In several cities, groups have organized to secure community control in city school systems. They are aware of the importance of procedures and requirements in plans for reorganization. They have been moving toward an ideal model of independence. The legislation proposed by these groups calls for supervision of local districts by state departments of education, based on the desire to remove the local district entirely from the city structure.[30] Their goal is a system as independent as possible, with city participation kept to a minimum. Such independent status increases the chances for creating a center of power in the local community. Development of an internal

[30] In the midst of the controversy at Ocean Hill-Brownsville, the governing board asked to be made an independent district under the state commissioner. The board considered this the only solution to the problem of local constraints. *New York Times*, Sept. 14, 1968, pp. 1, 18. See also Independent Harlem School District, "Proposal for Establishment of a Community Controlled Educational Data System for Harlem" (processed; 1968).

balance of power within the local district then becomes the primary concern. Relations with government are reduced to pressuring the mayor and other political leaders for funds and to coping with a remote state education establishment that has, so far, appeared to be more sympathetic to local interests. Relations with professional staff and teachers' organizations would then be limited to the community schools, giving the local district a decided advantage in its control over the basic resources of the system.

Local Balance of Power under Community Control

While school professionals will maintain a strong base of power in any school structure, two new conditions are likely to occur in the community-controlled school districts in ghetto areas. First, there will be, at least initially, less reliance on and trust in the professionals by parents and community leaders and, second, the more traditional types of school professionals will probably not monopolize administrative and classroom jobs. Rather, people from outside of the system with minority group backgrounds will be utilized. In addition, there will be greater acceptance of the role of the paraprofessional.

Local school boards will be anxious to use and test their new powers. They will expect to be involved in matters traditionally considered a part of the administrator's domain. Particularly in the area of personnel selection, the local board is not likely to want to yield any of its newly acquired prerogatives, even to its own administrator. There is no question but that the local boards will want a strong role in the appointment of principals and teachers. The local administrator (superintendent) will certainly want to follow the tradition of choosing his own staff and having it responsible to him; this would include principals and assistant principals. In the three demonstration districts in New York City, local boards insisted upon holding interviews for all staff appointments, although they recognized that the unit administrator should have some authority in the selection of "his" staff. Teachers were also interviewed by personnel committees of each board.[31]

[31] Interviews and field observations were conducted in the three districts from January to September 1968.

In trying to achieve a proper balance of power, the local board and its administrator will be faced with many of the same problems that have confronted city boards and their administrators. But because the power of the local boards will be so new and untested, there will be a stronger desire to use it, and administrators will have to be able to cope with this situation. For example, in the Two Bridges demonstration project in New York City, the resignation of the first local administrator was due in large part to his unwillingness to accept a less influential role.

In ghetto areas, the struggle for power will also have racial overtones. The professional will face problems even though he may be a member of the ethnic or racial group of the community. Of the three experimental projects in New York City, the two dominantly black and Puerto Rican projects are far less trusting of traditional professionals than is the other district. In all three projects, there is almost constant concern that the administrator will act without proper consultation of the board, even in matters that appear inconsequential. While the administrators in these districts are dedicated to community participation, their tendency is to act independently,[32] partly because it is easier but also because they have a vested interest in developing their own power base. Strong administrators are anxious to control jobs and expenditures in order to enhance their own positions. Administrators will use these powers to enlist support from individuals or factions on the board. In poverty areas, the power to distribute jobs and funds to board members and their associates can be an important resource. In each of the demonstration projects board members have been placated by judicious use of this power.

In the white middle-class communities, local control is not likely to reduce deference to school professionals. This is supported by the actions of the Two Bridges district, as distinguished from the other two areas, where the selection of the local administrators was based on more traditional values. However, personnel selection procedures will probably be broader than under a centralized system. Because

[32] Again, McCoy's role in the Ocean Hill-Brownsville dispute in September 1968 was clearly one of strong leadership, not of reticence. See the *New York Times* coverage for that period. The Two Bridges administrator has indicated his concern that he be the source of board action and in several instances has discounted directives from the local board.

of the increased possibility of influencing fundamental aspects of the system, new participants may also emerge in these communities but not as quickly as in ghetto areas. In ghetto areas, where parents have been alienated from the schools, the change will be more drastic. This is evident in the attendance at meetings and the activities of new participants in the demonstration districts. Election turnouts, although low by some standards, were high for these districts. While there has been no systematic effort to quantify parent participation, as measured by contact with school officials, interviews with residents of the three districts indicate that there is an apparent increase in parents' visits and confrontations over those in the old system. This has been encouraged by the open-door policy of the locally selected principals, the regular appearance of board members at the schools, and the receptivity of unit administrators to such contact. Certainly, if increased participation were to be measured in terms of degree of involvement in the policy process, the change in the demonstration districts would be considered significant. In all three districts there has been wide community involvement in the implementation of Title I programs of the Elementary and Secondary Education Act of 1965 and in the evaluation of teachers and principals. Board members have been more directly involved in the policy-making process than in any other local district in the city.

The political leverage of board members in relation to the administrator can be especially significant on questions other than those of school policy. Under the community school arrangement, school personalities cannot help but become important community leaders. The potential political advantage to be gained from a role in school affairs can be used for furthering local political careers. Thus, individual board members and the administrator will often be competing for community approval and recognition.

The administrator in the local district may be confronted by a conflict of his own loyalties—to professional standards and to community goals and interests. Balancing these two aspects of his own involvement is not an easy task, but traditional professional standards must be made compatible with the community's needs. Many administrators will be unable to function in these new roles.

The resistance of organized school administrators to local control is probably closely related to this conflict of loyalties.

Every locally selected principal is clearly a candidate for local administrator. Some may seek to increase their chance for the position by playing to the local governing board, or a faction on it—including undermining the incumbent administrator. Such alliances should be anticipated. But a good administrator will be able to channel these efforts constructively. The likelihood of such an occurrence will be greater where a faction of the board is also seeking to undermine the administrator.

Under centralized school systems, field superintendents are relatively weak, and administrators and principals are not particularly responsive to their demands.[33] The experience in the demonstration districts in New York City suggests that principals must be chosen locally and that both local district administrators and principals must have sufficient powers to control educational practices.[34]

The board itself will probably develop factions, most likely along class lines. The administrator will have to cope with these divisions. (In the three demonstration projects this has not been especially difficult.) However, divisions broaden the array of policy choices and sometimes lead to frustrating but worthwhile deliberations. In general, local boards will be more unified if the neighborhood is homogeneous. But there should be some provision, through election procedures and organization of the board, to guarantee diversity, if only to provide for the different points of view between parents and other community members.

Local boards will gradually develop a sound working relationship with their administrators and staff. It is essential, however, that the boards and not the professionals hold the power. The traditional idea of stressing a long-range policy role for the board and a day-to-day role for the administrator may not be valid under community control. If the aim is to secure wider participation through the

[33] The administrative organizations in six big-city schools are described in Gittell and Hollander, *Six Urban School Districts*, pp. 52–84.

[34] In interviews, the administrators have suggested that this is necessary to carry out the programs and policies of the local governing boards. In many cases, principals who were appointed prior to the creation of the local district board have been a major obstacle to instituting change.

community and the board, professionals will have to adjust to a more supportive role in the policy-making process and a shared role in traditionally administrative functions. Those administrators who can accept and work with this weighted balance of power will be most successful. The effectiveness of the administrator and his ability to work with the board and the community in this capacity will certainly be a key factor in the success or failure of the district. If too much of the procedure of school policy making becomes routinized, as it is under the centralized structure, then the validity of local control as a concept must be questioned.

THE LOCAL BOARD AND THE COMMUNITY

There will be a great tendency to presume that community participation and control is fulfilled by the creation of a local school board, its election locally, and the delegation of some power to it. In fact, the community school concept demands the development of mechanisms and procedures to insure that people, particularly parents of school children, will continually be involved in school affairs. The local school plan must utilize paraprofessionals more extensively in the schools; it must devise daily, weekly, and yearly programs that relate to community interests and needs; and it must be a model for participatory democracy, using the individual school as a basis for participation and school governance.[35] School committees can be the training ground for new board members and can serve as a source of ideas for the local school board. School and district committees should also act as community overseers of board and staff actions. Local boards should develop procedures through which these community groups can be heard on a regular basis and become a significant part of the policy-making process.

Many of the existing agencies in the community—political club houses, civic groups, and neighborhood councils—can and should be concerned with educational needs. Leadership in ghetto communities will come from the poverty agencies. For example, in the three demonstration districts in New York City, local poverty groups initiated the school projects and participated on the school boards. If nothing else, the poverty program has produced a whole new cadre of local leadership and support, and the local community

[35] See Community Planning Council, "Anacostia Community School Project."

school district can stimulate still another layer of leadership and organization.

Recruitment of people representative of community interests to governing board membership is made difficult by the amount of time that board membership demands. The traditional civic concept of unpaid board membership developed by a middle-class community and for a limited concept of the role of a school board is not practical in a system of community control. In lower-class communities, civic responsibility cannot include extensive service in unpaid jobs. Many capable and interested persons will be unable to serve since the added telephone, travel, and food expenses are too burdensome for most people in these communities. Last year, members of the governing boards in the New York City demonstration projects spent, on the average, from 25 to 40 hours a week on school matters. Significantly, several members are or were employed by local poverty agencies; other members, such as ministers, had the time to devote to these responsibilities. But one member who is a blue-collar worker missed five days of work in five months and is fearful of losing his job. His contribution to the deliberations of the board has been extremely valuable, but it is unlikely that he can continue to serve. The housewives who are board members, and they are a majority, are also under great personal strain. All of them have young children and can barely afford baby-sitting costs. In the three demonstration projects, the board members displayed sophistication in dealing with problems close to them, about which they have intimate knowledge and great sensitivity. Unless means are developed for guaranteeing the participation of these community people on local school boards, the new balance of power may never come into existence. Great pains must be taken to assure wide recruitment for local boards. This may require a form of payment or at least an arrangement for covering expenses. Payment may be necessary if the participation of new elements in the community is desired. This applies not only for board members in ghetto areas but also for school committee members and governing board trainees.[36]

The elected local governing boards will have the same motives for maintaining power once they are in office as do office holders in

[36] See Mayor's Advisory Panel, *Reconnection for Learning*, p. 17, for a discussion of community school boards.

other political systems. Without a well-conceived and structured community base, the balance of power will become narrow and closed. Those community organizations that supply the leadership will function as the major sources of power, exercising influence through key board members. In the early stages of decentralization and community control, those who run for local governing board positions are likely to be politically active and, possibly, somewhat militant. Later elections will attract more school-oriented candidates. However, it should be noted that in ghetto communities the schools are an important source for jobs and political power. Board membership, therefore, will be a valued political position. A broad education campaign and training program should be considered vital parts of any movement toward community control if community interest is to be aroused. Involvement should not be left to chance.

The homogeneity in ghetto areas may result in a monolithic attitude, at least in the early stages. Because of the particular problems in ghetto communities, this can be an asset to program development. Where ethnic differences do exist, they may be a source of competition or conflict. In fact, local control is likely to produce greater ethnic clashes in such communities.[37]

THE TEACHERS' ROLE

The teaching staff should contine to play an important role under community control, both through unions and teachers' organizations and, perhaps more significantly, through leadership in individual schools. Their role in policy making is likely to include such areas as curriculum (where it is almost nonexistent under centralization) and regulation of suspensions, dress, student government, and other pupil policies. In some communities, the initial period of reorganization may produce some overt clashes between the community board and the staff, particularly with reference to the traditional civil service concepts and protections. The teaching

[37] Such clashes have developed between Chinese and Puerto Rican groups in the Two Bridges area, and between black and Puerto Rican groups in the Ocean Hill-Brownsville and I.S. 201 areas. They are not particularly serious but have undoubtedly been intensified under local control.

staff will provide the pressure for retaining personnel protection. It is hoped that a compromise position can be established which will allow greater flexibility but will also guarantee security for teachers.

The process of teacher bargaining with community interests through the local board should be significant in the development of the local district. If supplemental negotiation by the local district is provided for, the process will be even more relevant. The balance of power will then be shifted to the local area.

The fear that the community will act arbitrarily in the hiring and firing of teachers has only limited justification. State procedures and civil service regulations are an important constraint on local action. The teachers' organizations and contracts provide a further limitation. Most important, the short supply of teaching staff and the vast needs of the community give the teachers a decided advantage in disputes on these issues.

The strong clash between the United Federation of Teachers and the Ocean Hill-Brownsville and I.S. 201 districts in New York City suggests that similar conflicts will arise in those cities where the union is a powerful force in the central structure. However, the position of the teachers' union in Washington, D.C., in favor of cooperative action indicates that the character of union leadership and membership is not uniform. In Washington, 75 percent of the teaching staff is black; this is clearly a factor in their decision to support efforts toward community control over decision making. In cities where the union or teachers' organization has not become a prime policy maker, teachers may be more willing to negotiate contracts on the local level.

Under community control, the role of teachers in the policy-making process can go beyond the areas of salary and fringe benefits. In a cooperative environment, they can become a vital instrument of professional policy making. They can become active in curriculum development and teacher training, either through advisory committees or by direct participation on local boards and faculty councils in each school. In the local district, they can be a source of significant policy inputs and program review. Accordingly, the structuring of teachers' committees and advisory groups in the local district should be given priority. This need not diminish their power;

in fact, in cities with weak teachers' organizations, their power will increase. In any case, it will provide a more flexible situation.

INTERGOVERNMENTAL RELATIONSHIPS AND COMMUNITY CONTROL

The degree of power that state and local agencies command will be determined by the formal structure of the community-controlled education system. Both the city and the state will counterbalance the local power structure. Even under a plan for complete local control, state education departments will set standards and make policies that will influence the actions of local governing boards. If citywide education boards are eliminated (which is unlikely), the state agencies will become more involved in urban education matters. The state influence will be largely professional, with power exercised through the state commissioner and his staff. In addition, state legislatures will continue to be involved as overseers of educational policy for the state as a whole. State participation will balance the more parochial view of local districts.

The mayor, under any circumstances, will continue to be held responsible for educational needs and problems throughout the city.[38] Even in cities where central school districts are fiscally independent, the mayor has been held responsible by the public for the actions of the school system. The creation of local districts will not change this attitude.[39] However, it might be desirable to create some mechanism of appeal to the city level through the mayor's office. It is likely that local control will be established under some central city structure, under either a board of education or the mayor. Therefore, local board power will be constrained and influenced by citywide standards and policies. Most local boards will try to expand their own powers through continual pressure on the central agency. Even a plan providing a minimum of local participation (as was adopted for the three demonstration projects in New York City) will

[38] For a discussion of the role of the mayor in school policies, see Gittell and Hollander, *Six Urban School Districts*, pp. 116–19.

[39] While on several occasions the UFT leadership and the Board of Education of New York City have accused the mayor of interfering with the school system in the September strike, they both looked to him for resolution of the conflict and at the same time blamed him for not coming up with the solution. *New York Post*, Sept. 25, 1968, pp. 1, 3.

result in increasing pressure for more local power. The central and local districts will create a new arena of political interchange on school policy, with each moving to influence the actions of the other. This can only be a healthy injection of new life into the policy-making process of the school system.

No plan of local control can avoid or eliminate a prominent role for the city and state. The problem is to assure a viable local source of power that can properly balance the larger and more professionally oriented interests. This can only be achieved by providing, within the system, those mechanisms that will be receptive to a shifting balance of power.

ROBERT F. LYKE

Representation and Urban School Boards

Currently numerous people are arguing that the urban school board is not sufficiently responsive to citizens in the community. They charge not only that board policies poorly reflect the interests and demands of citizens but also that the attitudes of the board members are unsympathetic and cynical. This criticism is made with increasing frequency by citizens active in community organizations (many of which are largely or entirely Negro) and is, in turn, being repeated by many of their academic and ideological supporters.

The feeling that the urban school board is unresponsive has caused a crisis of legitimacy in many northern cities. Citizens whose demands are unmet and who detect lack of sympathy and understanding among board members no longer accept their defeat in silence. With some, the lack of confidence in the board has reached such proportions that they feel justified in escalating their own attacks: complaining has changed to picketing; dramatic protests have been displaced by boycotts, sit-ins, and other acts of dubious legality; and, on occasion, verbal assaults have become physical attacks. Dissatisfaction with school boards and educational policies has been one of the prominent grievances of citizens in communities where civil disorders have occurred.[1] Because of this dissatisfaction it is not surprising that a principal motivation of the Mayor's

[1] *Report of the National Advisory Commission on Civil Disorders* (Government Printing Office, 1968), pp. 11–12, 236. Referred to as the Kerner Report.

Advisory Panel on the Decentralization of New York City Schools was to design a system that would be "responsive to the deep and legitimate desire of many communities in the city for a more direct role in the education of their children."[2]

The origins of this crisis of legitimacy are well known, at least in general terms. The migration of nonwhite groups to urban areas has created a distribution of political power such that the newcomers are dominated by whites. Although nonwhites gradually gain positions of influence and authority, the time-lag permits misunderstanding and distrust to develop. Within the public schools this problem is exacerbated for four reasons.

First, the percentage of public school students who are nonwhite always significantly exceeds the percentage of total population that is nonwhite, emphasizing the distinction between the pupils and those who make decisions about their education. De facto school segregation caused largely by segregated housing patterns groups these pupils together, magnifying their problems and discontent.[3]

Second, public school bureaucracies are structured to emphasize professional competence, which in the twentieth century has delayed internal changes and raised barriers against pressure from parents and community leaders.[4] For example, teachers and principals are protected in their positions of authority and influence by state and local laws that require new employees to meet high standards in order to gain positions. As a result, disproportionately fewer nonwhites have been able to become educators.

Third, educators have not fully appreciated the social and economic characteristics of their nonwhite students; consequently, they have had difficulty adjusting teaching techniques and school programs to the needs of these students.[5]

[2] Mayor's Advisory Panel on Decentralization of the New York City Schools, *Reconnection for Learning: A Community School System for New York City* (1967), p. vii. Referred to as either the Bundy Report or the Mayor's Advisory Panel.

[3] Kerner Report, pp. 237–38.

[4] For a detailed study of this problem in New York City schools, see David Rogers, *110 Livingston Street: Politics and Bureaucracy in the New York City Schools* (Random House, 1968). Herbert Kaufman's "Administrative Decentralization and Political Power" (a paper presented at the 1968 annual meeting of the American Political Science Association; processed) discusses this issue as it affects public administration in general.

[5] For a graphic description of the impact of these problems on Boston city schools, see Jonathan Kozol, *Death at an Early Age* (Houghton Mifflin, 1967), and Peter Schrag, *Village School Downtown* (Beacon Press, 1967), Chaps. 3–4.

Finally, but no less important, the crisis in legitimacy has been nourished by the increasing political activity of American Negroes and the general ideological crisis that is the aftermath of the civil rights struggle of the 1950s.

Knowledge of these broad problems, however—particularly because they are broad problems—is not the same as knowledge of how to increase responsiveness of urban school boards and to end the crisis in legitimacy. In particular, knowing how the crisis originated does not indicate whether these problems can be solved by retaining a centralized school board that is reformed in certain ways (either by changing its membership or by giving it more authority and resources with which to work); whether the centralized board must be abolished and a system of decentralized school boards adopted; or what form a school board, be it centralized or decentralized, should have. Additional information is needed to explain why urban school boards are unresponsive to citizens in the community.

The School Boards Speak

To help answer these questions I studied relations between school board members and community organizations in two medium-sized cities on the East Coast. Large cities such as Boston, New York, and Philadelphia were purposely avoided so that the findings would have wider application. Both cities, however, have had disputes similar to those which have been so prominent in the larger cities. Four years ago in Alpha[6] there were demonstrations and sit-ins to protest the poor condition of a Negro elementary school. Currently, there are demands for more emphasis on black culture and for more rapid integration of the elementary schools, which are becoming increasingly segregated. There are angry protests that school officials and board members are inaccessible and that citizens may not present their grievances at board meetings. In Beta, there was controversy over the assignment of pupils to elementary schools located between white and nonwhite neighborhoods. At present, there is protest from the Negro community over the possible closing of a predominantly Negro high school. In both cities, the school boards

[6] The names of the cities and respondents were altered at the request of those interviewed.

have been attacked as unrepresentative. Negroes comprise approximately 40 percent of the cities' total population and approximately 70 percent of the public school enrollment.

In other respects, however, the two cities are quite different. Alpha is predominantly industrial and the population is largely lower-middle class. The main source of revenue for the public schools is the local tax on property values. The single board of education consists of nine members, all elected for six-year terms in citywide, partisan elections. Currently, all nine members of the Alpha board are Republican, as they have been for the past fifty years (the Democratic candidates normally get 25 percent of the vote). One member is Negro. The background and orientation of most board members is markedly local.

Beta, on the other hand, is more commercial and has a larger middle-class population. The single board of education consists of five members appointed by the governor for four-year terms. Board members are a mixture of Democrats, Republicans, and nonpartisans, and one is Negro. The background and orientation of board members is distinctly national.

Research was conducted largely by open-ended interviews of board members and leaders of community organizations and was focused on two questions: first, what reasons do board members give for not responding to the demands of citizens in the community and second, what factors in general facilitate or retard the responsiveness of public bodies in the field of education? It will be demonstrated that answers to the first question, which is discussed in this section, indicate that no centralized urban school board can adequately respond to the demands of citizens at the present time. This is partly due to the nature of urban social systems and partly to the characteristics of community organizations, which differ from traditional interest groups. Answers to the second question, on the other hand, give information about the type of decentralized school board that will be responsive.

It is interesting that board members, who were asked to describe their attitudes and actions during serious community school board controversies, are quite frank to acknowledge that they do not respond to the demands of the citizens in their community. All the board members interviewed recognized that citizens were making demands that they did not fulfill, and all but a few would admit that this lack of response on their part contributed to the dissatisfaction evident in the community. Yet *all* board members felt the need to justify their lack of response. Four explanations were predominant in their replies.

DEMANDS ARE IRRELEVANT

Most board members feel that on questions of educational policy the demands of community organizations are irrelevant. Boards of education, they claim, ought to provide good education at reasonable costs, irrespective of what citizens maintain. If community organizations push for what the board considers desirable, all the better; if they do not, their demands should be rejected:

> We should run the school district for the benefit of the children and taxpayers and let the chips fall where they may.

> The school board is duty bound to help all; its only obligation is to make the schools better.

> [Black history] is a good idea; it's relevant to their situation and ours; it's irrelevant that they are demanding it.

Similarly, one board member responded to a question about Negro protests over the closing of an almost all-Negro high school with the remark:

> It isn't a matter of ignoring their wishes or acceding to them. We rely on the experts.

This position is not as undemocratic as it might first appear. None of the board members who made these comments argued that they should ignore the complaints and suggestions of citizens who come before board meetings: what they contended instead was that the advice of experts (typically the superintendent, though occasionally outside consultants) should be given more weight. The citizens should be used as sources of information about possible educational problems; their views, however, might be unbalanced or wrong. In discussing an old elementary school with dark halls and small lavatories, one Alpha board member commented:

> About these improvements the spokesmen want—they aren't made because we don't feel they are educationally supportable.

It is significant that only one board member felt that the emphasis on black history and culture in the school curriculum resulted merely from community pressure:

It came because of the continual demand for it; we couldn't hold out against them forever.

What is surprising is that board members feel little inclination to accede to the demands of neighborhood groups merely to buy them off; none suggested, for example, that a program in black history and culture should be implemented in the hope that protestors would go away. This is partly because most board members feel that the spokesmen for community organizations have insatiable demands (discussed later); there is no point, they feel, in compromising with people who keep raising the ante.

Quite aware they are rejecting the demands of minority community groups, most board members believe they do so only to promote the citizens' long-run interest. The citizens are either pressuring for what is not an educational improvement (as the board member above explained away requests for building improvements) or are considered ignorant, as this comment about a critic of the schools indicates:

Reston wants nothing but agitation. The Negroes have no practical concept; they don't know whether the children are behind or ahead.

THE SCHOOL BOARDS ARE LIMITED IN TASK AND INFLUENCE

The second type of reason cited by board members for not adapting public policy to the demands of community organizations is that board members can play only a limited role and that some problems are beyond their ability to handle. All board members draw a distinction between their job and the job of the educators:

The school board doesn't run the schools; the board acts as a financial body in charge of schools.

We need more of a professional approach than a board approach.

If you select a good superintendent and staff, you automatically get good schools.

One board member felt that reliance on staff recommendations was the rule, despite what members sometimes said. In discussing why the board rejected an offer from a youth group to tutor ghetto youngsters, he commented:

Customarily the school board will accept the recommendation of the superintendent and his staff. In this case the board voted to back up the superintendent and there's a big public outcry. Then the members had to say something to justify their stance, and this had no relation to why they acted.

Abdicating responsibility to the professional educators is not seen as an evasion. The board members are hesitant to assess what appear to them as technical problems; at most, they feel they should turn complaints and questions over to the superintendent.

Board members also feel limited in another way. They are not optimistic that what they do will have much impact on the overwhelming problems they encounter:

I don't think there's any solution within the next ten or even twenty years.

Whites are moving out anyway. The city today has more problems than just schools. The population migration figures are the result of diverse pressures. I don't think the school board can hold this at all.

Integration is a losing battle—we can't do it.

To act is considered just as futile as not to act, so board members prefer to resist making even a gesture, since the costs of significant change are high and the rewards are temporary:

A lot of complaints are justified but it's tough to know what to do. Charlie Reston's group came and complained that the Douglas School was a mess of broken glass and strewn toilet paper. Well, I'll tell you what happened: we put in new windows and stocked up on toilet paper but the next day things were the same. The kids run wild with anything left in the johns and they bust fifteen or sixteen panes a day. How can we stop that?

This pessimism affected board policy to quite differing extents in the two cities. In Alpha, where both educators and board members have a local background and orientation, problems of education for minority groups generated mostly despair. Members tended to feel that improvements would come only by changes in home life and through the aspirations of the students. They felt no special obligation to help these students beyond what they did for other, more advantaged ones, and they never mentioned programs undertaken elsewhere. In Beta, on the other hand, the pessimism was restricted to an appraisal of how quickly problems would be eased. The board members were proud of special programs that educators had implemented, were aware of work going on elsewhere, and were willing to increase compensatory work if it might be useful.

COMMUNITY ORGANIZATIONS ARE IRRESPONSIBLE

A third reason mentioned by board members for not responding to the demands of community organizations is that the organizations do not act responsibly. Board members feel that the organizations' leaders are antagonistic and make unfair demands. A frequent complaint is that the leaders disrupt school board meetings. They are verbose, arrogant, and unorganized.

I have no objection to sitting until 1 or 2 A.M. if we get something done, but eight would say the same thing as the first and it would take two hours.

We're glad for suggestions, but they want to run it.

Were he to come with a different attitude, he would get a lot further.

These people who are trying to get involved—now it's not shaking up—it's harassing. Educators are now doing all they can do. The people won't sit down—they are just shouting it out—they have no spokesmen.

The Alpha board has had such unruly meetings that it has adopted what is known as the Choker Rule, requiring people who want to speak before the board to notify the secretary in writing in advance and then to limit their remarks to five minutes. Naturally, the rule infuriates community organization leaders who see it as nothing more than a device to curtail criticism. But board members comment:

I voted against [the Choker Rule] as a permanent fixture. I feel anybody who is a citizen and taxpayer has a right to speak—but we've had meetings when we've feared someone would get hurt.

The Choker Rule was necessary, for they were definitely going to make the school board stay all night.

Organization leaders are also seen as aggressive and needlessly militant:

Their demands are overplayed. These groups are a bunch of agitators.

Rose is nothing but a professional agitator. I think he has created more problems than the Negro has. He's idolized only by the fifteen- and sixteen-year-olds.

This could have been handled differently, by coming into the board meetings. Picketing wasn't required, for they had a just gripe.

The Reverend Love, he overdid his role and we overdid ours. It got more attention than it deserved.

None of the board members would disagree with the comments of this board chairman:

There's two ways of doing it. There's not a man in Dayton County from Judge Singer on down that I can't sit down and talk with. When I fight, I walk into their office. Now the demonstrations were good but to a point, but then they smashed my car and walked around my house. They might be pressing without stopping to think. It's got to be worked out.

Demands for improvement of schools in ghetto areas tend to be dismissed by board members who, without denying that problems exist, resist what they feel are appeals for special treatment:

Leave this "black" out and go to the schools as a whole, and they'll be a lot more successful.

The Supreme Court decision applies to Negroes as well as whites.

In rejecting any emphasis on black history or black culture, one board member said:

I don't think that race of any type should be propagated in the schools. Historical events should be pointed out, of course.

One Negro board member complained:

We must arrive at prejudice at a different way than they're doing. I refuse to favor the Negro; I am therefore an Uncle Tom. They say this of anyone who tries to be fair.

Some Alpha board members complained that it was basically unfair to institute compensatory programs for ghetto children:

You have so many parents. They've got six or seven kids and they don't care. They go out and sit on the taxpayer.

The Negro is predominant in the schools but the whites pay the most taxes. Nobody wants to be his brother's keeper at this point.

The charge of irresponsibility of organization leaders is, of course, overplayed. Board members are not as critical of people toward whom they are basically predisposed, even though such people make special appeals or at times are unruly at meetings. Furthermore, the few who do judge them critically tend to make special allowances:

Harry Edmonton, of course, is a racist, though I just don't know how many in his group are. But, look, he is basically a nice guy—have you met him?—and rightly concerned with what's going to happen in Alpha. You can't blame him for that.

The label of irresponsibility is applied to all opponents, from the militants to those who are merely persistent. But the tactics of the community organizations permit board members to rationalize rejecting their demands, a point that is not insignificant. More important though, these tactics make it easier for board members to justify to others in the city their opposition to the demands of the community organizations, thus helping to strengthen opposition to nonwhites.

Not surprisingly, board members frequently feel that they cannot get through to the leaders and members of the community groups:

> They have representation, but they are dissatisfied with the representation they have. And those who are dissatisfied—I don't know how to put this —don't have an education to understand.

> They are hard to communicate with; they don't seem to understand.

> If the Negro community had the proper leadership and had the proper respect and understanding, then we can sit down and talk and we'll get a lot further. The trouble is the spokesman for them—he don't [sic] know how to speak.

> It's actually—you need good communication and good understanding and the colored don't have it.

This feeling of poor communication is shared by leaders of the community organizations. The two sets of participants rarely contact each other outside of the official board meetings; they do not meet informally nor do they telephone or write each other. Board members are not particularly eager to increase communication:

> They must see our principals, I think. That's what they are there for.

The community leaders also feel that more contact would not do any good: why talk with people who always reject your suggestions? That the only confrontation occurs at board meetings tends to reinforce the suspicion of board members that the spokesmen desire publicity as much as dialogue.

COMMUNITY ORGANIZATIONS ARE ILLEGITIMATE

The fourth reason for the lack of response to the demands of community organizations is that school board members feel that, in many ways, the community organizations are not legitimate. For example, a frequent complaint is that the organizations are not an accurate reflection of the community:

The rank and file of the Negroes of Alpha still like the neighborhood school. They want gradual change and don't want radical change.

Those who come before the board want integration, but others want to preserve the neighborhood.

The average Negro doesn't want this agitation.

The middle class is as much concerned as the radicals but they don't say as much. It just isn't natural.

The petition was signed by 700 people, but—huh—I haven't seen it.

The charge is similarly made that the organizations underrepresent the most important group, parents:

The Hayward PTA Executive Committee has no parents of Hayward students on it!

If we just had to work with parents, I'm certain we could have worked things out.

A lot of these people who want to represent parents really don't represent them.

Nonparents are hard to satisfy; parents are easy to satisfy.

In opposing a desegregation plan that would require elementary students to walk farther, one board member commented:

I was brought up with the idea that you have to have parents interested in the schools. By making them walk farther you will kill parent-teachers' organizations. How can we reach the community then?

A number of board members believe that the community organizations are not interested in education per se; if they are not merely concerned with building an organization for personal power, then they are aiming at ideological victories which are difficult to relate to problems of running schools:

The newer generation with their militant attitude—they just don't seem to care about an education, with the exception of a few.

The parents won't come in on vandalism. They don't complain about the rocks being thrown through windows. They could at least make an effort.

The most serious charge, however, is that the leaders of the community groups are without a following, that is, they do not even have much support in the community:

The more interest shown the better it is all around, but there's this danger: Rose—he came here to agitate; he comes nearly every meeting night and wants to talk; the school board would be making a mistake if we felt that in any way he represents the rank and file of the citizens.

Board members are especially critical of neighborhood leaders who are newcomers or who appear to be acting in a professional capacity:

Rose hasn't been in Alpha too long.

All those pickets they had—*they* weren't from Alpha; they were sent down from the college.

Reverend Love—well, he's been trying to build the Westside Association up for some time.

Several board members commented about a particular social worker:

He's paid $25,000 a year to agitate.

Being "outsiders" or professionals is a serious offense to board members concerned about working with parents, if with anyone, but the complication, as some members see it, is that these spokesmen without followers are attempting to build their organizations by disingenuous appeals:

I have no objection to [courses in black history] as long as there is sufficient demand. It is, of course, an artificially stimulated demand.

Rose does this to win a following—though I don't know why anyone needs fifteen-year-olds running after him.

In short, the crisis in legitimacy that community organizations experience with respect to urban school boards is matched by a similar crisis among board members with respect to community organizations. Board members see the organizations as making demands, and feel that they should bring only complaints and suggestions. Furthermore, many of the demands involve policy changes which board members feel are either beyond their competence or are not adequate to reduce the overwhelming problems faced in urban public education. Board members also label the community groups "irresponsible," meaning that their spokesmen are antagonistic and that they make unfair demands. Finally, the organizations are considered illegitimate, since they are run by outsiders and professional organizers and have small, unrepresentative memberships.

Board members' perceptions of the size of community organizations were accurate more often than not. In these two cities such organizations are of three main types: (1) racial associations founded and run by Negroes, which are filling the void created by the collapse of civil rights organizations in the early 1960s (a number of these are avowedly militant, black power groups); (2) area organizations founded and generally still run by ministers or social workers, white as well as nonwhite, which are relatively moderate in program and action; and (3) ad hoc organizations founded by parents, which rise quickly over an issue and then, despite their names and intentions, collapse into inactivity. In Alpha and Beta all of these organizations were in what can best be called formative stages: they were either new or were considered by their leaders to be "just revitalized." Active membership in these groups does not exceed a dozen people, though on particular occasions (such as a demonstration) fifty or even several hundred supporters might appear.

With the exception of the area organizations, in which the professional leaders are trying to transfer control to people in the community, the community organizations are caught in a vicious circle over the question of their own legitimacy. Lack of actual community support causes the school board to doubt their representativeness and to break communication with them. This break is seen as a hostile act by the leaders of the organizations, who then stage confrontations to build up membership. The confrontations, in turn, cause even more doubt among board members, and this eventually provokes sharper conflict over the next issue.

To organization leaders the central question is not how many members they have, or whether the membership is a microcosm of the community, but what are governmental institutions such as boards of education doing to permit community control. As one leader commented:

> Of course we're small. But people aren't going to join us as long as they are harassed by Superintendent Vosburgh and the school board.

To these people then, community control—or at least the genuine response of the school board to demands of community leaders—must come before extensive participation can be expected. To board members, on the other hand, a response to these organizations as they are presently constituted would be undemocratic—it would grant authority to groups that lack legitimacy.

The Boards' Viewpoint Examined

The answers given by board members explaining their lack of response to the demands of the community organizations indicate that no centralized urban board of education is likely to be very responsive. To begin with, one cannot argue that a centralized school board with more authority or financial resources would take a different position, for both the Alpha and Beta boards had sufficient authority and finances to implement most of the demands made on them. One of the most frequent demands, that board members listen more closely and patiently to the complaints of the citizens, could presumably be satisfied without the expenditure of any additional funds. Furthermore, none of the board members mentioned, even when pressed, that lack of authority or funds was the principal motivation for their actions.

Similarly, the answers indicate that a centralized school board would not be any more responsive if its composition were changed to reflect more closely the social and economic characteristics of the population in the community. Members of the Alpha and Beta boards had markedly similar views about responding to citizens' demands despite the diversity of their racial, social, and economic characteristics. While some members were more understanding than others, and some less caustic in their appraisal of the activists, none felt that as a matter of policy their board ought to be more responsive than it was.[7] Placing more Negroes on the board would not necessarily change responsiveness.

Why do members of centralized urban school boards react this way to demands from the community? Why are they not more responsive? The basic reason is that centralized school boards in most cities face social systems that are markedly heterogeneous. The con-

[7] That social and economic characteristics of board members cannot be used to predict policy positions has been confirmed in other studies. See Roy Caughran, "The School Board Member Today," *American School Board Journal*, Vol. 133 (December 1956), pp. 25–26, and Peter Rossi, "Community Decision-Making," *Administrative Science Quarterly*, Vol. 1 (March 1957), pp. 420–43.

stituency of a centralized urban board is composed of virtually unspecifiable clusters of people who differ with respect to race, religion, economic status, and culture; indeed, to speak of a "community" at all is a mistaken and misleading use of words. If board members were to respond to the demands of one social group, they would be pressured to respond to the demands of others. To permit one community organization to have influence over educational policy would stimulate demands for similar influence from others. Even establishing open, definite communication channels with all the citizens would reduce board members' power to reject demands that are parochial or disruptive, since they would then have to explain their actions. In a homogeneous community, a school board is not faced with these problems. While it might not agree with all demands from community groups, at least it would not be attacked by competing groups if it compromised and acquiesced to some of them. Moreover, in a homogeneous community a school board is more likely to anticipate the demands of community groups when initially shaping educational policy.[8] In a heterogeneous community, however, a centralized board that attempts to respond to demands of community organizations will only lose what control it has over policy formation.

Boards of education are more vulnerable to competing pressures from community groups than are other local government bodies.[9] Because of the size of the education budget and the ideological implications of the programs, the public schools draw the interest and concerns of nearly all social groups in the city, whereas other government functions concern only a relatively small number. Furthermore, school board members are only part-time officials, many of whom have had little previous political experience, thus as a group they lack the time and expertise to handle the demands made on them.

It is also important to recognize that the community organizations involved in the crisis of legitimacy are different from other in-

[8] See the author's "Suburban School Politics" (Ph.D. thesis, Yale University, 1968), Chaps. 8–9.

[9] For a description of how some government officials draw upon and manipulate various social groups to gain power for themselves, see Wallace S. Sayre and Herbert Kaufman, *Governing New York City* (Norton, 1965), pp. 253–63.

terest groups in city politics, including other interest groups involved in school affairs. Traditional interest groups, such as teachers' organizations, companies that sell school supplies, or labor unions, rarely are open or salient: they favor select or limited membership; they hold private meetings (if they hold meetings at all); and they prefer to bargain privately with school officials or board members. These groups do not attempt to appear representative of the community as a whole and are interested in only a limited number of goals (such as higher salaries and better job guarantees or profitable contracts). Community organizations, on the other hand, are quite different. By their very nature they are open and salient: they attempt to build large, nonselective memberships; they hold public meetings; and they argue their positions before the school board in open, publicized meetings. They try to appear representative of the community as a whole and are concerned with a wide variety of issues. School board members find it much easier to respond to the demands of the former groups: since negotiations are generally unpublicized and follow regular procedures, board members can control the bargaining and anticipate the outcomes. When dealing with community organizations, however, board members cannot limit publicity or establish regular bargaining procedures; consequently, they lose control and cannot anticipate the outcomes. Shaping public policy to the demands of one group arouses competing demands from others, and in such open, hostile situations it is difficult to work out compromises. Moreover, traditional interest groups frequently have a monopoly of some services or goods that a school board needs (such as trained personnel or supplies at reasonable cost) and thus they can force the board to negotiate with them. Community organizations, on the other hand, rarely have been able to muster comparable threats; a school board that refuses to negotiate with them loses nothing but good will. For both these reasons, centralized urban school boards often respond to the demands of traditional interest groups while ignoring those of community organizations.

It is sometimes charged that urban board members do in fact respond to community groups and that the current controversy results only because they are not responding to the demands of all groups equally and fairly. In particular, it is charged that urban school boards respond to demands of the dwindling numbers of middle-class whites still remaining in the cities, and that significant gains for Negroes have had to come from boycotts, court cases, and pressure by federal and state governments. In Alpha and Beta, however, this is not true. Board members as a whole have little contact with any community organizations, and the few who do generally do not agree with all of the organization demands. Board policy in both these cities is often quite similar to the policy preferences of white community organizations, but this is because those preferences, being for the perpetuation of the status quo, are both easier to implement (since they involve less political cost than policies of change) and are seen as more reasonable (since established practices become legitimate over time).

In summary, members of centralized school boards do not respond to the demands of citizens in the community because they consider these demands as either irrelevant or unreasonable and regard the community organizations as irresponsible and illegitimate. Partly because board members' conceptions of these organizations are accurate, it is unlikely that their attitudes will change or their policies will become more responsive. Neither increasing a centralized board's authority or resources nor appointing members that better reflect the social characteristics of the community will change the situation. Because they face a heterogeneous constituency with conflicting community organizations, board members prefer to minimize community influence rather than face continual, conflicting pressures.

The Crisis in Political Representation

If centralized school boards cannot be sufficiently responsive to the demands of local citizens, how can the current crisis in legitimacy be ended? Would a system of decentralized school boards be better? To answer these questions, it is necessary to examine the problem of political representation in public education and to try to identify those factors that affect the responsiveness of boards of education.

In her superb study, *The Concept of Representation*, Hanna F. Pitkin argues that political representation consists "simultaneously of both formal, 'outer' institutional aspects and substantive, 'inner' purposive ones."[10] The former are various concrete organizational techniques, such as regular, free elections, that historically have been used to secure the intention of representation. The latter, or the substantive aspects of representation, are metaphorical expressions indicating that the people are "present" in the actions of their government in some complex manner. Of course, people are not literally present—after all, the whole point is to have someone else represent them—but in some certain if difficult to specify way their demands and interests must be reflected in government policy. As with all institutions, tension exists between the substantive component—the realization of the peoples' demands and interests—and the organizational components, which may or may not adequately insure the substantive goals.

The formal aspect of representation on urban school boards is clear: in Alpha and Beta, as well as in other American cities, the boards are either chosen in regular, free elections or they are appointed by an elected official. But as the crisis of legitimacy in these same cities indicates, the formal components are not presently securing the substantive ones. Numerous citizens feel that urban boards are reflecting neither their demands nor their interests in the development of educational policy. While board members may claim that the solutions presented by leaders of community organizations are not viable or legitimate, the widespread frustration and discontent are evidence of the lack of substantive representation. The formal representing institutions simply do not provide adequate means for urban citizens either to direct or control educational policy.

This problem is most clearly seen in those systems where board members are appointed, for the appointers—be they the mayor, the governor, or municipal judges—do not campaign for election on issues of educational policy. The norm "keeping politics out of the schools" makes it difficult for the appointer to interfere more than occasionally with educational policy in any overt way and permits board members to rebuff covert attempts. Besides, if there is controversy, most appointers would just as soon avoid involvement.[11]

[10] (University of California Press, 1967), p. 236.

[11] Events in New York and Philadelphia in 1967–68 have prompted mayors to take a more active role in education politics. It remains to be seen whether their activity is

Matters are not much different in elective systems, whether partisan or nonpartisan, since board elections are characteristically devoid of issues and debates. Typically, the emphasis in these elections is on the personal qualities of the candidates, and discussion of local educational policy rarely is significant.[12]

Of course, through elections citizens do have some influence over policy formation, for technically they can replace either appointees or board members whose educational policy is unpopular. This control, however, is minimal and imprecise, and it is difficult for community leaders to force tests of strength over particular issues. The elections do not permit concerned citizens to hold political leaders accountable, and this in turn produces the current frustration that is so disturbing.

Why does education politics lack sufficient substantive representation? Why are the formal institutions not insuring that the demands and interests of the citizens are sufficiently reflected in public policy? By comparing urban education to other policy areas, two reasons for the difficulty in achieving substantive representation become apparent.

First, educational systems lack institutions that could supplement the formal ones that already exist. Political parties, for example, play a negligible role: typically, they are restricted to controlling nonprofessional positions for patronage and, in some cities, obtaining contracts for supplies and materials (this is the case both where board members are partisan and where they are nonpartisan). In other municipal policy areas, however, the parties are more active: they provide continual, salient organizations for the communication of grievances and suggestions, and they help, alternatively, to make legitimate the response of the bureaucracy. Active parties provide a mechanism by which public officials have contact with

---

only temporary, based just on the prominent conflicts that have closed the schools. But it could be that controversy will be so rampant over the next decade that mayors will take an active part in fashioning educational policy.

[12] Despite there being well-publicized incidents to the contrary, the frequency with which school board elections are fought over issues is quite low. See, for example, Richard F. Carter, *Voters and Their Schools* (Stanford University, School of Education, Institute for Communication Research, 1960), pp. 7, 16; Roscoe C. Martin, *Government and the Suburban School* (Syracuse University Press, 1962), pp. 51–58; and the author's "Suburban School Politics," Chap. 7.

the community; the parties recruit officials and then support them in encounters with citizens. The official is not left facing a potentially hostile community by himself.[13]

Second, there is a lack of diversity among the political representatives who fashion educational policy. All board members are either elected by the same constituency or are appointed by the same agent. In other policy areas, however, representatives are frequently selected by different processes. In city councils, some councilmen are elected by district while others are elected at large; or, more commonly, the councilmen are elected by district while the mayor is elected at large. Most cities, even those with strong mayor systems of government, elect some administrators in addition to the councilmen and mayor. In these policy areas the elected representatives come from different constituencies and consequently adopt different public positions; citizens who do not find their substantive demands reflected by one representative may find them reflected by another. Conflicts in the community have a greater chance of being reflected in conflicts among the political representatives. Therefore, if citizens do not find their preferences reflected in public policy, at least they can identify some public officials who support their views.

The impact of these two characteristics of the politics of urban education is, thus, twofold: it is difficult for citizens to ask questions and present demands, and it is difficult for school board members and school administrators to legitimize controversial decisions. Communication is awkward, and in times of controversy this only compounds frustration and distrust. The numerous social groups that have concern and interest over public school policy lack effective ways to express themselves.

To some extent, American educators have recognized this problem, for periodically they suggest, and sometimes implement, institutions to improve communication with the community. The most common such innovation, of course, is the parent-teachers' association (PTA), though other variants have been tried: citizen

[13] For the general impact of nonpartisanship on local political systems, see Edward C. Banfield and James Q. Wilson, *City Politics* (Harvard University Press, 1963), p. 165, and Robert C. Wood, *Suburbia: Its People and Their Politics* (Houghton Mifflin, 1959), pp. 161–66.

advisory committees, community school councils, parent-teacher conferences, and so on.

It is doubtful, however, whether these innovations by themselves can significantly improve substantive representation. Since typically they originate and depend upon either board members or school officials, they are likely to lack legitimacy in communities where citizens are already hostile and suspicious. Changing the style of political activity is not likely to convince critics that in fact changes in substance have occurred. Beyond this, it should be recognized that these innovations depend upon the cooperation of board members and educators, which in serious disputes is not likely to happen. Thus the problem of substantive representation remains.[14]

[14] Of course, it can be argued that public policy should not be a simple reflection of the demands of the community. In fact, in some circumstances, good representation probably requires that the representative be permitted to exercise independent judgment (see Pitkin, *The Concept of Representation*, Chap. 7). For example, professional educators often have demands and interests that conflict with those of the community. For both professional and political reasons, members of boards of education often choose to support the superintendent and other educators in disputes with citizens, a stance aptly illustrated above by the Beta board member who commented, "we rely on the experts." In policy areas that administrators are considered to have technical competence which laymen are chary to judge, it would be difficult, if not foolhardy, to support the citizens consistently and ignore the professional staff. Nonetheless, the tendency of board members to abdicate effective authority on educational policy to administrators and teachers is a significant restriction on substantive representation.

Furthermore, state and federal laws and administrative regulations have always limited policy enactment by local boards of education, irrespective of the desires and interests of local citizens. These restrictions can provide endless frustration in a state such as New York, which has extremely detailed laws and regulations. In a strict sense, perhaps, these limitations do curtail local representative government since local, popular mandate may be overruled elsewhere; however, these restrictions are democratic within the larger decision arena and, quite obviously, are a permanent feature of our federal system.

Whether these qualifications which limit the extent to which policies reflect local demands are ultimately in the long-run interest of all citizens is, of course, difficult to establish. In some form the points mentioned above have traditionally been incorporated within democratic theory, so that it is quite reasonable to maintain that simple reflection is not what representation is about.

Recognition of these restrictions, however, does not mean that citizens' demands and interests should be ignored. For one thing, citizen communication ought to be encouraged as a source of information about problems of policy implementation. For another, good representation presumably requires that the restrictions be sensibly explained to the citizens by either the educators or the board members. Role conflicts of this sort for representatives are discussed in J. Roland Pennock's "Political Representation: An Overview," in J. Roland Pennock and John W. Chapman (eds.), *Representation*

Decentralization as a Solution

After discussing why centralized urban school boards resist responding to community demands, and considering why substantive representation is so undeveloped in the political system of urban public education, it is appropriate to discuss a current proposal that many thoughtful people believe will end the crisis in legitimacy: decentralization of urban school boards.[15]

Will decentralization sufficiently improve formal representation mechanisms to insure adequate substantive representation? Will it enable the new boards of education to respond to the demands of the community? The answers to these questions depend to a great extent on the particular design of the decentralized system: whether there are enough individual districts to encompass only small populations; whether all board members are elected by citizens of the district or some are appointed by an outside authority; whether the decentralized boards have significant authority to form program policy and to hire, transfer, or dismiss personnel; whether revenue is adequate to permit the much-needed reform; and so on.

In general, the more authority decentralized school boards have, the easier it will be for them to reflect the demands of citizens within their respective areas. The boards will find it difficult to respond to such demands if they must first clear policies with centralized institutions. For example, a centralized board of education in the very act of granting approval to local board action will attempt to establish policies that are consistent throughout the city. Similarly,

(Atherton Press, 1968), pp. 3–27. According to Pennock, representatives have "a special obligation to look after the desires and interests of the people" (p. 12) but this doesn't preclude independent action in matters of conscience and the like. Beyond this, there would appear to be a number of matters in which neither laws and regulations nor educators' final judgments ought to be paramount; in these matters the desires and interests of the community should be given precedence. The public schools are not simple pedagogical laboratories, and teaching cannot be isolated from political and social controversies.

[15] Careful distinction must be made between a decentralized system of urban school boards, which is discussed here, and administrative decentralization within a system that is governed by a centralized school board. While the latter structure would undoubtedly solve some problems now facing schools in large cities, by itself it does little if anything to increase substantive representation.

centralized administrators are likely to dismiss local policy that differs from their own preferences by charging that special interests are using local boards to violate canons of administrative rationality. Likewise, a centralized teachers' union will undoubtedly support local educators against criticism and demands from the various communities.

It should be recognized that decentralization will preclude some policy options for local boards and that this will, in some districts at least, frustrate local demands. Bussing pupils beyond the local community in order to promote racial integration will be more difficult, since white districts will be able to resist pressure to participate from the centralized board. Similarly, decentralization might make it harder to obtain special funds, either from the federal or state governments, which now are more readily obtained by larger districts.

The decentralization proposals of the Mayor's Advisory Panel, as described in its *Reconnection for Learning*, are likely to frustrate the responsiveness of local boards to the demands of citizens in the community; in fact, in serious controversies, community tension and distrust may grow higher than they presently are. The proposed method of selecting local boards is quite cumbersome and will result in such vague lines of responsibility that the citizens will be unable to vote rationally. According to the report's recommendations, six members of the local board would be elected from the community and five appointed by the mayor. The six elected members, however, would not be elected directly but by a district assembly composed of delegates elected by parents of students at the individual schools. Similarly, the mayor would appoint only people who were nominated by the central education agency, which would replace the present centralized board of education.

Having five of the eleven members appointed by the mayor will dilute local control since the five need only to obtain the cooperation of one elected member to form a majority against the other five elected members. Furthermore, having a board composed partly of members who are appointed by an outside authority would make it difficult for voters who are dissatisfied with board policy to bring about change. It would not only be hard to influence the selection of members by the mayor, but also it would not be easy to identify the policy positions taken by locally elected members, all of whom will negotiate and compromise with appointed members, often in private.

The Mayor's Advisory Panel argues that this divided selection is necessary: first, to insure that the decentralized districts retain the advantages that the city as a whole can offer, and second, to enable minority groups too small to elect a member to have some representation. But neither of these arguments is a necessary or sufficient reason for adopting the cumbersome procedure that the panel urges. If there are advantages in retaining some central coordination, they should either be persuasive enough that individual decentralized boards would willingly cooperate, or they could be insured by explicit requirements of the central education agency (or the state legislature or education department), which would override local preference. Ironically, the proposal of the Bundy Report does not insure such central coordination: after all, the local boards could ignore recommendations as long as the six elected members voted together. Second, minority groups too small to elect members to local boards could be given effective representation. By creating different constituencies within the local district and making the representation process more professional (see the discussion of these points in the following section), the selection procedure could still be confined to local elections.

Having indirect elections for the six local seats would make it difficult for citizens (or parents, if the electorate is to be so restricted) to vote rationally. Citizens who are dissatisfied with board policy, for example, would not easily be able to determine how to vote for delegates to the district assembly. The delegates might not compete with one another (why should they if they have no authority to establish policy?); they might not distinguish their positions on the matters that concern the citizens; or, as is most likely, they might not take a position at all.

The Bundy Report raises three objections to direct elections: first, the danger that political parties would dominate the elections; second, the difficulty of persuading qualified people to become board members if they would have to campaign; and third, the likelihood that few ghetto residents would actually participate.

The first criticism is not persuasive. Nonpartisan elections, even in localities where political parties are otherwise strong, rarely are significantly influenced by party activity.[16] Furthermore, party influence would undoubtedly be stronger under the proposed indirect elections, partly because the voters and the delegates would have to rely upon some organization to insure policy accountability and partly because parties can have greater influence over the small number of delegates in the district assembly than over the larger number of voters. The second point is also invalid. People who want to serve on local boards but are adverse to campaigning would be weak board members in the very way that decentralization was designed to be a strengthening measure: they would not have adequate contact with the citizens during the campaigns and would find no compelling reason to do so once elected. While there are people who dislike campaigning, it is difficult to understand how they can be considered good representatives. Finally, if the panel fears that low turnout in board elections is probable,[17] it is hard to see how they could then justify any local election, even that of the district assembly. Actually, turnout would probably be higher in direct elections since votes would be more meaningful. Substantive representation and responsible government can be more readily achieved by local, direct election of all board members.

The awkward dispute in New York City at the beginning of the 1968–69 academic year gives further insight into the type of decentralized system that will best be able to respond to citizens' demands. First, decentralization will be frustrated to the extent that administrative lines of direction and control remain ambiguous. In the Ocean Hill-Brownsville district, such lines were indeed vague:

[16] See Charles Adrian, "A Typology for Nonpartisan Elections," *Western Political Quarterly*, Vol. 12 (1959), pp. 449–58, and the author's "Suburban School Politics," Chap. 2. Where political parties are closely competitive in other elections, voting results may be quite similar to those in partisan elections, but this is due to the cohesive value preferences of the voters, not to direct party activity. See Oliver P. Williams and Charles R. Adrian, "The Insulation of Local Politics Under the Nonpartisan Ballot," *American Political Science Review*, Vol. 53 (December 1959), pp. 1052–63.

[17] While turnout in ghetto areas during elections is generally low, it is doubtful that turnout in local elections anywhere can be considered significantly better. In nonpartisan school elections held in a New York suburb, the mean turnout across a fifteen-year period was only 10 percent of the turnout during a presidential election, and obviously was even less as a percentage of the possible voters (see the author's "Suburban School Politics," Chap. 7). Significantly, the board in the Ocean Hill-Brownsville experimental district was elected by 25 percent of the eligible voters.

essentially, the educators had two bosses—the local board and the New York City Board of Education—that frequently disagreed and issued conflicting orders. Second, decentralization will be thwarted insofar as the authority of the local board depends upon the discretion of the centralized board. In New York, disputes between the two (which will invariably occur, given a centralized board of any influence) were complicated by the centralized board's withdrawing authority from the local board, which neither settled the substantive issues nor assuaged an already tense community. Appeal processes must be maintained, of course, but they should be directly between the local district and the state commissioner of education. Finally, a distinction must be made between the difficulties that decentralization would cause and the difficulties that implementation of decentralization would cause. The latter problems, such as transferring of teachers and altering curricula, are presumably temporary problems which, while difficult, cannot be ascribed to the system of decentralization per se.

By and large under a decentralized system the willingness of school board members to respond to demands of the citizens will increase significantly. In part, this will come simply because members of decentralized boards will be from smaller districts: they will have closer ties to the separate communities and will be able to understand and appreciate citizen complaints. Moreover, if members on the decentralized school boards must run for reelection in their districts, then presumably in the long run they will be forced to respond to local demands more than centralized board members, whether appointed or elected.

Most important, substantive representation will be improved because decentralized school boards will not face as heterogeneous a community as does the centralized board. As was pointed out earlier, the primary reason that centralized school boards try to limit communication with community organizations and do not respond to community demands is that in a heterogeneous community such practices would lead to chaos in the policy-formation process. Numerous groups with irreconcilable and intractable demands would pressure the board, and the members' control of school policy would become unpredictable and tenuous. With decentralized school districts, however, this is much less likely to happen since most, if not all, decentralized urban districts would be significantly less heterogeneous. The separate boards could respond to pressures in each of their own communities. Local control would permit variation in local policy.

Other Reforms

While decentralization of urban school districts would significantly improve substantive representation in education politics, decentralization by itself is unlikely to be the complete answer. In fact, for several reasons decentralization might entail some political practices that could thwart good substantive representation.

First, as in all electoral systems, the representatives rarely, if ever, receive an explicit mandate from the voters. Candidates do not take clear stands on the issues, and, more often than not, issues themselves are given little attention. Voters in turn do not always respond in terms of their issue preferences: some support candidates of similar racial or social characteristics, others support the ones with the best personal qualifications, while still others vote merely to throw incumbents out of office. In general, it is difficult to translate support for a candidate into support for a particular political position, even in a nonpartisan election. Furthermore, many issues arise between elections, when no formal ways of assessing community preferences are available. Thus, even a decentralized school board will find times when it cannot accurately respond to the preferences of citizens in the community.

Second, decentralization could be dangerous in the same respect that it is otherwise strong: the reduced social heterogeneity within individual school districts. Relative homogeneity will permit board members to establish closer contact with the community and will encourage more response to citizens' demands. However, increased homogeneity may decrease the visible symbols of conflict in the community, thereby decreasing the incentive to participate, and may also hamper the formation of interest groups based on minority elements within the new districts, permitting a new Establishment to form and become dominant. The former possibility is based on the assumption that people participate in local politics when they have something to protest rather than merely to exercise power. By removing the obvious symbols of antagonism, especially when improvements are made in the schools, people in the community may feel participation in meetings and elections to be less essential.[18] The latter point assumes that interest groups of all sorts can form more readily in larger districts, partly because larger districts have greater absolute numbers of people with a particular interest and partly because resources for organization, such as newspaper coverage, are better. Local politics, particularly in the field of education, depends heavily on the presence of on-going interest groups,[19] and decentralization may (depending on how district lines are drawn and how stable communities are) inhibit their formation and impact.

As mentioned above, one of the fears of the Mayor's Advisory Panel was that participation would be so low, particularly in the ghetto areas, that only a small number of people would be setting educational ploicy. To some extent, this argument over the amount of participation misses the point. The crucial question is not whether more people become active in school politics but whether community participation is sufficiently diverse to both support and challenge the position of educators and board members. Much of the participation in suburban school politics, for example, simply supports the educators (which is not surprising since it is organized and led by them) and thus fails to have the impact that it should in a democratic system of government. In short, increased community participation may only be a subtle way of forming a new Establishment group, one that appears legitimate because the active people in the community support it. Democracy, however, demands that attention be paid to the preferences of the inactive people as well, and any administrative system that makes it difficult for them to express their opinions must be regarded with skepticism.

Should these doubts about the effectiveness of decentralization discourage attempts to establish such a system? Should we continue with a centralized school board, maintaining that its drawbacks are

[18] Unfortunately, there is very little concrete information on the reasons for participation in local politics. While most studies show that people who feel powerless do not frequently participate, others indicate that even those with a sense of efficacy typically must be goaded to action by some striking event. Most participation in suburban school politics occurs at times of sudden, emotional public controversy, which is rare. See the author's "Suburban School Politics," Chap. 7.

[19] *Ibid.*

less serious and more visible than those of decentralized boards? Given the morass into which urban public education has fallen and the rampant discontent of ghetto communities, the answer is clear: we must decentralize school boards nonetheless, but attempt to prevent the likely defects.

To promote maximum substantive representation, a decentralized school board should be directly elected by citizens within the individual districts. In addition, three reforms should be made. First, an Ombudsman ought to be appointed by each decentralized board to help citizens with their complaints.[20] Most of his work would involve incidents with school administrators and teachers, but some would deal with disputes over board members' contact with the community (for example, he could handle the dispute over Alpha's Choker Rule). The Ombudsman would have to be independent of the educators, though he and his assistants should be familiar with teaching and administration. He should be able to assure the educators that the regularized handling of complaints and suggestions, especially by someone who shields them from a hostile public, will work in the long run to their advantage.

Operating perhaps from a store-front office and branches, the Ombudsman would be charged with listening to complaints, probing educators and board members for explanations, and, where necessary, working out compromises. Should the resolution of a dispute be unsatisfactory, he would be empowered to bring the matter up in public before the board. The Ombudsman need not interfere with the development of a sound teacher-parent relationship, but would always maintain an alternative channel for communication. His greatest service would be to translate citizen protests into reasonable demands and official responses into legitimate answers.

A second reform is to elect some board members, perhaps five on a nine-member board, from election districts smaller than the whole school district. These smaller election districts might be modeled on elementary or junior high school attendance boundaries, though this would not be mandatory. Such an election pattern would force elected board members to pay closer attention to the demands and

[20] For background and bibliography on this government innovation, see Stanley V. Anderson (ed.), *Ombudsmen for American Government?* (Prentice-Hall, 1968).

interests of different neighborhoods,[21] thus enabling the citizens in these areas to present their cases better. All citizens would then have alternative channels to express their preferences. Minority groups too small to elect members in at-large elections could more readily win positions on the board. While the whole purpose of this reform is to make policy more responsive to the demands of particular neighborhoods, undue parochialism would be avoided by the necessity of compromising with members elected from other smaller districts, and the necessity of persuading members elected from the district as a whole. The different electoral bases would engender differences and stimulate public debate on the board, a change certainly to be welcomed.

Finally, representation should be made professional by having the representatives be professionals: they should be full-time, paid legislators. Perpetuation of a board of unsalaried amateurs is an anachronism for twentieth-century cities with gigantic school budgets and overwhelming social and economic problems. Presently, board members can devote only part of their time to school affairs since they are usually extraordinarily busy people (with the possible exception of those who are retired, who should not be running urban school systems in the first place). Being offered a salary (perhaps $25,000 in New York City) for the position, board members could devote full time to their job, not only overseeing the work of the administrators but also contacting and listening to the citizens. A second advantage of this reform is that the salary would attract more candidates, not only increasing competition for board seats but also broadening its social base. The aristocratic donation of one's time to the community is, to be sure, commendable, but it tends to exclude those groups that do not have the resources and traditions that encourage this type of participation. The most important effect, however, is that salaried board members would fight to keep their positions, and in doing so would maintain closer contact with the community. Having to depend on reelection to keep one's job forces a representative to listen closely to citizen complaints.

The objection will be raised, of course, that the salary might at-

[21] Banfield and Wilson, *City Politics*, pp. 89–96.

tract board members who are primarily motivated by the monetary reward rather than good education or good government. While this may be the case, it is not obvious that such people would make worse representatives than the present members, who are motivated by desire to exercise power or to perform civic duties. Furthermore, it would be difficult not to improve on present members with respect to their knowledge of educational problems at the time when they joined the board; moreover, under this plan, new members would learn more quickly.

These three reforms will hardly be a panacea for the shortcomings in substantive representation in urban school districts, but they will help more than the other proposals currently being discussed. Their most significant feature is that they better enable dissatisfied citizens to contact and influence board members and school officials, thereby helping reduce citizens' discontent. The reforms can bring improvements without requiring attitude changes either by school officials and board members on the one hand, or by community leaders on the other, changes which are most unlikely to occur. The reforms could be instituted by the state government (the electoral changes) or local governments (the Ombudsman) without having to stimulate the participation of numerous people in the community, always an uncertain procedure. Finally, none of the reforms would be expensive to implement, not an unimportant consideration.

RHODY A. McCOY

The Formation of a Community-Controlled School District

The educational conditions in New York City's Ocean Hill-Brownsville district are deplorable. The six elementary school buildings are obsolete, overcrowded firetraps. The teaching staff is 50 percent substitutes with a higher than 30 percent yearly turnover. Of the 58 percent of the students who are academically below level about 6,000 are three or more years behind. No experienced principal has ever been assigned to fill a vacancy in this district; only new ones, who gain experience through trial and error, get trained, and then leave. Parents have been deceived, degraded, and denied information or redress of their grievances by teachers, principals, and other administrators while their children have consistently maintained a pattern of failure. Moreover, any real community involvement in the schools has been discouraged by school personnel, though the failure of students in school has been blamed on the parents. The Ocean Hill-Brownsville community has a higher unemployment rate than any neighboring area; it has the largest percentage of welfare recipients; it has a frightening narcotics problem that is largely ignored by the health authorities. Many buildings in the area are uninhabited, while absentee landlords wait to reap profits from Model Cities resales. The inadequate service of the Department of Sanitation makes the neighborhood's physical appearance horrendous. In the midst of all this squalor, there are many black homeowners in the area who attempt to maintain middle-class standards.

The people of Ocean Hill are, in fact, disadvantaged not only because they are economically poor and racially separated but because they have been denied equal employment opportunities. They are disadvantaged because their parents were "raised" under the separate but equal concept which was a sophisticated form of slavery. They are disadvantaged because of America's inability to resolve its racism. As a result of city housing patterns, even the more middle-class residents are lumped together with the welfare population.

Ocean Hill's people have had little experience with the processes of participatory democracy. It is a tribute to their basic commitment to human values that in a short year and a half they have been able to educate themselves to the point where they can make the city give them at least the rudiments of reasonably decent neighborhood services, including the start of a thoroughly reorganized and remodeled educational system. The outside observer of the efforts to redo the schools of Ocean Hill must remember that this was a divided and conquered neighborhood. Having undertaken to change the schools, the people are also persistently changing themselves into actively concerned citizens. A major effort has gone into the uniting of the various community elements, a process that continues to the present.

Why Community-Controlled Schools?

For too many years educational policy making and implementation have been in the hands of the educators. This situation takes on more meaning, particularly in the ghetto areas, when the policy implementors are neither community people nor ethnically representative of the community. In addition, they are not community-minded or sensitive to the socioeconomic trends in the community that affect the pupils' education and parental attitudes toward schools. Moreover, these implementors are, as a whole, job-oriented personnel. This condition may be acceptable if the level of productivity is satisfactory, but when those who appear job oriented do not produce, then their failings become more relevant.

Like the gyp furniture stores that entice the poor with dreams of fashionable purchases at apparently bargain prices, job-oriented teachers or administrators utilize the Madison Avenue technique of selling an inferior product to a receptive audience.

Team teaching is an example of such salesmanship. The first publicized results of team teaching were based on a program operated in a superior school, staffed by select, experienced teachers and supplemented with many extra services. The team teaching plan was implemented in urban schools with inadequate resources and children with special, unforeseen needs. Staffs were professionally and personally unprepared for the demands of the new technique, and the plan was not flexible enough to allow for the divergent needs of ghetto children. This program was the product actually foisted on the parents. They were forced to buy it for its purported gains. As in many such situations, realism was lost, and ultimately the parents were even made to feel the blame and sense of inadequacy that the professionals passed on to them as part of the package deal.

The top policy makers—those who design education and give instructions for its dissemination and implementation—are out of contact with the grass roots people—parents, children, and community-based school personnel. They have forced what they believe to be good and sound educational programs upon a school population that may initially be receptive but is inadequately prepared to carry them out. The inequities between the powerful and the poor are clearly defined. In effect, the professionals say, "You have it, but you can't do a damn thing with it, and without us (the professionals), you don't even have a hope."

Thus, the stage is set for a revolution. People—black people—want control over their schools for self-determination, for building a strong self-image, for individual and community development, for restoration of confidence in education, for economic stability, for recognition, and for survival. Community control means community growth and development, and the school is the hub of this growth.

The community is forced to make a decision as to whom it will entrust with this facet of development, what degree of control it must have over the process, and which controls it is willing to relinquish or share. Therefore, it must establish and then explicitly articulate what its needs, desires, goals, and expectations are. In accordance with these, it can proceed to decide upon plans for the education of its children.

Origin of the Independent School Board

From the time of the formation of District 17 in Brooklyn, people in Ocean Hill and the upper end of Brownsville were totally unrepresented on the local school board. In September 1966, interested parents and community leaders from these areas began to form what has become known as the Ocean Hill-Brownsville Independent School Board, District 17. This group set out to achieve three principal objectives: (1) to stimulate an almost inactive parents' association in the schools in this section; (2) to seek out interested teachers who wanted to work together with the community for the improvement of education; and (3) to form at each of the schools, school-community advisory boards consisting of parents, teachers, and community persons to participate in the running of the public schools. The schools included in this project were Junior High Schools (J.H.S.) 271 and 178, and Public Schools (P.S.) 144, 137, and 87.

A steering committee of parents, teachers, and community people was created in January 1967 for the opening of Intermediate School (I.S.) 55. The group wrote a proposal that would give the community a definite voice in the running of this new intermediate school. The community was particularly anxious that a principal be selected who would make learning possible for the early adolescent-age children of the area. They also asked for a voice in the selection of teachers, a voice in the formation of curriculum, the use of nonprofessional neighborhood staff in the school, and whatever other innovations would insure better education. The proposal was mailed to Bernard Donovan and members of the Board of Education, and the community awaited a response. After four months none had come.

By late April, the community was in contact with Mario Fantini of the Ford Foundation. Since J.H.S. 271, I.S. 55, and their feeder schools were at the farthest tip of District 17, and since the community there had organized around the issue of better education and was without proper representation on the local school board, it was agreed that the parents, community people, and teachers of the eight schools involved should formulate a proposal for decentralization that would establish the eight schools as an experimental unit. An official representative from the United Federation of Teachers (UFT) was also involved.

Fantini then arranged a meeting between the community people and Donovan, who urged the group to formulate the proposal and promised to meet afterward with all the parties concerned. At the second meeting with Donovan and Fantini, which was also attended by the UFT representative, the group discussed the proposal, point by point. Donovan explained that the proposal was substantially acceptable, but that in accordance with state law, certain parts would have to be discussed with the Board of Education and the state Education Department. It remained unclear whether the unit administrator would have to be a New York City principal or merely a person with New York State certification. Donovan said that he would discuss this point with the Board of Education. It was also left unclear whether the governing board in cooperation with the unit administrator would directly select principals for the various schools or whether the superintendent of schools had to participate in the selection, agree to it, or both. At the first meeting, Donovan stated that he would not offer these schools any more money than he could offer any other special service school. However, at the third meeting, he said that it was possible to secure additional money for these schools, though not as much as had been requested—which was at least a budget equivalent to the quotas in the More Effective Schools (MES) program. In addition, Donovan announced that the Board of Education agreed in concept to the experimental school unit in the Ocean Hill-Brownsville section and urged the community, supported by Ford Foundation funds, to prepare both teachers and parents for the formation of such a governing board.

Selection of the Unit Administrator

The unit administrator was selected from several applicants, each of whom had state certification as a principal or superintendent.

Candidates were both white and black; some had from fifteen to twenty years of experience. The steering committee spent from one to two hours with each candidate, questioning them on their experience, professional education, and educational philosophy. Relevant questions were asked: "Would you 'hold back' a student who could not read?" "How many times would you hold him back and what programs would you plan for him?" Questions like these obviously were matters of gut-level concern to the committee and reflected their educational experiences as well as their worries about the person they were to select. The candidates were viewed in terms of their ability to communicate with the various elements reflected in the group: professionals, parents, and community people. It was with primary focus on this quality—sensitivity to the aspirations of the community—that the decision was made. The person chosen needed the ability to hear both community and professional people and to translate what was said into clear terminology so as to be understandable to the whole group.

Another vital factor was the type of prior experience the candidate had and what he had accomplished, tried, and initiated. Had the candidate worked in a deprived area? What was his level of responsibility? What were his objectives and what had he done to achieve them? The candidate obtained a plus if he demonstrated initiative, innovative ideas, and concern for a district's problems rather than the desire for a well-paid career. The candidate gained additional consideration through statements that indicated sensitivity and awareness of the plight of minority group members. This concern was not to be limited to the philosophical level but also had to show the promise of personal involvement. Often the questions were acutely sensitive and controversial. The candidate had to demonstrate his ability to make decisions, take a position, defend it, and if necessary accept rebuke or another point of view. Was the candidate at ease, sincere, or going through the staid or traditional educator's interview? How much information did the candidate volunteer? What was the depth of his understanding? Would he, or could he, take a position contrary to that of the interviewing body or did he espouse what he felt the body wanted to hear? How much of a traditionalist was he? Did he reflect the status quo?

The interview, though not formally structured, was conducted through questions that gave the candidate a real sense of what working with community boards and people who were potential policy makers would be like.

As a candidate-elect, I took exception to many of the positions of the interviewers and volunteered information that questioned their knowledgeability. Immediately afterward I felt that I had "blown" the job. I made demands of the interviewers that I felt had to be met if our working relationship was to be a fruitful one. I feel now that I was accepted partly because of my own security—they recognized my accomplishments—and partly because the demands I made of them clearly indicated that I intended this to be a partnership.

District Staff Selection

The first step was to find the best-qualified people in specific disciplines to develop a team that could immediately structure areas of success. The most important criteria were the selection of people actively pursuing effective educational change, as well as having been successful in their pursuits of quality education, and the selection of people who, along with ability, would ethnically represent the population of the community. Any good administrator must establish a following of competent people in special disciplines. Briefly stated, I sought to find personnel whose beliefs were in consonance with the objectives of the program; personnel who could accept and shoulder decision-making responsibilities; and indigenous community people with skills and competence who were either overlooked or who had been relegated to positions of minimal stature in this segregated system, positions not in accordance with their ability. In addition, educators were carefully sought who could feel secure about "bucking" the Board of Education system when they had to.

These criteria of selection are particularly vital in the study of this one district. It must be remembered that we were to attack the most crucial problems under unique circumstances and had to work for solutions with maximum facility.

It's interesting to note that I was given free choice in the selection of my staff. In return, strategically as well as because of the importance of not making a unilateral decision, I presented or recommended my choices to the governing board for their approval.

I recruited a former college teacher and dean, expert in the area of guidance, to be my assistant. He was black. He had his doctorate and had spent years fighting to achieve professional success. I was confident that he could assume full responsibility for this project in my absence and was capable of sound decision making. Furthermore, he was an individual who was acceptable to the governing board and the community. Under this give-and-take system, I also selected a member of the community to be the curriculum director. His background was in language—the Spanish language that was representative of our population from the first grade through college. He was also an accomplished musician. This candidate's potential intrigued me and since he was not part of the system and had never worked in public education I believed he would introduce fresh insights and innovations.

I kept in the forefront of the selection process the requirement that all staff members had to have a sense of, as well as appearance of, dignity, speak the subcultural language of the various sections of the community, not be afraid of the so-called militants, and be devoted to this new task.

It is important here to discuss the problem and its limitations that affected the selection of the above personnel. I was told by the superintendent of schools that I would be given a number of positions for my staff proportionate to the size of the district as compared to district superintendents' staffs of larger districts. My experience in New York City schools made this most distasteful since I was aware of how ineffective most district superintendents' staff members were. Moreover, I was concerned that the size of the proposed staff would be inadequate, considering the vastness of the district's needs. I refused to accept the superintendent's decision, and he finally agreed that I would be given a dollar allotment, not specifying salary or number of positions.

I immediately made my plan operative. The two key people, my assistant and the curriculum director, were to be titled "assistant administrative directors," effectively outranking the principals. This was done to give them decision-making authority in order to insure that changes would be made when needed, after consultation with the principal and the governing board representative of each school. "Supervisor of libraries" was another title created, designed to give decision-making authority to this staff representative.

It is interesting to note that these positions were made so that the teachers and administrators molded in the archaic Board of Education system would be more likely to implement the mandates of these people because of their rank. My title was created by the superintendent of schools and the salary set to circumvent the merit system. I was told that I had the same powers as the regular district superintendents, yet on various occasions I was either defied by staff (teachers) who were uninformed, or my orders to transfer or reassign personnel within the complex were rescinded by the superintendent of schools. In certain cases, the United Federation of Teachers even balked at my attempts to move teachers within the complex.

PRINCIPALSHIPS

The chronology here is important. First we were informed that there were three vacant principalships, then four, then five, then three, and finally there was complete uncertainty. I prepared to fill vacancies anticipated as a result of community action. I wanted to create a process of selection that would involve the individual schools in the community. I had all prospective candidates appear for one week (for which they were paid) to talk to people in the community—to possible governing board members, to college people I selected, to students, and to others. I wanted the governing board members to know why one was selected and another rejected and to understand the framework of personnel selection. The principals were expected to bring to the schools a high level of competence and a special subject discipline that would complement the organization. The organization was designed to be my professional resource group working in concert with my staff. I had to be sure that these principals would not be "yes" men but rather independent people, able to assume responsibilities and make decisions. I made mental assignments of certain candidates, based on my assessment, whom I could recommend for principalship. This process worked extremely well.

I recommended to the governing board a Puerto Rican principal, certified by the state, for appointment to a particular school (which, incidentally, did not have the largest Puerto Rican pupil population of the schools in the district). The recommendation was based on my feeling that he could work with the parent-teachers' association (PTA), which had been organized for several years. This was the move that gave national publicity to our area. The community people also chose this principal for their school. I recommended to the governing board a black principal (state certified) for J.H.S. 178; he also was the people's choice. I recommended to the governing board a principal from the New York City civil service list, white and Jewish, for a small school. This appointment showed the city that no discriminatory practices were used: we selected personnel from a variety of sources. Yet the Council of Supervisory Associations claimed coercion since this man waived his position on the list so that another principal could be appointed in response to a community request in another district. This was part of the lawsuit brought against our district. I recommended to the governing board a black principal with a background in special education and psychology (who also was Jewish) for an elementary school, one of the largest in the city and one with the severest problems—staffing, attendance, and the like. Finally, I made a further recommendation of another competent person for a principalship to complete not only a balanced cadre but to unify totally the community.

These selections, however, also marked the beginning of the overt hostilities toward the project by vested interest groups and antidecentralization advocates. Ironically, the resulting conflict accomplished several important steps: (1) the entire community and city became conscious of the problems in education; (2) the issue of black versus white as it related to personnel matters was now out in the open; and (3) parents became inquisitive, sought answers, and began to assume active, and occasionally militantly active, roles.

OTHER SUPERVISORY PERSONNEL

It was typical of assistant principals requesting reassignment to delay notifying the district board until all the principal parties—the Council of Supervisory Associations and the Board of Education—had agreed to the reassignment. The probationary supervisors who were asked to leave by our governing board were reassigned in grade, a clear violation of the law, which was the result of such a compromise. These illegal acts are effected when the white power structure so desires and particularly when the black community must be put in its place or shown the power of the white community.

Despite having benefited from this consorting, they still blocked us from appointing assistant principals, from the civil service list or from other sources, to replace those who had left. To leave the schools and education in the hands of perpetual and perennially malfunctioning professionals is criminal. Their very presence prevents this district from effecting sound educational programs.

Chronology of Administration and the Factors of Influence

At the earliest contact with the steering committee, and continuously through the life of this project, it seemed reasonable that sensitivity, perception, and communication skills on my part would be the most vital links for progress and cohesion with the community. Therefore, my first task was the establishment of business-like and serious work modes. I instituted and still continue office hours seven days a week from 7:30 A.M. until whatever hour in the evening the business of the day is concluded. My office was and is open to anyone. I spoke clearly on issues that were vital for the community and for improved working conditions for teachers, such as an open-school atmosphere.

Once the tempo was set, I sought the cooperation of the principals. They meet in my office every morning at 7:45 and most are found in the community after hours and on weekends. After hours includes attendance at all community meetings. As a policy, their schools and offices are open to parents one evening a week.

For deepening contact with the parents and community people, I suggested meeting in small groups, recording everything observed in the community and the schools for reference, discussion, improvement, and evaluation. At the beginning, it was the PTA presidents and selected community people who were to serve as electioneers. I wanted them to become involved in education, adopt an attitude reflecting this involvement, and carry it into the community for further development in fertile soil. In workshop settings with this group and in larger public meetings, I would discuss any aspect of public schools that was germane—from personnel, to school buildings, to laws, to agencies with an impact on education. District problems became more relevant and came into focus for the community members. People began to come in to ask questions, to demand action, to explain their interests. At one school, we spent days obtaining adequate traffic lights for Atlantic Avenue and Rockaway Avenue. One group of parents demanded the establishment of special classes for both bright and slow children in their school. The parents never had this opportunity before—a listener, an implementor, a person of concern working in their midst, from the Establishment, against the Establishment. The parents' voice returned.

One danger I was constantly working to minimize was the pressure of individual demands. I tried to have people think of common needs, to view the schools as an interdependent totality—a whole school system. This was one of the positive areas of endeavor. We backed away from charges against a teacher, a principal, or talking for just one child; rather, we focused on the needs of our district, of Ocean Hill-Brownsville. This, I fear, had an ominous effect on, or appearance to, the teachers, for in public meetings they constantly went back to individuals and specifics about individuals. This strategy, in my opinion, later proved worthless to them.

That several incoming PTA presidents found these procedures more effective was testified to by larger membership and attendance at PTA meetings; they thus made their organizations heard. These processes also helped those who campaigned for election to the governing board to be more effective.

After the election of seven parent representatives to the governing board, the problem of unifying the board was paramount. Members were asked to appear on the mass media and as a result gained confidence in their abilities, demonstrated their commitment, and developed their public and self-images. Some were offered trips to other communities in and out of New York City as consultants on decentralization. This gave board members insight and depth with regard to problems and their responsibilities. Others were organized into a curriculum committee and discussed with educators in New York City and Albany the problem of discipline. All of these activities were designed to obtain maximum involvement and image-building. I do not suggest that it was easy. The selfish attitudes and desires to emerge as leaders had to be carefully handled to maintain a viable unit. The addition of the community representatives (a professional, two clergymen, an assemblyman, and a person representing a community agency) gave the board the sophistication and maturity it needed. The then acting unit administrator was versed in the subculture of the majority of the board and capitalized on this in order to unify it and bring before it vital issues to which the members could now address themselves as equal partners, respecting each other for their contributions.

Procedures had to be developed and established to facilitate the board's functioning. For example, to assure a wide range of community involvement we set as policy that all paraprofessionals, in order to be hired in this district, must be interviewed by a committee consisting of the PTA president of the school, the principal, and the district's school-community liaison officer. This reduced the possibility of patronage, and made more likely selection of the people who were interested in the education of children. This process was employed on a school-to-school basis. At that time, there were no governing board committees, since the bylaws were not yet formulated.

Another procedure was to have all prospective professional employees appear before the entire governing board for an interview. The board asked questions as to why they were acceptable and why they were not. Soon it was able to evaluate and make decisions, some of which were in consonance with my recommendations and others which were not. In the latter instance, I would recruit more candidates. As a matter of policy when there was a split faction on any issue, I would request its withdrawal for reconsideration and resubmit it with modifications at a subsequent board meeting. When individual board members had specific interests I would discuss these with them, always in the presence of another board member who I was sure was acceptable to the member involved.

In areas of program and curriculum, I would prepare informational documents for presentation and would usually bring in individuals who either were to be responsible for the program or who were expert in the discipline. When I was in doubt about any issue that was relevant to the community, before a presentation I would discuss it with the people from the various factions in the community, then with the college representative on the board, and, if necessary, with professionals outside the district. I always insisted that principals attend board meetings and oriented them to observe the internal, interpersonal group dynamics, believing this would be meaningful to them in their relationships with their governing board representative.

Many times the allocation of funds or the placing of programs in selected schools drew flak, but once the rationales were offered, they were either accepted or modified to meet community interests. This frequently happened. As the project developed it became a matter of procedure and policy that the governing board requested adequate information upon which it could base decisions and adequate time in which to deliberate these decisions. The individual governing board members listened to both individuals and groups in the community and brought their interests and demands to me for response, reaction, and formulation for presentation to the whole governing board. The community-at-large was and is invited to regular open meetings of the board (held in addition to the scheduled monthly meetings) where fact sheets are presented, opinions from the community are elicited, and their responses and reactions recorded. When possible, these reactions are translated into forms suitable for implementation.

The question of the militants is always raised. I encourage the principals and my district staff to become involved in communications and dialogue with members of the black student movement in our district. I recently had a meeting of key staff and student militants at my home for an entire day, 9:00 A.M. to 9:30 P.M., to discuss our role in a mutual relationship as they conceived it. It was a profitable venture, for it established that as a team, white and black, our interests were mutual and we were sincere. This will continue. I have had representatives of this group sit in on my staff conferences and attend my monthly principals' conferences. They have also been involved in the district schools. For example, a small group, whom I admire and respect, volunteered to "round up" all truants each morning, take them to their schools, and hold guidance sessions with them. They attend governing board meetings and public meetings—and are heard. Their actions are accepted critically by the more conservative community element. But they must be involved and accepted since they are part of the community. Because they are also part of a national movement, many of their peers visit our meetings and express their point of view. I listen carefully to this pulse; it is part of our future in this community. However, I cannot establish one instance where their presence affected any decision of our board. I might add one comment here that I feel is important. Youth representation on the governing board is an immediate goal. It is essential that their voice be heard so that community education will be relevant and have a more representative and positive foundation. The process of education will be dependent on consultation with the youth. They must have a voice in self-determination.

The Principals

The principals have had continuous problems of adjustment and I suggest they are still having problems. They have made substantial adjustments but not with the rapidity I had hoped. However, the basic factor is that they enjoy the complete confidence of the people who have elected them, despite obstacles and problems.

I am sure that because of their desires to succeed, their professional commitment, the challenge, and the continuing pressure they do not always realize that this confidence exists. The principals, especially those who are from a public education system, are not yet visionary educators; rather, they are effective practitioners. They have ventured forth, but because of pressure they have withdrawn to some degree. When the principals (and I have them organized as a professional committee—an arm of my office) propose an idea that may be in conflict with those of the community, they seldom persist with vigor. I often find myself in an awkward position as they withdraw. For example, several principals requested after-school programs—one as a means to hold teachers, one for tutorial purposes, one for cultural enrichment. I presented their request to the governing board for approval and funding. The board attacked the idea because postprograms were of no value. It was alleged that few pupils attended, teachers' performance was poor, and there were other items of higher priority. When called upon to justify their claims, the principals either made a poor presentation or withdrew their idea. I took the initiative and reactivated the issue by appealing to the governing board representative of the schools in question for support. The principals then "came alive" and their requests were granted with modifications. Now the principals know how to obtain programs. I do not suggest that it is easy, but it is a process that must be followed through.

The principals have been in a bind, so to speak, since they are exerting every effort to recruit staff and involve people in the activities of their schools. This then makes the principals vulnerable to their staffs. One of our objectives is to get principals to accept the fact that teachers should run the school or have a major part in its policy making. Once this is acknowledged and an open-school atmosphere is established, we will be more in tune with community involvement. It is not inability to change that is the problem for the principals but rather reluctance in the light of pressures. Principals have allowed teachers to transfer or have dismissed them without the approval of the governing board. This has created a degree of conflict. Several principals see board approval as an invasion of their rights instead of being part of the process. I have been forced to rectify this on one occasion by returning teachers to a school where they had been dismissed by the principal. The principals have other areas of conflict that result from the UFT contract. They know of the impending problems involved in reorganizing the school and are usually at a disadvantage since they do not wish to create conflict with the staff. This is another feature the community is against; that is, positions for teachers as reward for UFT membership rather than based on performance.

Another problem area for principals is their reluctance to involve staff in decision making when it is necessary because of the principal's inexperience, poor performance, restrictions from the system, or unfamiliarity with community concern about specific teachers. Thus, the principal often assumes an almost dictatorial role, despite the fact that he desires a new role for the staff. Most principals now have developed relationships with selected or key persons on their staffs who can keep them tuned to the staff's pulse and assist them in making recommendations.

The Teachers

The teachers are divided into several groups and play overt and subterranean roles. Those in the overt group are usually the black teachers; most are young militants who have won favor with the community by their demonstrated loyalty, their help in the community, and their organizing and support of community positions. They usually make demands that conflict with the existing UFT contract which we are obliged to adhere to. This group is growing in number in each school and their demands are increasing. These demands can also be a result of the backlash of years of deprivation and denial, due in turn to their small numbers and antiwhite or anti-UFT sentiments. There are many white teachers who are freely accepted as colleagues by this group, by virtue of their allegiance as well as their commitment to community control. Therefore, when issues arise that are antiwhite in implication, the principal, though he may be black, is in an awkward position because these young teachers demand militant leadership. I was confronted with such a problem by the principal of an intermediate school: he asked me to set a policy for him on the wearing of a dashiki, an African garment which the white teachers objected to.

There is a second group of teachers, predominantly white, who feel they are employed only to teach their subject matter and want to do just that. They adhere to the requirements of the Board of Education and live within the contract of the UFT. They leave immediately after school. Unless they are requested to attend meetings after hours, they rarely do. They do not yet recognize the authority of the existing governing board but continue to see the principal as the only responsible agent. In cases where they do recognize the board, they have little or no contact with its members or its operations. These teachers also avoid the governing board members that visit the schools.

The Paraprofessionals

The paraprofessionals have an impact on the decision-making process since all of them (120 at present) are indigenous community people. For the most part, they have been trained in specific skill areas and have a high degree of competence. Most are at least high school graduates; many have one or more years of college. As a result of their training, the fact that they have children in the schools, and their full acceptance of the concept of community involvement, they feel confident in discussing programs, teachers, school conditions, and the like. These people serve as information links to the community and the community now knows more about what takes place in the schools than do the educators. The question that arises is, when they pass school information on to the community rather than to school officials, is it because they are employees or because they are still not confident in the system?

The teachers are concerned over the presence of this group. Some teachers feel that the paraprofessionals are teacher replacements and either ignore them or show some open resentment. Others feel that the paraprofessionals display social antagonisms. But the paraprofessionals have found some teachers, very few, to be committed. They are new and resourceful teachers hoping to improve the education of their students.

The paraprofessionals will often appear at a governing board meeting and offer suggestions, criticize proposals, and make demands. The latest demand is that they work the same hours as teachers; and they have decided to become unionized. The paraprofessionals now appear to espouse the position of the Establishment, a position certain to prove interesting since their existence is a result of opposition to the Establishment.

The Establishment

The Establishment—the Board of Education and the UFT—has its tentacles deep in the administering and decision-making process of the district. When a proposal is suggested we must be concerned about existing controls exerted by this power. If we wish to move teachers within the complex, the union rejects the move or does not assist in the implementation of the directive. The lack of cooperation on such occasions indicates their aim—failure for the project—and has been a strategic mistake.

The psychological "warfare" conducted by the Establishment has had a demoralizing effect on my staff. Delayed payrolls, personnel omitted from the payrolls, delays in examination and certification of staff, and inabilities to reach decisions on personnel are examples of its tactics.

When I wanted to reassign a particular principal, the Board of Education countermanded the order. This kind of action, or reaction, in highly sensitive areas causes the white versus black flags to be hoisted. While such a move is obviously part of the political strategy, it also indicates complete insensitivity to the peculiarity of our district, its needs, its objectives, and its desires. The need to assign personnel to effect programs and operations is crucial, yet it must have Board of Education approval. The actions of the bureaucracy, however, make it impossible to function effectively. The delay in payments of the paraprofessional staff has created distrust in our people since they are led to believe we have the power to make change. The press coverage implies that the board and the union are sympathetic and cooperative, yet their actions contradicting their supposed philosophical positions are not reported in the press. The governing board has no confidence in the support of the Board of Education. This is a result of the central authority's actions: not recognizing the validity of the governing board, delaying delegation of authority to the board, and, more recently, refusing to transfer the controversial nineteen professionals out of our district.

The constant contradictory statements and actions by the Board of Education and the union in the present crisis destroy all confidence, and thus we make decisions to force issues and to give us command of the right to make education meaningful for our children. We voted to keep our schools open during the citywide teachers' strike. We voted to close our schools on Friday, April 4, 1968, the day after Dr. Martin Luther King's assassination. The Board of Education has refused our request to name our new school in honor of Dr. King. This causes our decisions to be packed with emotionalism rather than objectivity. We feel that these decisions have been some of our best.

The issue concerning the transfer of teachers is of primary importance. We notified the teachers that they were no longer to remain in our district and were to report to the Board of Education Personnel Bureau for reassignment. This was done after repeated requests to the superintendent to take some action. The law is specific—we need not bring charges against the teachers. Yet the Board of Education was unyielding, and it marshaled public opinion as it never had against any of our previous actions. After we reluctantly complied, the ruling stated that if we had only sent our request to the superintendent of schools, without preferring charges against the teachers, he could have transferred them easily. The very actions we took legally to move a dissident group are now sounding the death knell of our attempts.

Outsiders such as the mayor's office, the Ford Foundation, the state commissioner's office, and the colleges have played crucial roles in our development. I will address myself to each one separately, but first I want to point out that a community group of lay people out of touch and denied access and involvement with the city needs assistance and guidance.

This weakness was preyed upon to the advantage of the city. The mayor's office either gave no help, made decisions about us without consulting us for facts, or gave advice that led to more polarized problems. To acknowledge a mistake afterward is apparently a sin of commission.

The Ford Foundation has been vital to our project by providing consultants, resources, funding, interest, and commitment. This view may be contrary to that of many of our community members, considering our need for expediency and urgency. However, in spite of the foundation's bureaucratic processes, at least one of its staff has lived up to commitments promised, with minor modifications.

The state commissioner of education of New York has offered encouragement, but offered it in ambiguous language.

We have had practically no assistance from the colleges with whom we have been involved. One college in particular felt that involvement would have created a negative effect upon the university, especially since we have been involved in so-called controversial issues. It is hard to translate to parents the role or lack of role of a publicly supported city college whose function is to provide educational services to the community. How can we explain to our people that a city college feels it must cater to the wishes of a white majority at the expense of a black minority that has been denied access to it for years?

Conclusion

Finally, I would like to encapsulate two basic matters. First, my experience in this district has covered a wide spectrum, working with parents, professionals, city officials, politicians, and other agencies' representatives interested in urban affairs. The exposure has broadened my insights and sharpened my repertoire of skills. As a result, I am aware of all the groups that shape education, their contributions, and the resultant pattern that emerges. I am now more fully equipped to effect change. I am equally sure that this new tool does not assure change but rather it begins to indicate the range of possibilities. Thus, I am prepared to move effectively to change educational processes for my pupils.

Second, as a result of my experiences, contacts, and inundation, I would suggest that careful examination be made of the following items, placed in suitable priority, called the Ocean Hill-Brownsville Ten-Point Program, as a recommendation for the resolution of the current crisis, and also as a platform for others who may wish to venture into a similar program.

1. *Due process.* A body of elected teachers will serve under, and along with, a committee of the governing board, to handle all personnel grievances. The decision of this group may be appealed to either the courts or the commissioner of education. This will serve to give teachers professionalism, relevant involvement, decision-making roles, and an opportunity to "link up" with the community.

2. *Personnel.* The governing board will establish the proper machinery to hire, appoint, and certify all staff in compliance with state regulations.

3. *Allocation of staff.* Because of the need for special educational programs, additional positions should be allocated to this district.

4. *Curriculum.* The right to create, develop, and implement curriculum germane to the needs of the pupils in this district is insisted upon. Any change in the existing state laws will be formally requested of the commissioner of education.

5. *Operations.* The present faculty in the schools of this district should remain intact and no attempt should be made to create conditions that would disturb the normal educational process.

6. *Administration.* Four training schools should be immediately established in this district in order to meet the needs of the staffs.

7. *Funds.* (1) A substantial allocation of funds for maintenance and repair should be given to the district immediately; (2) a substantial allocation of funds for educational programs should be given to the district immediately; (3) the accruals formerly returned to the Board of Education should be given to the Ocean Hill-Brownsville governing board; and (4) a voucher system for the disbursement of funds should be structured in such a way that the controls and signature be at the local level.

8. *Capital construction.* A commitment should be given to replace at least one building each year.

9. *Union negotiations.* Any collective bargaining agreements with the union should include a representative of the Ocean Hill-Brownsville governing board and other demonstration districts.

10. *Good will.* A written guarantee should be given the governing board assuring that its present staff of teachers will be paid and will be secure in their positions.

MICHAEL H. MOSKOW
KENNETH McLENNAN

Teacher Negotiations and School Decentralization

Collective bargaining for teachers has increased dramatically in recent years. Before 1962, no board of education in the United States was required by law to negotiate with its teachers, and only a handful of boards had signed written collective bargaining agreements. By 1968, however, ten states had passed laws requiring school boards to engage in some type of teacher negotiations. Over 1,500 school boards had written negotiations procedures. The two national teachers' organizations, the National Education Association (NEA) and the American Federation of Teachers (AFT), had made important changes in their policies on collective bargaining. The NEA, which a short time earlier had been slow to encourage collective action through negotiations, now supported the strikes of local affiliates.

Even more important, citizens and educators were astonished by the rash of teachers' strikes and work stoppages, including a three-week, statewide strike in Florida. In 1967, approximately 973,000 man-days of work were lost due to teacher strikes. Even if the fifteen-day New York City teacher strike is excluded from the data, the number of man-days lost increased fivefold from 1966.[1]

[1] Ronald W. Glass, "Work Stoppages and Teachers: History and Prospect," *Monthly Labor Review*, Vol. 90 (August 1967), p. 44. Data for 1967 were supplied by the U.S. Bureau of Labor Statistics.

The tremendous growth of collective bargaining in public education and the increased militancy among teachers have occurred concurrently with recent proposals to decentralize big-city school systems. As a result, school decentralization has become an important concern of teachers' organizations. The term "school decentralization" has been defined in various ways; here it will mean the delegation of decision-making power from citywide school boards and administrators to lower policy-making and administrative levels of the school system. Implicit in this delegation of authority is greater community control of schools by lay persons residing in local school areas.

School decentralization plans have many implications for teachers' organizations and collective bargaining. For example, the Bundy Report[2] recommends that decisions on hiring, promotion, tenure, and discharge be made by local community school boards. It also suggests that the citywide school board continue to negotiate the master collective bargaining contract, setting the salaries and working conditions of all teachers in the city. On the other hand, the New York State Board of Regents' proposal recommends that representatives of the local school boards serve as an advisory committee, while the central board negotiates the master contract with the union.

This chapter approaches the complex topic of decentralization and teacher negotiations as follows: the first section analyzes data on the topics now negotiated together with the results of a survey of teachers' attitudes toward decentralization. The topics that teachers want to negotiate and the levels at which decisions should be made are included in the survey. The second section examines the impact of alternative decentralization plans on teachers' organizations and collective bargaining.

Subjects of Negotiations

In 1966–67, about 25 percent of the public school districts in the United States had written agreements that covered about 41 percent of the elementary and secondary school instructional staff.[3] Only about one-quarter of these agreements, covering 13 percent of the

[2] Mayor's Advisory Panel on Decentralization of the New York City Schools, *Reconnection for Learning: A Community School System for New York City* (1967), p. 11. Referred to as either the Bundy Report or the Mayor's Advisory Panel.

[3] *Negotiation Research Digest*, Vol. 1, No. 10 (National Education Association, June 1968), pp. B-1, B-3.

total instructional staff, included terms and conditions of employment; the remainder established procedures for negotiations. The majority of the comprehensive agreements were in the state of Michigan. Since 1966–67, this type of agreement has spread rapidly.

Negotiations in public education presently take place on a school district-wide basis with some provision for consultation at the school level between the school principal and the "building chairmen," who represent the teachers. Table 3 lists the clauses most frequently negotiated by teachers and the percentage of teachers covered by each clause. Salaries and working conditions are the most common clauses, but those governing instructional programs are growing in

TABLE 3

Incidence of Selected Topics Included in Collective Bargaining Agreements with Public School Teachers, 1966–67

Topic	Percentage of comprehensive agreements with negotiated clause[a]	Percentage of teachers covered by comprehensive agreements with negotiated clause	Percentage of all U.S. teachers covered by negotiated clause
Salary and fringe benefits			
Salary schedule	100	100	13
Health insurance	62	89	12
Extra pay for special activities	76	75	10
Working conditions			
Teaching load or class schedule	52	81	11
Transfer policy	72	91	12
Teacher discipline or reprimand	44	47	6
Procedure for teacher evaluation	66	57	7
Instructional program			
Curriculum	23	33	4
Textbook selection	38	34	5
Class size	61	85	11
Teacher aides	46	35	5

Source: National Education Association, Research Division, *Negotiation Agreement Provisions*, 1966–67 Edition (National Education Association, 1967).

a. For purposes of analysis, a comprehensive agreement is defined as a collective bargaining contract that includes a salary schedule.

importance. Merely including a clause in a collective agreement does not guarantee its implementation. In some cases, widely accepted informal procedures contradict written agreements. Nevertheless, the inclusion of a grievance clause assures teachers the right to appeal administrative actions through a formal procedure and to demand adherence to the clause at issue. Once data become available, it will be interesting to see whether future agreements will reflect the current discussion of school decentralization.

Teachers' Attitudes

School decentralization proposals have been extremely controversial, partly because they involve major changes in the policies and administration of big-city school systems. The highly developed interest group structure in public school education has intensified the controversy. Because of the general concern over the issue, teachers' organizations have been forced to formulate policies on school decentralization, even though it is not certain that local union leaders have had enough time to assess rank-and-file views. As the 1968 AFT convention has shown, there is no unanimous position of the teachers as a group. As a result, it is important to understand teachers' opinions on decentralization since this will affect the nature of future negotiations if decentralization becomes a reality.

A preliminary survey was conducted to obtain the views of teachers on the current proposals. The results, though useful for speculations, cannot, of course, be regarded as conclusive.

SAMPLE AND METHODOLOGY

The sample was not randomly selected from a well-defined population. Instead, the questionnaire was administered to students attending eight summer school education classes at four locations in Pennsylvania. There was no identification of the respondents. Since the questionnaires were distributed with a personal appeal for participation, the response rate was high.

The characteristics of the sample group are shown in Table 4. Compared to the teacher labor force in large northern cities, the sample is overrepresented by young teachers. It is clearly under-representative of black teachers. About one-third of the respondents teach in suburban schools, thus making the sample considerably

TABLE 4

Selected Characteristics of Teachers in Survey Sample, Four Colleges in Pennsylvania, Summer 1968

Characteristic	Number of teachers
Sex	
Male	174
Female	142
No response	0
Total	316
Age	
Under 25 years	158
26–35 years	96
Over 35 years	62
No response	0
Total	316
Race	
White	284
Black	26
Other	4
No response	2
Total	316
Type of school district	
Large city (over 1,000,000)	74
Small city (50,000–1,000,000)	71
Suburban	101
Rural	50
No response	20
Total	316
Racial composition of student body in teacher's school	
More than 50% black	75
Less than 50% black	220
No response	21
Total	316

different from the teaching faculties in big-city schools. Because of these sample characteristics, any conclusions drawn from the responses must be considered tentative.

The questionnaire explored the teachers' views in two major areas. One group of questions focused on the extent to which employment and educational policy issues should be decided bilaterally or unilaterally, and how these issues should be decentralized for decision-making purposes. The other group of questions, involving similar issues, attempted to determine each respondent's preference between collective bargaining and unilateral decision making.

RESULTS

The respondents were asked to assume that the Philadelphia school system would be divided into ten local districts. They were presented with a list of some thirty personnel and educational policy decisions. For each decision, respondents ranked the three most important decision-making levels.[4]

The responses to the question are analyzed in Tables 5, 6, and 7. Table 5 presents the responses to ten selected decisions grouped according to three decision-making levels: central, local district, and local school. These decisions were selected as representative of the major issues currently receiving public attention in discussions of school decentralization. The responses are not weighted; all are counted equally regardless of the rank of "first," "second," or "third" given by the respondent.

Clearly, the most important finding shown in Table 5 is the teachers' dissatisfaction with central-level decision making. This result supports the contention that teachers feel the educational bureaucracy in large cities is incapable of adequately dealing with a number of important policy and administrative decisions. For example, "selecting district superintendents" was the only decision that respondents preferred to be made at the central level.

[4] As shown in Tables 6 and 7 the decision levels were as follows: central level: (1) central school board, (2) superintendent of entire system and his administrative staff; district level: (3) local community board, (4) district superintendent and district-wide administrative staff; school level: (5) principal, (6) teacher, teachers' organization, or both.

TABLE 5

Decision-Making Levels Preferred by Teachers in Sample for Selected Employment and Educational Policy Decisions, 1968 Survey

(*In percentages*[a])

Decision	Central level	Local district level	Local school level	Other or no response
Procedure for disciplining students	7	26	66[b]	1
Criteria for use of school facilities outside normal school hours	16	52[b]	30	3
Evaluating teachers	11	27	58[b]	4
Determining qualifications for teaching in so-called culturally deprived areas	19	40	35	6
Selecting paraprofessionals	19	39	37	5
Content of curriculum and courses taught	17	33	49[b]	1
Setting educational objectives for each grade level	19	32	47[b]	2
Actual hiring of teachers	29	41[c]	28	2
Selecting principals	41	44	13	2
Selecting district superintendent	51[b]	32	13	4

a. Percentages are based on the total number of times (948) that respondents ranked the decisions. Percentages may not total 100 because of rounding.
b. A statistically significant difference (0.01 level) was found for this decision among all three levels.
c. A statistically significant difference (0.01 level) was found for this decision between the highest-ranked level and the other two levels.

Although decentralization is a desired goal, the respondents, in most instances, prefer that decisions be made at the district level rather than at the school level. For teachers, the preference for decentralization is not synonymous with community control. They seem to feel that their own professional competence is more important in decision making than is the viewpoint of the community, as presented by local board members.

Table 6 provides a more detailed analysis of the responses within the three major levels. Respondents who favored the local district level had no significant differences in their preferences between the

TABLE 6

Participants Preferred by Teachers in Sample for Selected Employment and Educational Policy Decisions, 1968 Survey[a]

Decision	Central level			Local district level			Local school level			
	Central school board	Superintendent of entire system and his administrative staff	X^2 test[b]	Local community board	District superintendent and his district administrative staff	X^2 test[b]	Principal	Teacher, teachers' organization, or both	Other or no response	X^2 test[b]
Procedure for disciplining students	13	11	NS	24	16	NS	108	135	9	NS
Criteria for use of school facilities outside normal school hours	41	22	S	125	33	S	53	28	14	S
Evaluating teachers	10	14	NS	18	23	NS	139	91	21	S
Determining qualifications for teaching in so-called culturally deprived areas	31	39	NS	71	51	NS	28	81	15	S
Selecting paraprofessionals	26	38	NS	42	58	NS	62	52	38	NS
Content of curriculum and courses taught	19	35	S	37	40	NS	16	158	11	S
Setting educational objectives for each grade level	34	37	NS	38	44	NS	17	135	11	S
Actual hiring of teachers	58	62	NS	47	74	S	43	21	11	S
Selecting principals	60	63	NS	65	78	NS	1	36	13	S
Selecting district superintendent	148	53	S	52	17	S	3	22	21	S

a. For each decision, the preference of respondents is based on the total number of times (316) each level was ranked first in preference.

b. Chi-square test for goodness of fit. S = difference is statistically significant for responses within that level; NS = difference is not statistically significant. Level of significance = 0.05.

local community board and the local district superintendent for most decisions. The only exceptions were "criteria for use of school facilities" and "selecting district superintendent," where the local community board was preferred. Similarly, respondents favored the "actual hiring of teachers" to be done by the local district superintendent. For those respondents who preferred decentralization at the local school level, there was a significant preference for most decisions to be made by the teacher, the teachers' organization, or both, rather than the principal. The principal was preferred in the hiring and evaluation of teachers.

In Table 7, the rankings were weighted (first rank given a weight of 3, second rank a weight of 2, and so on) and the total numerical weight for all respondents provided a measure of importance of each decision level. The results of the weighting system for each decision were adjusted to assign the weights for the central level (central school board plus the superintendent of the entire system level) a base of 100. The weighted scores for each other level were recalculated using this base as a benchmark for the degree of centralization. Therefore, if any of the two other major levels (district level and school level) have scores of more than 100, some degree of decentralization is preferred.

A second question dealing with school decentralization provided responses on (1) whether certain employment and educational policy decisions should be decided unilaterally or negotiated, and (2) the appropriate level for making the same set of decisions. Respondents strongly favored negotiations with a teachers' organization on every decision presented. As shown in Table 8, only 6 percent of the respondents wanted salaries and fringe benefits decided unilaterally. The number of respondents favoring unilateral decisions increased slightly for some working conditions and "professional" topics, but it never exceeded 13 percent of all respondents. This overwhelming support for negotiations on a wide range of subjects was greater than expected, given the large number of respondents from suburban and rural communities.

When the results are analyzed by personal characteristics, however, some noticeable differences arise among groups of respondents. No differences were apparent on attitudes toward salary and fringe benefits, but about 30 percent of the twenty nonteacher respondents,

TABLE 7

Index of Degree of Decentralization Preferred by Teachers in Sample for Each Decision, 1968 Survey[a]

(*Weighted responses at central level = 100*)

Decision	Central level			Local district level			Local school level		
	Total	Central school board	Superintendent of entire system and his administrative staff	Total	Local community board	District superintendent and districtwide administrative staff	Total	Principal	Teachers, teachers' organization, or both
Procedure for disciplining students	100	50	50	303	148	155	1,163	581	582
Criteria for use of school facilities outside normal school hours	100	59	41	295	184	111	166	110	56
Evaluating teachers	100	36	64	264	86	178	596	350	246
Determining qualifications for teaching in so-called culturally deprived areas	100	41	59	198	100	98	176	77	99
Selecting paraprofessionals	100	40	60	191	77	114	183	107	76
Content of curriculum and courses taught	100	35	65	179	82	97	324	103	221
Setting educational objectives for each grade level	100	42	58	149	64	85	251	89	162
Actual hiring of teachers	100	45	55	130	55	75	80	57	23
Selecting principals	100	45	55	111	51	60	27	4	23
Selecting district superintendent	100	63	37	51	38	13	19	5	14

a. Each decision is compared separately using the weighted responses of teachers to calculate the index numbers. The data in this table cannot be compared vertically.

TABLE 8

Extent and Level of Negotiations for Selected Decisions

(*In percentages*[a])

Subject of decision	Total	Bilateral decision: Negotiated by teachers' organization and central board, superintendent, or both	Bilateral decision: Negotiated by teachers' organization and local community board	Bilateral decision: Negotiated by teachers' organization and school principal	Unilateral decision: Central board, superintendent, or both	Unilateral decision: Local community board	Unilateral decision: School principal	Other
Salary and fringe benefits								
Basic salary schedule	100	72	21	2	1	1	—	3
Hospital and medical insurance	100	75	14	1	5	5	—	—
Working conditions								
Teaching load and preparation time	100	30[b]	26[b]	32[b]	1	3	6	2
Procedure for discharging nontenure teachers	100	61	19	7	5	3	1	4
Teacher transfer within one of ten districts	100	38[b]	40[b]	7	4	7	2	2
Instructional program								
Curriculum	100	30[b]	35[b]	18	4	5	2	6
Textbook selection	100	18	28	33	2	4	4	11
Class size	100	31[b]	29[b]	26[b]	2	3	4	5
Decision to introduce teaching machines in specific schools	100	22	36	26	2	5	2	7

a. Percentages are based on the total number of decisions (316).
b. Using chi-square test for goodness of fit, differences are not statistically significant to 0.05 level. Differences are statistically significant for all other responses.

who were mostly school administrators (compared to 2 percent of all respondents), preferred unilateral determination of teaching load and maximum class size; almost 40 percent of the same group opposed negotiations on procedures for removing disruptive children from classes. Similarly, about 25 percent of teachers employed in big-city school systems rejected negotiations on special programs to improve quality of education, decisions to introduce teaching machines, and procedures for removing disruptive children. The response favoring unilateral determination on some of the above professional decisions from teachers employed in integrated schools appeared to be significantly different from other teachers. These responses rejecting negotiations, while only a small minority in most cases, indicate some dissatisfaction with teachers' organizations and the results of collective bargaining.

Table 8 also shows the desired level of negotiations for selected decisions. The respondents preferred central negotiations for salary and fringe benefits and decentralized negotiations for most decisions involving working conditions and instructional programs. In areas such as teaching load, class size, and procedures for textbook selection, a relatively large number of respondents favored negotiations at the school level.

Teachers employed in rural school districts preferred more centralized negotiations than those employed in big-city systems. Where decentralization of negotiations was preferred, rural teachers tended to choose the principal more frequently than did big-city teachers. Since more big-city teachers favored the local district board as the negotiating unit this probably indicates some disenchantment with school principals. Only slight differences were evident between the responses of teachers who were education majors and those who were not. The latter favored slightly more centralization on most issues and noticeably more centralization on topics such as procedures for discharging nontenure teachers and deciding curriculum.

Married female respondents compared with single female respondents favored more negotiations with the local district boards. No reason for this difference is suggested, but it would be interesting to test the hypothesis that teachers with school-age children tend to favor greater community involvement.

Given current discussions of racism, it is unfortunate that the sample included only twenty-six black respondents. The black teachers surveyed showed slightly more preference for decentralized bargaining, but the small sample limits the reliability of this finding. Teachers employed in schools that are more than 50 percent black also showed a slight preference for greater decentralization.

On some issues, teachers chose increased community participation through the local community board. A significantly greater number of respondents preferred district administrators to hire teachers rather than the local community board. On the other hand, more respondents (no significant difference) preferred the local board to determine qualifications for teaching in so-called culturally deprived areas. Respondents clearly favored decisions on educational objectives and curriculum to be made by teachers, teachers' organizations, or both.

In most cases, the professionals in the district superintendent's office were ranked equally important with the lay members of the local community board. Where increased community participation is favored, it appears that the teachers are suggesting that the community is as well qualified as the teachers to make decisions. If decentralization has an impact on collective bargaining, it would seem that the rank-and-file teachers' organization members would not object to negotiations on selected issues at the local district level.

The Impact of Decentralization on Negotiations

The behavior of employees during a period of major change in their work environment has frequently been discussed in industrial relations literature. From the employee's point of view, possible changes in the organization and performance of the productive process are almost always viewed as a direct threat to job security. Selig Perlman has described the employee's view of the job market as displaying a "manualist psychology," in the sense that workers feel that job opportunities are always exceeded by the number of job seekers. As a result, workers are willing to accept union control over the allocation of scarce jobs.[5]

[5] Selig Perlman, *A Theory of the Labor Movement* (Macmillan, 1928), pp. 237–53.

The employee's pessimistic view of the labor market encourages him to support job-control techniques, such as establishment of jurisdictional boundaries, restriction of entry, make-work practices, and development of seniority procedures. In short, the employee's reaction to a dynamic employment environment is "job-conscious unionism."

The use of job-control techniques is not confined to blue-collar employees. Many white-collar groups, including professional organizations, make extensive use of such techniques. Licensing restrictions on out-of-state dentists and attorneys are notable examples. Similarly, changes that threaten the content or existence of the employee's job are likely to be received with some resistance. It is not surprising, then, that teachers view decentralization proposals with some apprehension. Employees frequently view their job as a "property right" based on the future value of the job. The concept of property right emerged as part of the guild system, and in many industries it has become an established feature of the industrial relations system.[6] More recently, the concept has been recognized through transfer-right clauses in many major collective agreements in private industry. Legal recognition also has been given to the concept through a number of arbitration decisions and court cases.[7]

The tenure system in public school education is likely to reinforce the job-property view among teachers. Any reorganization that does not protect their present conditions of employment is likely to lead to additional conflict. The controversy associated with decentralization should be distinguished from the increasing number of strikes in education over the past two years. The recent strikes have mainly been concerned with recognition and salary issues. On the other hand, the conflict generated by decentralization is likely to be over the administration of the existing contract. For example, the dismissal of nineteen teachers by the local board of the Ocean Hill-

[6] For a review of the concept of job property rights, see Simon Rottenberg, "Property in Work," *Industrial and Labor Relations Review*, Vol. 15 (April 1962), p. 402; Arthur R. Porter, Jr., *Job Property Rights* (Kings Crown Press, 1954); and William Gomberg, "Featherbedding: An Assertion of Property Rights," *Annals*, Vol. 333 (January 1961), pp. 119–29.

[7] A number of court cases have dealt with aspects of job property rights. The controversial Glidden doctrine reviews some of the recent legal developments. See *Glidden*, 288 F.2d. 99.

Brownsville school district in New York City is an extreme manifestation of the problem of new officials administering existing rules and regulations. If the new district board's interpretation of the contract is different from the previous interpretation by the central board of education, conflict is likely to emerge.

The problem of interpreting an existing agreement is magnified since school boards and teachers' organizations frequently rely on unwritten, informal agreements that develop over time. The legal force of these agreements is based on the past practices of the parties to the agreement. It is possible that the contract does not cover a particular procedure simply because it has never become an issue during negotiations, and the past practice for handling this procedure has always been followed by the central board. Will the district board be bound by this past practice? Any attempt to change the procedure will surely result in employees' resistance.

UNION STRUCTURE

Every teachers' organization has a vested interest in the organizational structure of the school system in which it is located. One of its functions is to represent the employment and professional interests of its members. School decentralization proposals have an immediate impact on the American Federation of Teachers and its affiliates because they represent most teachers in big-city systems. The National Education Association and its affiliated associations, which mainly represent teachers in suburbs and smaller cities, had not expressed, as of June 1969, official positions on school decentralization. Whenever the NEA does react to decentralization, however, its actions are likely to resemble those of the AFT. Both organizations are placed in similar positions and subjected to similar pressures when they negotiate for teachers.

The initial attitude of the AFT toward decentralization has been extremely cautious and at times negative. Its response is understandable and even predictable given the institutional needs of an organization representing a group of employees. In the bargaining procedure, leaders and staff members of a teachers' organization become accustomed to working with the board of education and its administrative staff. The organization has established methods for contacting members, preparing demands, conducting negotiations, and administering the written collective bargaining agreement. The leaders have developed informal procedures and contacts in order to accomplish their goals.

A decentralization proposal, which effectively is a plan to change the environment in which the organization operates, is bound to meet initial resistance. Traditionally, institutions resist change, and teachers' organizations are no exception. Leaders are skeptical because change can weaken an organization, and they have a vested interest in the status quo.

Once the union's initial period of caution ends and pressures for decentralization continue, the union and its affiliates must examine the proposals and refine their positions. The AFT is now at this stage, and different attitudes toward decentralization have emerged among affiliates. At the 1968 convention, the national leaders publically favored more community participation in running the schools as long as due process and the rights of teachers were protected.

> We must continue to insist upon the integrity and dignity and fundamental rights of teachers. At the same time, difficult as it may be, we must make greater efforts to involve community leaders in what we are doing. Where community leaders have a sincere interest in the quality of education and are not merely capitalizing upon the admitted deficiencies of the schools in order to promote obscure organizational aims; where there are such forward-looking leaders we must bend over backward to work with them and to share with them our thinking, our judgment, and our activities.[8]

At the convention, the Philadelphia local proposed a resolution strongly opposing decentralization, but the New York City, New Rochelle, N.Y., and Washington, D.C., locals all favored some form of decentralization.

If a school district is decentralized, the organization serving as bargaining agent probably will have to make some structural changes. Collective bargaining in all big-city school systems is highly centralized. Representatives of the teachers' organization and the school board establish system-wide conditions of employment and personnel policies. Once the central board delegates decision-making power to local boards, the teachers' organization will want to negotiate with the local boards.

[8] President's address delivered by Charles Cogen at the Annual Convention of the American Federation of Teachers, Aug. 19, 1968.

Some bargaining may still take place with the central board, but the organization will have to assign staff or rank-and-file representatives to bargain with the local boards or administrators. These representatives could work out of the central office of the organization which would facilitate communications among bargainers. Alternatively, they could also work from separate offices in each of the newly formed districts, in order to be closer to the teachers they represent. Members employed in each district could negotiate the contract or serve as an advisory committee to the negotiator.

The changed structure of the organization will affect collective bargaining. In general, if local district level bargaining is controlled directly by teachers employed in the district, negotiators will be more responsive to the wishes of the teachers in the district. This high degree of responsiveness probably will result in greater differences in the terms of the agreements among local districts. It will also be harder for the leaders of the organization to obtain a common set of proposals for negotiations with the central school board. Moreover, ratification of the central agreement will be more difficult because additional factions will develop within the union.

A trend toward local district bargaining will also require the organization to change its structure for administering its collective bargaining agreement. With one system-wide agreement, all grievances and questions of interpretation eventually were cleared through the central teachers' organization. Individualized local district agreements will make it much harder for the organization to coordinate contract interpretation throughout the city.

Decisions on whether to take a grievance to arbitration and pay the accompanying costs probably will remain with the system-wide organization if it continues to control organization funds. It is unlikely that the organization will delegate financial control to the local level because of the need for a strong, system-wide organization to coordinate bargaining and strike activity. This need is widely recognized by local unions in the private sector, and teachers' organizations are likely to follow the same pattern.

STRUCTURE OF NEGOTIATIONS

The structure of collective bargaining is largely influenced by the legal bargaining unit. In urban educational systems, bargaining units are system-wide and exclude nonteaching personnel and administrators. The rationale for this unit jurisdiction is that there is no community of interest between teachers and nonteaching personnel. It is, of course, possible to argue that smaller bargaining units based on geographic boundaries should be recognized. With centralized decision making and a history of citywide school jurisdiction, however, at present there is no legitimate reason for separate bargaining units based on geographic location within the city. Similarly, it is unlikely that separate bargaining units based on either level of school (elementary, secondary) or educational program (vocational, academic) would be established even though there is a community of interest and a functional relationship among these groups of teachers.

Consequently, the bargaining structure is highly centralized in urban school systems. Within any teachers' organization, however, a number of factions are likely to exist. The leadership of the teachers' organization must integrate these factions, which may be based on geographic location, grade level of school, subject specialty, and more recently, race, into the bargaining structure. Failure to do so may result in political problems for the organization leadership through loss of power or loss of members, who may turn to a rival organization. Although highly unlikely, it may be possible for the dissidents to seek a decertification election and establish a separate bargaining unit.

The introduction of a decentralization plan will not affect the organization's legal responsibility to act as bargaining agent for all teachers in the city. Reorganization of the bargaining structure, however, will become an administrative necessity. The extent and nature of the reorganization will depend on the new locus of personnel and educational policy decisions. Table 9 presents five decentralization plans and the structure for decision making on selected personnel and educational policy topics.

If salaries and working conditions as well as educational policy matters are decided at the district board level, as suggested in the Adams-Morgan community school plan, the bargaining structure will tend to be decentralized. The leadership of the teachers' organization along with teachers' representatives from each district will negotiate separate contracts with each district in the system.

TABLE 9

Proposed Levels of Decision Making for Selected Personnel and Educational Policy Topics under Five Decentralization Plans, 1967 and 1968

	Decision level				
Decentralization plan	Salaries and working conditions	Selection of teachers	Obtaining tenure	Curriculum	Textbook selection
Mayor's Advisory Panel in New York City (Bundy Report, November 9, 1967)	Central	Local	Local	Local	Local
Adams-Morgan Community School Board, Washington, D.C. (April 4, 1968)	Local	Local	Local	Local	Local
New York City Board of Education (August 17, 1968)	Central	Central and local	Local	Local	Local
New York State Board of Regents (March 29, 1968)	Central	Local	Not specified	Not specified	Not specified
United Federation of Teachers (December 20, 1967)	Central	Central	Local	Local	Local

Under this type of decentralization plan, there is a greater possibility that in the future bargaining units may be separated according to district demarcation. On the other hand, if only a limited number of decisions are delegated to the district boards, the structure of negotiation will remain fairly centralized with a single uniform contract covering all districts.

At present, all negotiations are conducted at the central level with some consultation at the school level. The results of the survey suggest that under decentralization teachers prefer to negotiate salaries, hospital and medical insurance, vacations, transfer within the entire system, and standards for promotion and discharging teachers at the central board level. However, most respondents felt that decisions on the transfer of teachers within a district, curriculum, and special programs to improve the quality of education in individual schools should be decentralized to the local district board.

If the decentralization plan is developed according to the preferences indicated in the survey, a bargaining structure that handles some issues on a citywide basis and some on a district-wide basis probably will emerge. This structure would be analogous to the master agreement-local agreement procedure used for industry-wide bargaining in private industry.

Collective bargaining has traditionally been considered a bilateral process, but this view has recently been challenged in public employee bargaining. For example, it has been shown that bargaining in public education can assume multilateral characteristics because there are more than two parties to the negotiations. Third-party groups, usually operating on the fringe of the negotiations, are able to impose a cost (economic, political, or otherwise) on the parties to the agreement. Negotiations, therefore, are no longer limited to the teachers' organization and the school board but in some cases involve the indirect participation of community groups.[9]

Decentralization of the school system is likely to make the emerging multilateral bargaining structure even more complex. Inevitably, negotiations will include participation by representatives of the local district board on the employer side. This will affect the nature of interest group activity at the local level.

The interest group structure in the entire school system consists of "national" organizations, including civil rights organizations, with a variety of goals, and purely local organizations, such as parent-teachers' associations, whose interests are primarily focused on educational issues. The effect of decentralization will be a redistribution of power at the local district level. Local affiliates of national organizations will acquire more power and local groups will be encouraged to express their views on teacher negotiations. As a result, the number of groups attempting to impose a cost on the parties directly involved in negotiations will increase. In the short run, this will undoubtedly complicate negotiations.

[9] See, for example, Kenneth McLennan and Michael H. Moskow, "Teacher Negotiation and the Public Interest," in Seymour L. Wolfbein (ed.), *Emerging Sectors of Collective Bargaining* (forthcoming).

CONTENT OF NEGOTIATIONS

In a school system, it is economically sound to negotiate some personnel provisions on a system-wide basis irrespective of decentralization. Economies of scale can be achieved in the administration of fringe benefits, such as hospital and medical insurance, life insurance, and so on, when large numbers of persons enroll in these plans. System-wide coverage for these fringe benefits is also preferable since teachers' mobility among local districts will not be impeded. City school systems that participate in statewide examinations, such as New York City, should probably have a uniform school calendar, at least to the extent that all students in the city have the necessary preparation time prior to the statewide examinations.

The timing of negotiations would be affected if the master-local agreement procedure is adopted. The master agreement negotiations would precede local discussions so that details of the master agreement involving district problems could be dealt with at the district level. Local negotiations would most likely begin simultaneously in all districts once the master agreement is ratified.

According to our survey, the respondents favor hiring at the local district level. This may not be acceptable to the leadership of the teachers' organization. The crucial question as far as a teachers' organization is concerned is who determines the hiring standards. The Bundy Report suggests that a New York State teaching license be adequate to teach in New York City. The report recommends that the present Board of Examiner's licensing requirements be abolished and that the district board be authorized to set any other criteria for hiring teachers in their particular district as long as they meet the minimum state requirements.

It is unrealistic to expect any union to accept this feature of decentralization without considerable resistance. The Bundy Report in effect suggests the "lowering" of entrance requirements which would result in a larger available supply of teachers. Restriction of entry is used by unions and professional associations to reduce the quantity of labor and to improve the organization's bargaining power to raise wages. Elimination of entry restrictions is never viewed with enthusiasm by the members of the particular profession; teachers are likely to be no exception.

The level at which salaries are negotiated is another critical feature of decentralization plans. Some of the teachers surveyed felt that salary scales for extracurricular activities, including tutoring, should be negotiated at the district level. There was almost unanimous agreement among the respondents, however, that basic salaries should be negotiated at the central board level. From interviews conducted with a number of AFT leaders, it appears that teachers' organizations will strongly resist any attempt to give district boards the authority to negotiate basic salaries.

A differential salary structure has much merit since it provides for the allocation of manpower among the various districts within the entire system. Only one of the proposed plans favors decentralized negotiations over salaries. Although short-run salary differentials may develop under this plan, it is likely that in the long run the union will be able to negotiate uniform salary schedules in all districts. The district that is willing to pay the highest salary will become the pattern setter. Some interdistrict differentials can be achieved by having "extra pay" features, such as longer preparation periods or smaller class size, negotiated at the local level. The master agreement-local agreement probably is the most convenient method of obtaining these differentials.

BARGAINING POWER

Bargaining power, which is an essential element of collective bargaining, has been defined in terms of each party's cost of disagreement as follows: A's bargaining power is equal to the ratio of B's cost of disagreement on A's terms to B's cost of agreement on A's terms.[10] Accordingly, anything that increases B's cost of disagreement or decreases B's cost of agreement causes A's bargaining power to increase. Although it is not possible to quantify these costs, the definition is helpful in analyzing the effect of decentralization on the relative bargaining power of the parties involved.

The Bundy Report retains the existing system of citywide bargaining on salaries and working conditions. District school boards are given the power to allocate funds within their total budget after fulfilling contractual obligations incurred by the central school

[10] Neil W. Chamberlain, *Collective Bargaining* (McGraw-Hill, 1951), pp. 220–21.

board. This division of authority places district boards in a difficult position. They are given responsibility for operating the schools, but the cost of the most important item in their budget—salaries and fringe benefits—is completely outside of their control.

According to the Bundy Report, the district boards probably will exert strong pressure on the mayor and the city council to enlarge their budgets. This pressure will increase the strength of the central board and its total allocation from the city. As a result, the cost of teachers' demands relative to the total funds for education will decrease and the teachers' bargaining power increase.

Further changes in the teachers' bargaining power will depend on the actions of the district boards. If the district boards place pressure on the central board to avoid a strike, they will increase both the central board's cost of disagreement and the teachers' bargaining power. On the other hand, if the local boards do not express concern about a work stoppage, the central board will fear a strike less than it did before decentralization. The district boards provide a buffer for the pressure from citizens which ordinarily would be directed at the central board. Once a strike begins, the cost of continued disagreement for the central board will decrease if the district boards make other arrangements for manning the schools.

One feature of the multilateral character of bargaining in public education is that community interest groups may take action independently of the district board in order to keep the schools open during a strike. This occurred during the 1967 New York City teachers' strike and was threatened in the 1968 Philadelphia teacher negotiations. In Philadelphia, a coalition of interest groups representing the black community made plans to operate seventy-six schools located in ghetto areas. This threat clearly reduces the teachers' organization's bargaining power by reducing the cost of disagreement to the central school board. Since community groups will be more influential under decentralization, this form of pressure on collective bargaining will become more common.

An alternative to citywide bargaining is provided in Washington, D.C.'s Adams-Morgan Community School Board proposal that favors local community board control over salaries and working conditions. Under this plan, the local boards probably would have to negotiate these items with a single teachers' organization. The central teachers' organization would conduct separate negotiations with each district school board, or if local teachers' organizations are established, it would coordinate their bargaining efforts. This bargaining structure encourages whipsawing by the teachers.

In private industry, the union representing members in a multi-firm industry often refrains from striking all firms simultaneously. Instead, the union strikes the firm or group of firms that is most vulnerable to union demands. If it strikes a particular firm while other firms are producing, competition in the product market places tremendous pressure on the struck firm to settle even if the cost is extremely high.

After reaching agreement with this firm, the union starts bargaining with other firms, using the settlement as a base in the negotiations. If the union obtains a slightly higher settlement, it can continuously increase wages by whipsawing firms. When faced with this tactic, firms usually band together to negotiate standard conditions of employment for the entire industry.

If bargaining were decentralized in a big-city school system, the teachers' organization probably would bargain first with the district it thinks will agree to the best settlement terms. This district may have a large number of young residents with children of school age or it may be the most politically active. The criterion of product market competition would not apply because local school districts do not compete on that basis. The union would use the agreement reached in the "high salary" district as a starting point in bargaining with other districts. This structure enables the union to play to its own strength and to the weakness of its opponents. In the short run, the teachers' organization's bargaining power would increase because it is established and familiar with these tactics. Eventually district school boards would join together for bargaining and consequently reduce the teachers' bargaining power.

As this discussion has shown, decentralization will increase the bargaining power of teachers' organizations in the early stages of negotiations. Once a strike becomes imminent, however, the teachers' bargaining power will diminish under interest group pressure. This conflict between teachers and the community clearly distinguishes negotiations in public education from collective bargaining in private industry.

Urban teachers' organizations now find themselves in a paradoxical situation. For many years, they unsuccessfully attempted to participate in educational decisions. During this period, community groups often supported their requests for higher salaries and improved working conditions. Now that they have achieved decision-making power through collective bargaining, they are frequently criticized by the same community groups as guilty of perpetuating many of the social and educational problems of large cities. If school decentralization occurs, the changing decision-making structure will accelerate the trend for collective bargaining in public education to become the focal point of widespread community-interest group activity.

PART THREE

Organization and Financing

ANTHONY DOWNS

Competition and Community Schools

To an economist, many of the criticisms recently made against big-city public school systems have a familiar ring: they are identical with the complaints that consumers have leveled against monopolies for centuries. Since big-city school boards, administrations, and teachers' organizations are all essentially monopoly organizations, this similarity of discontent is no coincidence.

The classic antidote to monopoly is competition. By introducing alternative sources of supply, competition expands the choice available to consumers. Moreover, these alternative sources are likely to use different methods and approaches, or even to develop wholly new products. Thus, greater variety makes expanded choice really meaningful. Since consumers can shift their trade from suppliers who do not please them, suppliers have a strong incentive to provide what the consumers want. This attitude also means competitors regard innovations positively, as potential means of winning more business (if they can protect new ideas from instant duplication by other competitors). In contrast, monopolists usually view innovations negatively, as a bother designed to upset established routines for no good reason. Clearly, if greater competition causes these results in general, it might produce some tremendous improvements in big-city school systems.

Community schools could represent a limited form of competitive influence within such systems if these new types of schools were organized, operated, and related to other schools in certain ways.

The shifting of power in education from a single, monolithic administration to many decentralized boards would be quite similar to the breaking up of a monopoly into many competitors—that is, if consumers really had the power to choose among the competitors, and did not merely find themselves faced by many small monopolists rather than one big one. In this chapter, I will examine some of the possibilities, implications, and problems of introducing more competition into big-city public school systems, and will show how they can be related to community schools.

Requirements for Effective Competition

In order to provide the major benefits of competition, any system of production must possess certain fundamental characteristics. It is not possible to explore all of these here. Instead, five key characteristics will be described and related to existing conditions in most big-city school systems.

MEANS FOR CONSUMERS TO EVALUATE OUTPUTS

If consumers cannot tell a good product from a bad one, they cannot exercise consumer sovereignty to pressure the production system into giving them what they want. In our highly technological society, it is often difficult for consumers to evaluate the quality of products offered them. Is a Ford station wagon better or worse than a Chevrolet station wagon of comparable size and cost? Few people are expert enough to determine the answer. However, since both Fords and Chevrolets are readily available, consumers can directly compare certain measurable traits, such as size, design, and accessories. They can even hire experts to make impartial tests of more complex things, such as acceleration, braking, speed, and stability under loads.

Similar comparisons of more abstract products—such as schooling—require the same basic ingredients. That is, there must be well-defined outputs from different producers; those outputs must be measurable in some way; such measurements must be made; and information about those measurements must be available to consumers. Unfortunately, none of these conditions prevail in today's big-city public school systems. There are few agreed-upon definitions of what public school systems are supposed to produce; measuring those products that can be identified is extremely hard; they are rarely measured because doing so is expensive and potentially threatening to many teachers, administrators, and parents; and such rare information as does exist is usually a closely guarded secret.

Nevertheless, some information is available about the quality of education provided in different parts of the nation. It has generated strong discontent among many parents of children in low-income, big-city areas, especially those where ethnic minorities live, because it shows how poor are the results of public schools there as compared to other areas. But effective competition within, or outside, big-city public school systems can never be stimulated without vastly improving the quality and quantity of information evaluating the outputs of different schools and educational methods. How this can be done will be discussed later.

THE EXISTENCE OF ALTERNATIVE SUPPLIERS

Few "perfect" monopolies exist. Most consumers can usually find some alternative source of supply if they look hard enough, and users of big-city school systems are no exception. Parents living in big cities can send their children to private schools, buy entry into suburban schools without moving (in some cases), or actually move into the jurisdictional area of some other school within the big-city system or into a suburban system. But these alternatives are far more expensive than using the neighborhood public school. Therefore, low-income households cannot employ such alternatives. And even middle-income nonwhite households are restricted from moving into many all-white areas where superior schools are found. Thus, for thousands of households in big cities, there are no educational choices available except sending their children to that public school which has a district encompassing their residence.

Creating realistic alternative choices for these households will not be easy. Even placing control of local schools in the hands of many decentralized school boards will not expand real choices if each family must still use the nearest public school. Consumers—including the lowest-income consumers—must be able to choose among several, at least two and preferably more, alternatives if competition is to have any real effects. Therefore, individual schools must have attendance areas that overlap to some degree. For example, consider an area containing five elementary schools run by a single board of education. Each of these schools exclusively serves an attendance area surrounding it; that is, all students living in that area must attend that school, whereas no one living outside the area can attend that school. Now assume that control of these schools is shifted from a single centralized board into five decentralized boards. This does not create any expansion of choice for individual families if the same attendance policy is retained. However, such an expansion could be achieved by merging all five attendance areas into a single inclusive area, in which each family could apply to attend any school. Additional public schools (perhaps run by outside firms or agencies) could be introduced into the area and assigned attendance areas overlapping those of the original five schools. These expansions of choice would have to be accompanied by some scheme providing public payment of the extra transportation costs resulting from parents' sending their children to schools other than the ones closest to their homes. Otherwise, low-income families would be under economic pressure to continue using the nearest school, even if other options were theoretically available to them.

Inescapably, awarding consumers some freedom of choice creates uncertainty among producers concerning what "share of the market" each school will actually "capture." For example, if each of the five schools served 20 percent of all students initially, allowing consumers free choice might result in 40 percent applying for entry into one school, and only 10 percent into another. Coping with such an outcome raises difficult administrative and capital-planning considerations relevant to the next two requirements for effective competition.

FREEDOM TO OFFER SIGNIFICANTLY VARYING PRODUCTS

Multiplicity of outlets does not guarantee true competition concerning a given product; it must be accompanied by freedom among several producers to vary the nature of the products they offer. If every car dealer sold only red Ford two-door sedans all with the same accessories and at the same price, vastly increasing the number of dealer outlets would not expand consumer choice. Similarly, providing parents with the ability to choose among several schools for their children would not really increase their freedom of choice if exactly the same subjects, approaches, types of teachers, and materials were used in all the schools. True, individual personality differences among principals and teachers always produce some differences among schools, even when they are all governed by identical regulations. But a meaningful range of variation in educational contents and quality can be offered to parents only if principals of individual schools, or supervisors of relatively small districts, have real freedom to vary the products they offer consumers. Thus, decentralization of control over a significant part of what goes on in individual schools is an essential prerequisite for effective competition in education. Moreover, such decentralization must cover most of the key elements of educational contents. It is a sham to announce that individual principals or district superintendents are free to innovate and then retain centralized and standardized control over hiring and firing of teachers, teachers' salary levels, selection of textbooks, allowable classroom sizes, a large part of the curriculum, most administrative procedures, and capital expenditures for new buildings and equipment.

This means that competition among several schools for students cannot be the force that generates decentralized control of those schools. Allowing parents to choose among different schools might set up much stronger pressures accentuating those limited product differentiations that could be developed within existing centralized rules and regulations. But those rules and regulations must be greatly relaxed to allow wide variation among individual schools before competition can exert its maximum impact. To create fully effective competition requires overcoming all the frustrating and difficult obstacles that have so far blocked significant decentralization of control in most big-city systems.

Nevertheless, I do not believe it is feasible to wait for complete decentralization before initiating major experiments in greater competition. At least a few competitive units in which the local board, the principal, or individual teacher had significant autonomy could initially be set up outside the existing public school system, or as special, additional units supplementing it in certain areas. Similarly, competition among units within the system could be started even though only marginal decentralization of control existed (though this is inferior to the proposal just mentioned). But to postpone using competition until "perfect" decentralization is achieved is to forgo using it forever—even though it could be an immediate force exerting at least some added pressure to create greater decentralization of control.

CONSUMER CONTROL OVER SIGNIFICANT RESOURCES

In a free enterprise economy, consumers vote with dollars for the products they like—and against those they dislike. They can do so because they have the power to allocate those dollars to whatever producers they prefer (except for a few monopolies like the telephone company). Since the income represented by consumers' dollars is vital to producers, consumer-spending choices tremendously influence producer behavior. Similarly, if competition is to have any meaningful impact upon big-city public school systems, the consumers must have control over at least some resources used in their operation.

Some control is already exercised by school consumers. As voters, they decide on bond issues and sometimes indirectly upon other tax increases affecting the total resources available to the system. When a family moves from one place to another to gain access to better schools, it shifts its taxable resources into the new area. This increases the tax base there, and perhaps decreases it in the original area. It also moves its children from one school to another, and children are significant educational resources in several ways. First, they influence the total attendance figures used by each school as part of its formula for obtaining state aid. Second, the quality of education in each school is markedly influenced by the nature of the students attending it. In general, students from middle-income, upper-income, or other homes with strong cultural environments represent an educational asset to any school. But students from culturally deprived homes may represent an educational liability—considered solely from this viewpoint. Thus when parents move a child from one school to another, they affect both the financial and nonfinancial resources available to the two schools concerned.

Naturally, they also affect the demands placed upon those schools by their student loads.

But what about parents who cannot afford to move in pursuit of better schools, or are prevented from doing so by racial prejudice or some other force? If they are offered true choices among alternative schools, they can at least shift their children from one school to another instead of shifting their homes. However, this might result in a marked disparity between the number of students asking to attend each school and its physical capacity to handle them, as mentioned earlier. If 500 students apply to a school with a capacity for 100 students because it provides unusually desirable educational opportunities, how can the available places be rationed among the applicants?

At present, this problem is solved by setting boundaries so that the situation does not arise. But at the same time this eliminates any true choice among alternatives. Private schools often handle this problem by raising their tuition. But such price rationing discriminates against poor families and hence is inappropriate for public schools. The simple rule of first come, first served may be used, but this tends to favor students from the most intelligent and culturally advanced families, since they are more likely to plan ahead. The only remaining methods of allocation I can think of are random selection and use of geographic quotas. The latter can be illustrated by a system that divides the total attendance area into five parts with equal student population; classifies all applicants by location into five groups corresponding with these zones; sets a quota of 20 percent of total enrollment for each zone; and fills that quota from the applicants for each zone through random selection among them. If the boundaries of the five areas are carefully drawn in relation to the socioeconomic and ethnic traits of the population, this system can result in a well-balanced student body providing both ethnic and social-class integration in combinations likely to remain stable (that is, parents of one group will not withdraw their children to avoid the resulting balance).

Nevertheless, as long as any such rationing system still allocates the same proportion of total resources to each school as an exclusive district system, consumer choices are not really affecting the distribution of resources in the system. The worst school would still get

20 percent of all students, state aid, and other resources. Furthermore, parents whose children were assigned to that school would not really be exercising the kind of free choice vital to a truly competitive system. Many would have preferred to send their children to some other school, but it was too crowded. This brings us to the final requirement for a truly competitive system.

FREEDOM FOR CONSUMER PREFERENCES TO INFLUENCE RESOURCE ALLOCATION

A key long-run advantage of competitive markets is that they cause the production of those goods consumers like to expand and the production of those they dislike to contract or disappear. This same characteristic is essential to effective competition within big-city public school systems. Consumers must be able to use their power over resources to alter the long-range output of different types of education. At present, this is possible in theory when consumers move from one city to another. If most of the residents of city A were so repelled by its schools that they moved to much-preferred city B nearby, then the schools in city A would be forced to reduce their operations—and those in city B would expand.

Unfortunately, the economic ability to shift locations in search of better schools is unevenly distributed in society. Wealthier people can and do move to areas where the schools are reputed to be excellent. Those schools consequently expand. They can do so partly because the arrival of more middle-income or upper-income families within their attendance areas gives them the taxable resources they need for expansion. Furthermore, most students from such homes are positively oriented to education and benefit from relatively cultured home environments. Hence, their very presence in classrooms improves the quality of education. In contrast, poor students whose families cannot afford to move are left in the schools considered relatively undesirable. The departure of middle-income and upper-income students from those classrooms causes a higher concentration of students from relatively deprived homes, thereby lowering the quality of education. Moreover, rising concentration of poor families within the attendance areas of such schools reduces the per-student taxable resources available to support them. Thus, making alternative choices available to the wealthier families in society but not to the poorer—and to middle-income whites more than to middle-income nonwhites—tends to create long-run effects beneficial to the wealthier—especially whites—and detrimental to the poorer—especially nonwhites. What other tactics might help public school consumers gain the long-run advantages of competition without this undesirable result?

We have already described a system for allowing parents to express choices among five elementary schools all serving the same merged attendance area. But if all the parents who wanted to send their children to the best-liked school actually were allowed to do so, it might become extremely overcrowded. At the same time, the worst-liked school would be nearly empty. This would result in an inefficient use of invested capital, and might significantly reduce the quality of education in both schools. Yet adopting any system of student rationing that ultimately allocates 20 percent of all resources to each school does not result in any expansion of the most-preferred school or contraction of the least-preferred one. Expansion and contraction could be encouraged by either or both of the following tactics:

The first tactic is the use of a certain amount of flexible classroom and other school facilities that could be moved from one place to another. For example, if a school system consisted of 60 percent permanent buildings and 40 percent mobile classrooms, then the latter could be shifted around each year to accommodate parents' preferences for specific schools. Teachers and other resources would also be shifted correspondingly. This kind of arrangement could quickly be put into effect in cities with rapidly growing populations and school enrollments. A high proportion of the new physical capacity to be added each year could consist of portable facilities. In cities that already have fixed plants adequate for present and future enrollments, addition of such mobile capacity would represent a huge added expense and cause underutilization of existing capacity. However, in such cities, if some older facilities must be retired because of obsolescence, they could be replaced with portable units so as to arrive at the desired balance without added expense.

This tactic has two decided disadvantages. First, most parents—and many teachers—regard portable facilities as inferior per se and stigmatizing to the schools concerned. Second, moving such facilities—and other resources—each year would be expensive and might be administratively disruptive.

The second tactic is that of shifting control over the nature of education in accordance with the expressed votes of parents' attendance choices while still using the same buildings and classrooms. For example, assume there are five equal-sized schools in an attendance area containing 1,000 students. If 500 of these students apply to attend school X because its approach is so well liked (or for any other reasons), then the methods used in school X would be extended to at least one and perhaps one and a half other schools. This could be done either by expanding the administrative and curriculum jurisdiction of the principal of school X to these other schools or by putting pressure on the principals of the other schools to adopt the methods used in school X. Both of these tactics imply that some central agency exists within the system to perform these reallocations of resources or authority. They also imply that the methods used in school X can be extended almost instantaneously, or at least quite rapidly, to other schools without loss of quality. This is highly unrealistic, but it could be rendered more feasible if a longer period of adjustment were allowed.

Both of these tactics probably seem utterly impractical to the people who actually operate big-city school systems. Yet some version of them must be incorporated into those systems if competition is to have meaningful impact upon public education in large cities. Even now, there is an implicit assumption that each centralized school administration will somehow seek out and discover the most effective methods of education, and introduce them into the classrooms throughout its system. But it is precisely the failure to incorporate the most desired educational methods—and to reduce those least desired—that is one of the chief complaints against existing big-city systems. Moreover, a key response to this failure is the continuing migration of middle-class families with children from big cities to the suburbs. Consequently, even if big-city school administrators believe the responsiveness to consumer preferences indicated by the above tactics are impossible, many consumers clearly believe they are both desirable and possible—and act accordingly.

The Need for a Comprehensive Evaluation System

The preceding analysis emphasized the critical need for accurate and easily available information which evaluates both the educational performance of public schools and the methods of education used in them. Without such information, consumers cannot tell whether their children are really getting proper training or to what extent certain parts of that training are fine and others are terrible. Parents make such judgments now. But they do so only on the basis of personal impressions gained from comparing experiences in different schools with their friends and acquaintances or with the few national test scores that professionals release to them. Many parents in low-income neighborhoods do not even have these elements upon which to base accurate judgments. Therefore, it would be pointless to make the other institutional changes necessary to introduce competition into big-city public school systems without first creating an accurate and comprehensive educational evaluation system, putting it into operation throughout the school system, and making the results known to parents.

Such an evaluation system might also create pressures on individual schools, principals, local boards, and teachers to adopt those methods that have proved most effective in training various specific kinds of students. Knowledge of the success of certain approaches, and the failure of others, would generate both parental and professional pressure to expand the former and contract the latter. Hence, an accurate and widely publicized evaluation system could act as a substitute for the two tactics described in the previous section which seem both so necessary and so impractical.

Furthermore, an evaluation system of this type could greatly improve the efficiency of resource allocation within our enormous national education system. It is rather astounding that around $50 billion per year is spent on education in the United States and yet there is no systematic way of measuring the effectiveness of this giant expenditure. Few accurate measurements of relationships between costs and effectiveness are made anywhere in the system, and none are regularly applied, even to the larger parts, to measure comparative performance. As a result, widespread disparities in both effectiveness and efficiency appear and continue without any corrective action. It is widely believed that public schools in the South are generally inferior to those in the North. Many observers also believe that public schools in the East have higher academic standards than those in the West (especially in California). Yet even these conclusions are based mainly on a few national achievement tests in a narrow range of subjects, casual inspection of expenditure-per-pupil data, and personal observations. Admittedly, I am no expert on the nature of educational research, and I may be ill-informed about much pertinent analysis in this area. Yet I believe it is fair to conclude that existing methods of evaluating educational performance are grossly inadequate. They can neither identify nor encourage the adoption of many potentially huge gains in effectiveness from our current national spending on schools.

Accurate evaluation of educational effectiveness will be especially important if community schools become widespread in the United States. The shift of control over curricula to many decentralized school boards will probably lead to a wide variety of educational approaches in different cities, and even within each large city. Each school board will have a vested interest in claiming that its approach is successful. Unless there is some relatively objective way to evaluate these multiple approaches, neither parents, nor national educational policy makers, nor local taxpayers will know which methods are really working and which ones are failing. Admittedly, they do not know now either. Thus, the case for an accurate, comprehensively applied evaluation system will be no stronger under community schools than it is at present. But this case is already overwhelmingly persuasive.

Problems in Performance Evaluation Systems

One of the main reasons for which so few school systems have developed comprehensive and accurate means of evaluating their performance is the extreme difficulty of doing so. The need for good evaluation is desperate, but the need alone yields no clue as to how it can be met. In this section, I will identify some of the key problems involved, and suggest some potential approaches to solving them—or at least coping with them.

MULTIPLE ASPECTS OF EDUCATION

It is widely agreed that children who go to school should learn how to read, write, and perform certain basic mathematical skills with at least minimal proficiency. Their ability to do these things can be objectively measured by means of tests and compared with the abilities of other children of the same age and background. But schooling is also designed to have many other impacts on the children it affects. These include creating or bolstering self-confidence; inculcating certain basic democratic values; encouraging positive attitudes toward work; providing minimal skills and disciplinary habits relevant to work; and teaching basic skills of interpersonal relations. Measuring these things—indeed, just defining them—is extraordinarily difficult. In some cases, it may be impossible. Yet few educators believe that these nonacademic aspects of schooling are unimportant, and many believe they are more important than basic reading, writing, and arithmetic.

Therefore, no evaluation system should evade trying to measure the capabilities, and changes in capabilities, of students regarding these nonacademic aspects of education. Attempts should be made to develop clear definitions of the traits concerned, and descriptions of various states of proficiency concerning them. These will differ from place to place, especially if community schools become widespread. Nevertheless, the different participants in the education system—including teachers, students, parents, and counselors—should be asked to evaluate students using these criteria. Admittedly, subjective judgments may be prominent in such measurements, but trying to meet this problem head on will provide many significant insights, even if precise interpersonal or interschool comparisons prove elusive.

MULTIPLE DISTRIBUTION GOALS

Viewed as a whole, the nation's public school system (or that of any state, district, or city) expends certain resources in order to attain one or more of the following distributions of educational results:

1. *The minimum-citizenship goal*—there should be some basic minimum level of proficiency and capability for all students regarding the various aspects of education discussed above, especially those most relevant to democratic citizenship.

2. *The maximum-system-output goal*—the total capabilities of all students considered as a group (perhaps best measured by their total resulting productivity) should be made as large as possible within the constraints imposed by the total resources available to the system.

3. *The equal-opportunity goal*—all students emerging from the system (say, upon high school graduation) should have approximately the same capabilities for entering into the postschool portions of their lives.

4. *The maximum-individual-advancement goal*—each student should be given as much development of his individual potential as possible, within the constraints imposed by total available resources.

Undoubtedly, other worthy goals could also be identified. But I believe these four express the major system-wide objectives of education most commonly discussed in the United States.

These goals imply widely differing distributions of publicly supplied educational resources among various types of students and various geographic areas. This is true mainly because such resources are only one of the four basic inputs affecting the educational performance of particular students, as will be discussed later. The degree to which individual students possess the other three inputs varies widely in a rather systematic fashion. This variance is related to such factors as their parents' income and socioeconomic status, their geographic location in the nation and within metropolitan areas, and their ethnic nature. Consequently, pursuing each of the goals exclusively, without regard to the others, would result in very different allocations of publicly supplied educational inputs. At one extreme, the equal-opportunity goal would require a heavy concentration of resources among the poorest and most culturally deprived students. They would receive much higher per-student inputs than children from higher-income and more advantaged homes. The minimum-citizenship goal would also require concentrating more inputs per student among the most-deprived children. It might not result in quite as unequal a distribution, since the poorest-qualified children would not have to be brought up to the level of attainment with the best-qualified but only up to some minimum standard of basic achievement. In contrast, the maximum-system-output goal would concentrate publicly supplied inputs on the best-qualified students. This would result in the greatest total gain in technical proficiency per dollar invested.[1] The maximum-individid-

[1] Henry Levin argues that the highest marginal payoff would come from applying added resources to students from the most deprived backgrounds. He assumes that there are constantly declining marginal returns to investment in education. Since deprived

ual-advancement goal results in an indeterminate allocation pattern, since it really provides no precisely defined objective. If the goal is interpreted as equal advancement (in contrast to equal achievement), then this allocation would also probably favor the lowest-income and most-deprived students. It takes more dollars of publicly supplied inputs to advance such students a given amount in achievement than it does students from more advantaged homes.

At present, the allocation of such inputs greatly favors children from middle- and upper-income homes, especially whites, and penalizes those from poorer homes, especially nonwhites. This most closely resembles the allocation appropriate for the maximum-system-output goal. It is so unlike the allocation appropriate for the equal-opportunity goal that any major public emphasis upon that goal would call for radical revisions in the existing distribution of educational resources.

The existence of multiple goals and their call for such widely varying resource allocation patterns for publicly supplied inputs pose a difficult problem for anyone trying to design an educational evaluation system. Such a system should tell its users how well existing education methods achieve some set of goals concerning the performance of the educational system as a whole, as well as the performance of each district, school, or classroom. But which of these system-wide objectives should be used in making this assessment? Since any educational system should probably serve several goals simultaneously, the question really becomes what relative emphasis should be placed on each goal? Different groups of consumers would undoubtedly provide widely varying answers. Their answers would depend to a great extent on how each type of emphasis

---

children have had fewer total resources applied to their education (by their parents as well as by public school systems) than less-deprived children, the more-deprived children are not as "far out" on their marginal payoff curves as less-deprived children. However, I believe that the marginal returns from education are not constantly declining. Translating this jargon into English, it seems to me that children from affluent backgrounds who have already received considerable education can absorb a given additional amount of knowledge, or learn an additional amount of a skill, with less input from teachers or other publicly supplied resources than deprived children can. Admittedly, this is a purely subjective judgment on my part. See Henry M. Levin, "The Failure of the Public Schools and the Free Market Remedy," *Urban Review*, Vol. 2 (June 1968), pp. 32–37 (Brookings Reprint 148).

would affect the total share of publicly supplied inputs going to their children. Therefore, the evaluation system would probably have to be designed so that it could be used to assess the effectiveness of the system in attaining each of these four goals (and perhaps others) independently. This would allow each consumer group to arrive at its own conclusions concerning whether the system was allocating publicly supplied inputs properly.

MULTIPLE INPUTS AFFECTING EDUCATIONAL ACHIEVEMENT

Recent large-scale studies of educational performance in the nation's schools have dramatically shown that activities in those schools are only one of the basic factors influencing educational achievement.[2] In fact, it is useful to view the output of the educational process as resulting from at least four different inputs for each child: (1) genetically determined capabilities inherited from parents; (2) the child's home environment, both present and past (particularly during the first few years of life); (3) the school system and all its component parts (including teachers, buildings, other facilities, methods, systems of mixing students); and (4) the child's nonhome, nonschool environment, which will be referred to as the neighborhood environment. These causal factors could be broken down somewhat differently, but this classification is sufficient to illustrate the key points concerned here.

Educational achievement, however defined, is influenced by all four of these factors simultaneously. Thus, attributing it to only one factor is neither just nor accurate. For example, system-wide testing usually indicates that children in schools serving upper-income white neighborhoods score much better on most tests than those in schools serving low-income nonwhite neighborhoods. Yet it might be false to conclude that the former schools were doing a better job than the latter. The superior achievement of the higher-scoring students might be entirely attributable to the three nonschool factors. The schools serving the lower-scoring students could actually be doing a much better job than those serving the higher-scoring students, thereby causing the achievement gap between

[2] See James S. Coleman and others, *Equality of Educational Opportunity* (U.S. Office of Education, 1966), referred to as the Coleman Report. See also U.S. Commission on Civil Rights, *Racial Isolation in the Public Schools* (1967).

these two groups to be smaller than it would have been if both schools had performed with equal effectiveness.

Clearly, any useful educational evaluation system must be able to measure the impacts of the school system itself separately from the impacts of these other factors. Moreover, it should be able to measure the specific effects of various parts of the school system (such as training of teachers, quality of facilities, system of mixing students, attitudes of teachers, methods of instruction, and types of curricula). Only if it exhibits such sensitivity can an evaluation system enable those using it to make effective decisions on which publicly supplied inputs to alter and in what ways. But this kind of analytic separation of causal contributions to a single result is extremely difficult to build into any educational evaluation system. The widespread controversy among statisticians over the meaning of the Coleman Report perfectly illustrates this problem. To cope with this problem will require any workable evaluation system to have the following characteristics:

First, it must be used throughout a large part of the entire American school system simultaneously and in the same manner. Only in this way can a sufficiently large and varied sample be obtained so that the impact of a wide variety of individual factors can be isolated through standard statistical techniques. An evaluation system adopted by a single city might be large enough if that city was a big one. But if it is used only in one small suburban area, with a relatively homogeneous population in terms of socioeconomic and ethnic traits, then the evaluations it provides may not be measuring the performance of schools at all. This means that entire states would be much better units for the definition and administration of educational evaluation than individual school districts, and the entire nation would probably be the best base. However, it will be extremely difficult to get statewide or nationwide agreement on any specific method of measuring educational achievement—especially concerning those elements not easily subjected to written performance tests (such as success in building student self-confidence or imparting basic democratic values).

Second, a key part of the system should be comparing the performance of each group of children at different points in time. This would provide before and after results that would isolate the impact of the schools since—presumably—the other three factors will not have varied significantly between these testing points. In reality, children's capabilities change significantly merely because they get older and acquire better coordination and more general experience. But this could be largely offset by relatively frequent evaluation (at least once a year, and perhaps more), and by the next device described.

Third, major emphasis in evaluation should be placed upon comparisons among parts of the school system serving students from similar home and neighborhood environments. Thus, the performance of schools serving low-income neighborhoods should be compared with each other, rather than with the performances of schools serving upper-income areas. (This should not preclude the latter kinds of comparison, however, since they are necessary to certain system-wide effectiveness evaluations.) This would be analogous to dividing sailboats into specific categories or classes for comparing the performances of their crews. Such categorization should at least intellectually—though perhaps not emotionally—counteract some of the resistance to evaluation from teachers and administrators who fear that unfair comparisons will be made in criticism of their performances. (Unfortunately, many are equally afraid of fair comparisons.)

Fourth, the specific contents and procedures used in evaluation tests must be adapted to the particular experiences of students with tremendously varying backgrounds. Negro children reared in low-income urban slums do not have the same mental images, vocabularies, sense experiences, or even world outlooks as children growing up in wealthy all-white suburbs, on isolated Appalachian farms, or in borderline barrios where English is seldom spoken. Therefore, the techniques used to evaluate children's educational skills, and the impact of schools upon them, must be adapted to the particular experiences of the various types of children concerned. This implies that a wide variety of evaluation techniques and vehicles must be developed. It also seems inconsistent with the first characteristic for an effective evaluation system mentioned above: that it be used throughout a large part of the entire school system simultaneously and in the same manner. Admittedly, creating differently adapted evaluative techniques that still permit intergroup comparisons will not be easy. But reaching the moon was not easy either, yet sufficient national resources were applied to accomplish that task. And in my opinion the potential payoff for developing an effective educational evaluation system is vastly greater than the payoff for reaching the moon. Hence, an effort much greater than our present one should be devoted to this task.

DEFINING SYSTEM BOUNDARIES

Selecting the area to be included in any evaluation system will have a crucial impact upon the ways in which that system might be used to influence the allocation of publicly supplied educational inputs. At least two of the other three basic educational inputs are unevenly distributed through space. Thus, each school attendance area, or school district, contains a set of consumers quite different from the average composition of students in the nation or state as a whole. Families with home environments conducive to relatively high-level educational achievement tend to live in areas with other such families. Together they create neighborhood environments equally conducive to high-level achievement. Conversely, families with home environments that discourage high-level educational achievement also tend to cluster together. This produces neighborhood environments with similarly discouraging effects. Moreover, since most school systems use the neighborhood school principle to establish student mixtures, such spatial clustering means that students of each type tend to encounter similar type students in their classes. But classroom environment is a key ingredient in any school system. Hence the operation of the school system in such a residentially clustered society tends to further aggravate the inequalities of educational achievement resulting from home and neighborhood environments.

Insofar as the equal-opportunity objective is relevant to public education, it calls for an allocation that uses publicly supplied inputs to compensate for the inequalities resulting from the other inputs affecting educational achievement. But the practical implications of this conclusion for any given school vary sharply. They depend on whether that "system" is considered to be the schools in just one small community, an entire metropolitan area, a state, or the whole nation. At present, states provide a significant part of all publicly supplied inputs to local public schools. Most states do not allocate those resources to any well-defined and high priority goal (or set of goals). They largely leave the pursuit of such goals to individual school districts. The formula used to pass out state educational funds is based mainly (though not always exclusively) upon equal per-student distribution. Insofar as the sources of such state funds are regressive (as are property taxes and sales taxes), this approach aggravates income inequalities. But this aspect of the issue is too complex to explore here. However, it is clear that the basic duality of state funding for educational operations—collecting funds on a statewide basis but leaving the decision of their effects up to individual districts—has a profound impact upon the net inequalities of educational achievement in each state.

This result could be either reinforced or counteracted by future educational evaluation systems, depending upon what geographic areas they apply to. If a single evaluation system is used throughout an entire state, it will soon reveal profound inequalities in educational achievements. Experts know that these inequalities now exist. But there are few stark statistics that explicitly identify and measure them in the dramatic ways that a statewide evaluation system would. Political or legal pressure for much greater equality of results would be likely to emerge quickly from such a revelation. This might result in some effort to allocate state-supplied resources to compensate for the inequalities of distribution of the other causal factors described above. On the other hand, if all evaluation systems are strictly local in nature, they would use varying techniques that would obscure such statewide comparisons. The resulting pressures for greater equalization of educational opportunity would probably be much lower, as they are now.

In my opinion, every state should insist upon statewide evaluation of at least some key components of educational achievement. Since the state supplies a significant fraction of public school funds to all districts, it has the right—indeed, the obligation—to ask for some accounting of how effectively its funds are being used—not just whether they are being spent without fraud. Many states already require local schools to teach certain subjects or even use certain textbooks. Therefore, it is certainly reasonable for them to ask localities to appraise the effectiveness of their educational efforts by using certain standardized evaluation methods. As an added encouragement, the federal government should require every state that accepts any federal educational assistance to institute at least some statewide evaluation system on an annual basis, with results made public for each district and school.

LOCAL RESISTANCE

Most people do not like to have their activities scrutinized and evaluated by "outsiders." This seems especially repugnant if the results are to be made public and compared to similar examinations of other people engaged in the same activities. Such "auditing" of behavior may be both within the rights of the community that pays the auditors and highly beneficial to it, but these truths do not usually diminish community resistance. After all, any competent evaluation of an activity carried out on a large scale, like teaching in elementary and secondary schools, is bound to reveal that only a minority of those evaluated are superior in effectiveness. By definition, most will be rated as either average or below average. Thus, the majority have little to gain in terms of their own status and prestige, and perhaps quite a bit to lose. Even many parents, who stand to benefit most from evaluating the effectiveness of teachers, are often reluctant to subject the achievement levels of their own children to rigorous comparison with those of other children for fear of losing prestige or status.

This nearly universal resistance to evaluation occurs in many forms. The most obvious is opposing any evaluation scheme at all. More subtle is limiting the scope of such schemes. A third is insuring that control over the design and operation of the schemes is maintained by members of the organizations to be evaluated, so they can exclude the most threatening forms of evaluation. A fourth form of resistance is insisting that the results of any evaluation be kept confidential, or disclosing them to the public in such diluted forms that no individuals or schools can be pinpointed as incompetent or ineffective. The last form is demanding that no remedial actions be based upon the results of evaluation systems—particularly that salaries and other types of compensation be entirely divorced from effectiveness of performance.

In my opinion, the basic motive for all these forms of resistance is the dual fear of being revealed as ineffective, or being pressured to change in ways that might increase individual effort. However, this fear is rarely mentioned by those who support such resistance. Instead, they contend that the particular form of resistance they support is in the public interest. For example, it is commonly argued that outsiders should neither design nor control evaluation systems since they are not familiar with local problems, techniques, or educational objectives. Even more frequent is the contention that evaluation schemes cost far more money than the hard-pressed school systems can afford to spend.

It is these forms of defensive resistance, rather than any technical difficulties of designing or operating evaluation systems, that are now and will continue to be the major obstacles to widespread adoption of evaluation systems. Moreover, as teachers' unions become more widespread and more powerful, such resistance will greatly increase. Ironically, supporters of community schools are likely to be just as defensive about subjecting themselves to "impartial evaluations" as are the supporters of established school systems, who are now accused of ineffective performance—and for the same reasons.

How can such nearly universal—and intense—resistance to evaluation be overcome? I can only offer the following suggestions as possible tactics:

First, state and federal agencies responsible for providing funds to local school districts should insist upon use of evaluation systems with certain basic characteristics as a requirement for receiving aid. This would provide a strong incentive for adoption.

Second, evaluation systems should be designed and operated by persons outside the district public school administration, but that administration should have some voice in selecting the evaluators. They could perhaps come from local universities or consulting firms in which the administration has confidence, possibly because of previous experiences.

Third, the analogy of public auditing done by outside accountants should be used to persuade congressmen, other officials, citizens, and major public media that evaluation systems not only make sense but are necessary to protect the public's legitimate interest in using its money wisely. The growing understanding and support for planning, programming, and budgeting systems provides further intellectual underpinning for effective evaluation systems.

Fourth, proposed evaluation schemes should not be linked to

mechanisms that would translate evaluation results into changes in school behavior. Deciding what to do in response to such results should be left up to the parents, educators, and politicians in each district. Thus emphasizing only the provision of accurate data may reduce the threatening image of evaluation systems in the minds of those who fear any loss of local control over public education.

Finally, evaluation schemes could initially be restricted to community schools. The diversity of approaches likely to appear in these schools makes the need for some means of measuring their performance seem plausible. Also, their experimental character fits in well with the need for innovation in the design of evaluation systems. Even more important, the majority of existing educators will not be involved in running community schools; thus they would not feel threatened by evaluation systems aimed only at those schools. Using evaluation systems only in community schools could even have a vindictive appeal to those educators who believe that community schools cannot work. Even if community schools did fail to improve educational effectiveness directly, they would still be making an important contribution to overall educational effectiveness by opening the door to widespread employment of accurate evaluation systems.

SCARCITY OF RESOURCES

Most big-city public school systems are desperately short of financial resources. Therefore, they regard any diversion of available funds from educational programs to other activities as too wasteful or luxurious to contemplate. The argument that diversion of $\frac{1}{2}$ of 1 percent of all their funds into evaluation might result in a 10 percent or greater improvement in the effectiveness of the remaining 99.5 percent of all funds has so far failed to sway this resistance. However, I believe this is largely because there is so little evidence that effective evaluation systems can actually be designed. Once the possibility of creating and using such systems effectively has been demonstrated, school boards throughout the nation will be far more receptive to installing them. The initial, key task, then, is getting a few well-designed systems under way.

This is a "natural" situation for the use of foundation funding or federal experimental funding. Money for development of a large-scale evaluation system over a five-year period might be tied to money for some other kind of program which a big-city system especially desires. This would "sweeten" the package so as to make acceptance of an evaluation system more likely. One such program, which could also be used as a testing ground for the evaluation system, might be the development of prototype community schools on an experimental basis. Once an evaluation system was placed in operation, its success (or failure) at stimulating improvements in the schools concerned would greatly increase (or further reduce) the incentive of other school boards to launch similar programs.

Alternative Ways To Introduce Competition into Big-City Public School Systems

Assuming that greater competition in big-city public school systems is generally desirable, there are several specific ways to attain it. Some are mutually exclusive; but most could be used in combination.

WIDESPREAD AND WELL-PUBLICIZED USE OF EVALUATION SYSTEMS

The simplest way to create greater competition among public schools would be to design, install, and use educational effectiveness evaluation systems along the lines discussed earlier. Although such systems would probably encounter great initial resistance, their use would actually require no significant institutional or administrative changes in existing public school systems. They would generate greater competition solely by revealing to the consumers of education, and to all the professionals concerned, the relative effectiveness of each school, district, educational approach, or other element subject to measurement. Presumably, the persons in charge of those aspects that appeared to be least effective would receive heavy pressure from those they serve, from their own professional pride, and from other educational professionals to adopt elements revealed as more effective.

Competition through better information would be most furthered by evaluation systems that measured (1) the objective level of achievement of the students in each school (or even each classroom) related to analogous levels for all the other students in the system concerned, in the entire state, and in the whole nation, and particularly to other students in similar home and neighborhood environments; (2) the contribution to that achievement of the school itself, and of specific elements within the school (such as teachers, methods, student mixture); (3) the contribution of the school to the attainment of nonacademic goals of education; and (4) the effectiveness of various specific educational techniques in relation to their costs (not just in relation to their results, as is typical of existing educational evaluations).

As noted earlier, formidable technical and political obstacles inhibit immediate use of evaluation systems to stimulate competition in big-city school systems. Therefore, two types of compromises concerning evaluation systems appear necessary. First, any evaluation scheme that is at all sensible should be encouraged and initiated as soon as possible, even if it does not exhibit all or most of the desirable qualities described above. Second, there is no reason to wait until effective evaluation systems are designed before using the other forms of competition, as set forth below. It may be hard for parents to assess the quality of the alternative educational products offered them by competition without a good evaluation system. Nevertheless, any significant increase in competition is likely to produce desirable results and generate healthy pressures on present big-city school monopolies.

USE OF COMMUNITY SCHOOLS TO ENCOURAGE DIVERSITY

Community schools would also encourage a degree of competition within public school systems if they had at least two key characteristics. The first is a diversity of educational approaches. This would presumably arise if a wide variety of communities actually had control over significant portions of the curricula in schools serving them. The second is an evaluation system that would measure the effectiveness of these different approaches and promulgate the results throughout the system. Both of these attributes would generate some of the benefits of competition even if students are compelled to attend the school serving their area of the city rather than being given a choice of several schools. Again, knowledge of what worked and what failed should generate at least some pressure on schools that are failing to adopt the successful approaches used in those that are succeeding—or at least doing better.

USE OF OVERLAPPING ATTENDANCE AREAS

There are several ways that overlapping attendance areas, discussed earlier, could be used to create greater competition within an existing public school system.

Expansion of existing attendance areas. If attendance areas for several schools located close to each other were merged, then students anywhere in the enlarged area could attend any of the schools serving it. This would cause a concentration of applicants at the schools considered the best, and a shrinkage of applicants at those considered the worst. This approach would generate higher total transportation costs than the pure neighborhood school system. It might also require some form of student-rationing system other than geographic location. However, because simply merging attendance areas would not involve deliberately planned diversity, differences in quality within the system would mainly result from accidents of supervisory abilities. Most parents would probably continue to send their children to the school that was geographically most convenient, rather than encouraging them to go longer distances to find higher quality. Hence, the magnitude of the additional transportation costs involved, and the pressure to use nongeographic rationing, would probably not be great over the whole system; nor would the impact of the resulting competition become very significant.

Expansion of attendance areas plus creation of community schools. This plan is similar to the one above but would involve more deliberately planned diversity among schools. Hence, the ability of students to choose from among several reasonably proximate schools would represent a more meaningful choice. This might result in a greater convergence on certain schools regarded as superior, and more avoidance of those considered inferior. Consequently, the whole system would not be so dominated by sheer geographic convenience (though I believe that would probably remain the single most significant factor in parental choice of schools). Transportation costs would rise significantly, and the pressure to adopt some kind of nongeographic student-rationing system would also mount. Furthermore, the appearance of much greater diversity of educational approaches would create greater pressure to allow parents in any given area to send their children to schools located elsewhere, even though doing so would be less convenient. This would occur because some parents in each neighborhood would surely disagree with the particular educational approach or emphasis adopted by the community school serving that neighborhood. To insure proper freedom of choice, these parents would have to be allowed to send their children to some alternative schools. These alternatives could either be community schools elsewhere or schools still run by the centralized school administration, or both.

Community schools can either be entirely new structures (or at least structures newly used for schooling) added onto the existing system (in which case, the central authorities might still operate schools in almost every neighborhood), or conversions of existing schools into community-controlled schools (in which case, the central authorities would be running fewer schools). But in either case, use of enlarged attendance areas would be extremely important as a means of introducing and maintaining competition within the system.

Expansion of attendance areas plus creation of experimental schools. This approach is similar to the one just described except that the alternative schools would be run by innovation-oriented groups (such as private firms, universities, or local volunteers) rather than community-oriented groups—or perhaps in conjunction with the latter. For example, a community school board might select a basic approach to education, and then contract with a private firm to carry out that approach. This mixture of public control and private administration has already been endorsed by such educational experts as Theodore Sizer and Christopher Jencks.[3] It would provide many private firms interested in educational markets with a chance to show what they could do, thereby generating a new source of competition to existing public schools.

AWARDING PARENTS VOUCHERS TO BUY SCHOOLING

Milton Friedman has suggested that competition could be injected into public education by having educational services financed publicly but produced by a variety of private, profit-motivated

[3] See Christopher Jencks, "Is the Public School Obsolete?" *Public Interest*, No. 2 (Winter 1966), pp. 18–27, and Theodore Sizer, "Reform and the Control of Education" (processed; Harvard University, Graduate School of Education, 1967).

firms. The parents of every child would receive a publicly financed voucher of a fixed sum per child. They could then use this voucher to buy educational services from any approved supplier they wanted to patronize.[4] As Henry Levin pointed out in his excellent analysis of this proposal, it would undoubtedly increase the variety of educational services offered to parents, thereby enabling them to find more easily the kinds of educational services they wanted.[5]

But this scheme would also have two less desirable effects. First, it is vital for society as a whole to insure that all citizens receive a minimum quality education in certain skills and knowledge necessary for effective citizenship. Yet experience with other forms of private consumption shows that ignorant, low-income consumers can be exploited by unscrupulous producers who persuade the consumers to pay exorbitant prices for inferior-quality goods. To prevent this outcome from occurring in education, it would be necessary for public authorities to exercise some form of regulation over all private producers of educational services. Such regulation might become almost as extensive and standardized as existing public production of education.

Second, wealthier parents could add more funds to the voucher to buy better-quality services, but poor parents could not. Wealthier parents would evoke high-quality schools that would attract the best teachers and use the best facilities; poor parents would be compelled to give their children much lower-quality educations. Thus, direct price discrimination based on incomes would accomplish precisely the same result that geographic discrimination based on incomes now achieves. This might aggravate existing inequalities of educational opportunity rather than diminish them.

However, this second disadvantage could be offset by awarding a much larger voucher to low-income families than to high-income families, as Levin points out. He describes two methods: a sliding scale with payments varying inversely with income, and provision of such aid only to the lowest-income families. He rejects the first as politically unrealistic, but regards the second as politically possible —perhaps because it is essentially a novel version of the aid pro-

[4] Milton Friedman, "The Role of Government in Education," *Capitalism and Freedom* (University of Chicago Press, 1962), pp. 85–107.

[5] Levin, "The Failure of the Public Schools."

vided under Title I of the Elementary and Secondary Education Act of 1965.

For purposes of this analysis, I will assume that some form of providing either full vouchers or bonus payments to students from low-income households, and allowing them to choose where to apply such grants, could be used to inject a significant degree of competition into big-city public school systems. Every such voucher or bonus should be at least large enough to pay for the extra inputs needed to offset the disadvantages imposed on the child's education by deficiencies in his nonschool environment. In fact, any voucher or bonus should be made large enough to convert each low-income child from a liability into an asset, as seen from the viewpoints of the suppliers of education and of the parents of other children in the schools involved. Then, the voucher or bonus would create a surplus over and above the marginal cost of educating the low-income child. That surplus could then be applied to improving the quality of the entire school that accepted such a child. This would provide a positive incentive for schools to accept or even seek out such children. However, it is unlikely that society will presently pay the relatively large amounts needed to accomplish this outcome.

A voucher or bonus arrangement favoring low-income students could be used in any one of the three basic forms describing the use of overlapping attendance areas. That is, it could be employed in conjunction with an expansion of existing attendance areas into large and overlapping zones, or with a similar expansion plus the development of community schools, or with a similar expansion plus the development of experimental schools (which might be related to community control). In the last case, special schools catering only to students with vouchers or bonus payments might be developed. They would be able to use high levels of expenditure per student. In the first case, special schools with geographic quotas or bonus-student quotas could be developed. They could provide a socially integrated educational environment that would still take advantage of the added resources made possible by the bonus payments. But in all cases, the parents of low-income children would have to be allowed at least some discretion about where their children would use their bonuses if the benefits of true competition were to be generated.

Conclusion

Large bureaucratic organizations almost never make major changes in established behavior patterns unless strongly pressured by outside forces.[6] The most powerful form of such pressure is a direct threat to their continued existence, or to their current perquisites of office. This kind of threat can usually be created only by an alliance of all or most of the outside agents who support the bureaucracy. They must get together and demand that the bureaucracy change, or else they will remove or drastically reduce their support. But when the bureaucracy produces some vital service, they can reduce their support only by creating a competitive institution to provide that service. Competition has the advantage of generating sustained, almost automatic, pressure upon the organizations involved to keep adapting their production to consumers' wants, without constant vigilance by the consumers themselves.

Big-city public school systems are huge bureaucracies. Therefore, one of the potentially most effective ways of getting them to change their unsatisfactory behavior is to introduce significant elements of competition into their operation. It would be totally unrealistic to assume that most, or even any large fraction, of the existing school systems in large cities could soon be replaced by competitive systems created or run by outsiders. There are simply not enough qualified—or even unqualified—teachers to create truly parallel systems that could compete with existing public school systems across the board. Moreover, the additional capital investment required to build physical facilities for such an all-out system would be prohibitive.

Nevertheless, even a small dose of competition in certain forms could produce important—even radical—changes in the nature and quality of education in big-city public schools. The first and most crucial step is developing and using effective ways of evaluating the educational performance of public schools. Other devices may also be employed to generate the benefits of competition, with varying

[6] This definitive generalization is taken from a source in which I have an unusually high degree of confidence. See Anthony Downs, *Inside Bureaucracy* (Little, Brown, 1967), Chaps. II and XVI.

requirements concerning the amount of basic institutional change involved.

Community schools are currently being advanced almost as a panacea that will create the clearly needed changes in big-city public school systems. But unless community schools are designed and operated so as to increase competitive pressures within those systems, I do not believe they will have the desired effects. The pressure of competition is the crucial ingredient needed to force big-city school systems to adapt their outputs to what consumers want and need. Without such pressure, school systems will continue succumbing to the natural tendency of all monopolists: providing what is most convenient for them to produce regardless of its suitability to the needs of those who must consume it.

H. THOMAS JAMES
HENRY M. LEVIN

Financing Community Schools

While the political aspects of decentralization of big-city school systems have been discussed often, the financial aspects have been largely ignored. In order to fill this void at least partially, we will focus on a number of issues raised by the prospect of replacing the centralized school structure with decentralized community schools. From the viewpoint of resource allocation among schools in general, and financing schools in particular, there appear to be both advantages and disadvantages in community schools. We will discuss these strengths and shortcomings but will not pass judgment on the relative desirability of decentralization, since that decision must necessarily depend upon a larger number of considerations than purely financial ones.

Before the financing of community schools can be discussed, it is necessary to establish a workable definition of the term community school. Unfortunately, the heterogeneity of existing attempts to decentralize the big-city public schools hinders generalizations. For purposes of this chapter, community schools will represent those public schools in large cities that are subject to the governance of local, community-based school boards rather than a citywide central school authority.

This chapter will discuss several issues that relate to financing the decentralized arrangement. First, what should be the optimal size of the school district or community school? Second, how should these schools be financed and who should finance them? And third, who should decide how resources will be allocated within each community school district?

Economies of Scale

Until recently, it was widely accepted that small schools and small school districts were one of the principal obstacles to obtaining quality education for many elementary and secondary school children in the United States. The contention was that small educational units were unable to produce a full range of educational services at reasonable costs. Thus, the past three decades have seen the active consolidation of small school districts, a movement that was so effective that the 127,000 school districts that existed in 1932 have been winnowed down to fewer than 25,000. With the demise of the one-room schoolhouse operation, most observers thought that the problems of size had been solved; there was little concern that some school districts might become too large to operate efficiently.

The trend is only beginning to change, with large size being considered a prime suspect for the massive failure of the big-city public schools to educate disadvantaged children. Indeed, the advocates of school decentralization view the big-city school districts as too cumbersome to produce educational services efficiently. They suggest that the problems of administering such immense and unwieldy organizations are so great that "organizational sclerosis" sets in. As a result, the school system has become insensitive to the different educational needs among students and communities, and general educational effectiveness has deteriorated.[1]

Some school districts are considered too small to provide a complete set of educational offerings efficiently and others are considered too large. This implies that, in any school district, the average cost per student of producing a given educational outcome declines as enrollment increases until a minimum point is reached beyond which the average cost increases as enrollment continues to increase. Enrollments smaller than that at which the average cost is at a minimum prevent the district from realizing economies of scale because

[1] For a good description of "organizational sclerosis," see Christopher Jencks, "Is the Public School Obsolete?" *Public Interest*, No. 2 (Winter 1966), pp. 18–27.

the specialists and facilities required for producing a given educational outcome are underutilized. At enrollments larger than that corresponding to the minimum average cost, the existing organization and administration of schools becomes less efficient; diseconomies of scale arise and the cost per student for achieving a given outcome increases.

Given the decision to decentralize big-city schools, the existence of potential economies of scale in schooling is an important factor in determining the optimal size of the school districts: how small can schools and school districts be made before inefficiencies arise that increase the average cost per unit of output?

RESULTS OF SIZE-PERFORMANCE STUDIES

The size-performance relation can be studied separately by level of school—elementary, junior high, or senior high school—or by school district. Usually schools of a particular level have been taken as units of analysis because of large variations in the compositions of enrollments among school districts. Since per-pupil costs can vary significantly with the quality of educational services, only those studies which have accounted for the quality of inputs or educational outcomes as well as the size of the school will be examined.

What is particularly striking about the previous studies is either their failure to observe economies of scale in school operations or, indeed, their finding of a negative relationship between size and performance. The most comprehensive analysis of the effect of school size on costs has been carried out by Kiesling.[2] Kiesling examined the relationship between standardized test performances of students and school size while statistically adjusting for differences in school expenditures and student backgrounds. In addition, he carried out separate analyses for students at each of four socioeconomic levels. Using achievement tests in different skills as measures of educational outcome, Kiesling found a rather consistent negative relationship between high school size, as measured by average daily attendance and average test scores. While Kiesling looked for a nonlinear effect of school size on student performance, he found that the straight-line

[2] Herbert J. Kiesling, "High School Size and Cost Factors," Final Report for the U.S. Office of Education, Bureau of Research, Project No. 6–1590 (processed; U.S. Department of Health, Education, and Welfare, March 1968).

relationship was more appropriate. That is, over a large range of school sizes—less than 200 to almost 4,000 in average daily attendance—the apparent relationship between school size and student performance was negative. In his earlier study of school districts in New York State, Kiesling found no evidence of economies of scale at either the elementary or secondary level.[3] Moreover, under certain conditions the size-performance relationship was also found to be negative.

Kiesling's findings have been supported by the conclusions of several other studies that also detected no evidence of economies of scale. For example, studies of California school districts showed no unique relationship between the size of the school district and the test performance of students.[4] Moreover, Burkhead and his associates found no significant statistical relationship between school enrollments and several measures of educational outcome once differences in student backgrounds and school resources were accounted for.[5] The Burkhead analysis was carried out separately for high schools in Chicago, Atlanta, and a set of small communities. The measures of educational outcomes included test scores, relative changes in test scores among high schools between grades, dropout rates, and post-high school educational plans or actual college attendance of graduates.

Thus, all of the studies that have tried to relate school or school district size to educational outcomes have found either no relationship or a negative one between student enrollments and the level of educational output. These answers are not necessarily the final ones, for each of the studies acknowledges a number of methodological shortcomings that would qualify its conclusions. Yet, what cannot be ignored is the consistency of the conclusions—that while diseconomies of scale appear, economies of scale do not—despite dif-

[3] See Herbert J. Kiesling, "Measuring a Local Government Service: A Study of Efficiency of School Districts in New York State" (Ph.D. thesis, Harvard University, 1965). This is summarized in an article in *Review of Economics and Statistics*, Vol. 49 (August 1967), pp. 356–67.

[4] See M. C. Alkin, C. S. Benson, and R. H. Gustafson, "Economy of Scale in the Production of Selected Educational Outcomes" (a paper prepared for the American Educational Research Association Meetings, Chicago, Ill., February 1968; processed).

[5] Jesse Burkhead, Thomas G. Fox, and John W. Holland, *Input and Output in Large-City High Schools* (Syracuse University Press, 1967).

ferences in the techniques of analysis, samples of schools, measures of educational outcomes, and so on.

While several studies have attempted to relate average expenditures per student to school or school district size, only two have made any attempt to adjust the expenditure figure for differences in the quality of schooling. Since school quality is an elusive factor without a direct measure of educational outcomes, the quality adjustments in these studies must be considered speculative at best. Hirsch, in his study of per-pupil costs in twenty-seven school districts, found no evidence of economies of scale once school quality was accounted for.[6] On the other hand, Riew found that among a sample of Wisconsin high schools the minimum average cost was reached with enrollments of about 1,675 in average daily attendance. Unfortunately, Riew's particular measures of school quality and the limited range of enrollments in his sample prevent comment on the relevance of his finding except to say that his optimal high school size appears to be considerably smaller than that found on the average in large cities.[7]

A RECOMMENDATION

The absence of economies of scale for both schools and school districts when performance criteria are imposed on the analysis is a crucial finding.[8] Since there is little evidence of economies of scale and substantial evidence of diseconomies of scale, both among individual schools and school districts, we propose that no decentralized school district should be larger than the attendance area for its constituent high school. That is, the largest school district

[6] Werner Z. Hirsch, "Expenditure Implications of Metropolitan Growth and Consolidation," *Review of Economics and Statistics*, Vol. 41 (May 1959), pp. 232–41.

[7] See John Riew, "Economies of Scale in High School Operation," *Review of Economics and Statistics*, Vol. 48 (August 1966), pp. 280–87. The Project Talent sample of 94 big-city high schools showed an average daily attendance level of about 2,500. See Kiesling, "High School Size and Cost Factors," p. 97.

[8] Of course, none of these studies have included in their analyses the small rural schools or school districts that were the basis for the school consolidation movement. Such schools are not relevant for an analysis of big-city school decentralization since a typical elementary school in the city has a student population that is larger than the entire enrollment of many of the consolidated districts. For example, see Leslie L. Chisholm, *School District Reorganization* (Chicago: Midwest Administration Center, 1957), Chap. V.

should consist of a high school and the junior high schools and elementary schools from which its students are drawn. For example, an average high school size of about 2,500 for grades 10 to 12 would have a school district with about 8,500 students.[9] A school district of this size would be adequate to provide at efficient levels of utilization a complete set of educational services including the specialized services required for exceptional children. It is difficult to see how technological and administrative efficiency could improve by establishing larger districts.

But a school district of this size might be too large to obtain effective community organization, participation, and school governance. The population base required to support a school district with 8,500 in average daily attendance would be between 50 and 60 thousand persons. The meaning of community would certainly have to be stretched in order to be applied to a population this large.[10] The East Harlem block schools, where the community concept appears to be working effectively, have only 135 students at four locations.[11]

Paul Goodman has suggested another application of the community model: the establishment of "mini-schools" that would be attended by children between the ages of 6 and 11.[12] Each school

[9] The actual relationship between high school size and total district enrollment depends upon such factors as dropout rates, the age distribution of the population, and the prevalence of nonpublic schools at each level. In addition, the school assignment practice is critical. Some big-city school districts assign students to high schools strictly on the basis of the elementary and junior high schools attended; others give students the alternative of choosing a specialized high school (such as vocational, fine arts, technical, scientific); and some large cities practice open enrollment policies, permitting the student to choose any school that is not overenrolled.

[10] This contradiction is clearly reflected in the Bundy Report's proposal for New York City's schools. Under this plan some 30 to 60 school districts would enroll a school population of about 1.1 million students. Thus community school districts would have from 18,500 to 37,000 students enrolled, and the community would have a population base of between 125,000 and 250,000 inhabitants. Mayor's Advisory Panel on Decentralization of the New York City Schools, *Reconnection for Learning: A Community School System for New York City* (1967). Referred to as either the Bundy Report or the Mayor's Advisory Panel.

[11] See Peter Schrag, "Learning in a Storefront," *Saturday Review* (June 15, 1968), p. 71.

[12] Paul Goodman, "Mini-Schools: A Prescription for the Reading Problem," *New York Review of Books* (Jan. 4, 1968). Partially reprinted in *Current* (February 1968), pp. 52–54.

would enroll only twenty-eight pupils. The problems of obtaining community support for even a single school, however, suggest insurmountable difficulties in constructing a cohesive community for governing multischool units.[13]

Effective community control could be established and the organic identity of the high school district could be retained by instituting community control at the individual school level and forming a coordinating body to represent the governing boards of constituent schools at the district level (defined as a high school and its feeder schools). Under such a plan, the basic community decision making would be at the individual school level, where the similarity of interests and knowledge of the school is greatest and the size of the population base is small enough for the close communication necessary for effective and responsive government.

To facilitate a degree of policy continuity from the individual feeder schools to the high school, elected representatives from each community school board would form a coordinating council to align those aspects of school policies that would insure a smooth transition from the elementary schools to the schools serving higher grade levels. The coordinating council would also serve as a link between the decentralized school district and the modified central school authority. In this way the coordination of schools and communication among schools within a decentralized school district could take place without sacrificing the concept of individual community schools.

Criteria for Funding

Since decentralized school districts are obviously too small to raise their own tax revenues, decentralization will have its principal fiscal effect in choosing a pattern of expenditure. That is, the central school authority will still be responsible for obtaining revenues for the schools through its own taxing powers and through financial aid from higher levels of government. Yet, it would no longer determine

[13] For some insight into the early experiences at the Adams-Morgan community school in Washington, D.C., see Susan L. Jacoby, "The Making of a Community School," *Urban Review*, Vol. 2 (February 1968), pp. 3–4 and 29.

how that money was spent within each school. Rather, it would allocate a lump-sum budget to each community school, leaving the allocation of funds within each school to be determined by the community. Financial accountability would remain in the hands of the central school authority, but actual disbursements for each school could be authorized only by the governing board of that school. Under this arrangement the principal decision of the central school authority would be the determination of budget limits for each community school; the sum of the separate community budgets and the central authority's own budget could not exceed the total school revenue.

There are at least five guidelines that the central school authority might use in allocating the total school budget to constituent community schools. Three of these are straightforward and require little explanation.

First, the basic consideration for determining the size of the budget for each school should be the average daily membership of that school—an enrollment base—rather than average daily attendance. Some schools, particularly those in inner cities, have considerably lower attendance levels than enrollment levels. Yet books, supplies, physical facilities, and personnel are provided for all enrolled students, despite the overall level of attendance. For example, the teacher expense for a school is constant whether all the students or only 80 percent of the students show up on an average day. Thus, expenditures are more closely related to enrollment than to attendance, and should be reflected in community school budgets.

Second, the school level must be an important determinant of intracity budget allocation. Since secondary schools require higher concentrations of personnel and facilities than do the elementary schools, these implicit cost differences must be recognized.[14]

Third, the specific functions of the schools must be taken into account in allocating resources among them. In particular, special purpose schools require different financial consideration than do comprehensive ones. The most prominent examples of this are vo-

[14] For a reference to these differential costs, see Paul R. Mort, W. C. Reusser, and John W. Polley, *Public School Finance* (3rd ed.; McGraw-Hill, 1960), pp. 108–10.

cational schools, where per-pupil costs are considerably greater than those of other high schools.[15] Further, since even the comprehensive schools differ in their relative offerings of high-cost, specialized programs (such as programs for retarded, emotionally disturbed, and brain-injured children, as well as those in vocational education), these differences must be taken into account in setting individual school budgets.[16]

The other two guidelines for funding are somewhat more complex. The fourth criterion is that interschool budgetary decisions must consider that the costs of educational services differ among schools. The costs of obtaining personnel and other resources appear to be higher for schools in the inner city, those with a high proportion of disadvantaged children, than for other schools. In particular, teachers seem to prefer teaching in middle-class schools located in residental neighborhoods. Thus at the same salary level, the inner-city or slum schools obtain, on the average, lower-quality teachers than do schools in middle-class areas.[17] Moreover, it is likely that land and construction costs are also higher in the inner city and that the relatively higher level of student turnover in the inner-city schools leads to a higher textbook and materials cost per student. Many students who withdraw from a school within the school year neglect to return the textbooks and supplies that the school lent to them; the result is that other students who move into the school during the year must be provided with a new set of materials. Thus, these schools need more textbooks and other materials per student than do other schools. All of these differences lead to the conclusion that in order to provide the same level of educational services, the

[15] Careful analysis of costs among different programs suggests that vocational education programs cost from 40 to over 100 percent more than their academic counterparts. See Michael K. Taussig, "An Economic Analysis of Vocational Education in the New York City High Schools," pp. 77–79, and Arthur J. Corazzini, "The Decision to Invest in Vocational Education: An Analysis of Costs and Benefits," p. 102, both in *Vocational Education*, Report of a Conference Sponsored by the Brookings Institution, published as a supplement to *Journal of Human Resources*, Vol. 3 (Summer 1968).

[16] Since these special functions are often viewed as the responsibility of the larger society rather than of the community, the central school authority might simply remove them from the community schools and provide such services on a citywide basis.

[17] Some empirical evidence supporting the existence of this phenomenon is found in Henry M. Levin, "Recruiting Teachers for Large-City Schools" (unpublished manuscript).

inner-city schools need a larger budget than the middle-class schools.

Yet, the inner-city schools have an even greater burden: they are expected to compensate for cultural differences (disadvantages) in the backgrounds of their students. Lower-class students begin their schooling with lower academic performance levels than their more advantaged peers. Our society has recently undertaken the commitment to devote additional educational resources to such students in order to achieve greater equality of opportunity among students of different social classes at the end of the schooling process.

This now firmly established commitment prescribes a fifth funding criterion. The funding level of each school should be directly related to the degree of disadvantage of its student body. That is, those schools with a higher proportion of disadvantaged children must receive higher per-student allotments in order to subsidize the added resources required for compensatory education. An index of parental occupations might be derived from school records, and these would be converted to a scale showing the social class of the student body. Schools that rank low on the scale would receive substantially more dollars per student than schools that were high on the scale.

The actual relationship between degree of disadvantage and additional budget allocation should be determined by several factors. One of these is the social priority for equalizing opportunity; another is the effectiveness of compensatory expenditures in closing the gap between advantaged and disadvantaged.[18]

Since efforts to equalize opportunity among social groups benefit our entire society, there is a firm basis for expecting the federal and state governments to assume the main burden of the compensatory effort. The role of the federal government is further reinforced by the fact that many disadvantaged children in the large cities are the product of generations of educational neglect and deprivation in the rural South. Because their parents migrated to the cities, the educational responsibility for improving their opportunities now falls on the cities' schools, but the financial costs of compensating for past

[18] Some of the relevant issues are discussed in Samuel Bowles, "Towards Equality of Educational Opportunity?" *Harvard Educational Review*, Vol. 38 (Winter 1968), pp. 89–99.

neglect must be considered the burden of our entire society. Certainly, this rationale underlies the present national support of compensatory education financed under Title I of the Elementary and Secondary Education Act of 1965 and the Head Start program initiated by the Office of Economic Opportunity.

But the community school approach offers some distinct advantages over the present system in assuring that funds designated for compensatory education are actually used for that purpose. Title I moneys are allocated to states, and the states allot funds to the school districts. School districts are charged with using these funds to educate the disadvantaged. But under this arrangement, it is not possible to guarantee that Title I moneys are actually being fully expended on disadvantaged children. For example, states may be substituting Title I moneys for aid that would have been provided by state funds if Title I did not exist. Moreover, there is no readily available method of accounting for the allocation of Title I funds within school districts. That is, school districts may also be putting Title I moneys into programs for disadvantaged pupils that would have been funded locally in the absence of this aid. Thus Title I subsidies might be used as a substitute source of finances for existing programs. In this sense, it is likely that Title I aid enables the school district to increase allocations toward all programs, aiding advantaged children as well as disadvantaged ones.[19]

Since school finances within a district are not regularly accounted for on a school-by-school basis, the fact that cities have traditionally spent more on the education of advantaged than disadvantaged children has been obscured. For example, a school-by-school accounting for Washington, D.C., for the school year 1963–64 found that the median expenditure for predominantly white elementary schools was about $100 or one-third higher than the median expenditure for elementary schools whose enrollments were predominantly black.[20] Studies of other major cities have shown similar patterns of discrimination in the allocation of school resources.[21]

[19] A technical description of this effect is found in the appendix to this chapter.

[20] See the findings reported in the opinion of Judge J. Skelly Wright, June 19, 1967, in *Hobson* v. *Hansen*, 269 F. Supp. 401 (1967).

[21] See Patricia C. Sexton, *Education and Income; Inequalities of Opportunity in Our Public Schools* (Viking Press, 1961); also see Eric C. Thornblad, "The Fiscal Impact of a High Concentration of Low Income Families Upon the Public School" (Ph.D. thesis, University of Illinois at Urbana, 1966).

The community school arrangement has the distinct advantage over the existing organization of schools of permitting direct comparisons of school budgets and hence of compensatory education expenditure. Thus, a true social accounting of funds provided by higher levels of government for subsidizing compensatory education becomes possible. Not only can the additional money provided for the education of disadvantaged children be traced directly to the target schools for which it was intended but the results of these additional expenditures could be reviewed on a school-by-school basis.[22] In the present centralized purchasing arrangement for all schools within a city, no such social accountability among schools is evident.

Resource Allocation within Community Schools

Certainly one of the prime reasons for the strong support of decentralization by both educators and parents has been the desire to escape the institutional rigidity and uniformity that have been imposed upon individuals and individual schools by the central school administration. While most persons in favor of decentralization recognize that broad educational guidelines must be established by the larger society, they reject the assumption that the fine details of the educational process must be molded for each child at a highly centralized level, for it is well known that the effectiveness of particular educational strategies varies enormously among individual students and different groups of students.

Even under a decentralized plan, it is desirable that educational policies of broad social relevance be made at a highly centralized level. That is, those particular policies having implications beyond the boundaries of individual communities are rightfully determined through the consensus of a larger society than that of an individual community. These broader social issues involve setting the minimum educational content necessary for a meaningful role in society: the values and knowledge basic to an effective democracy and the skills required for full participation in the economy.

[22] Because it is not possible to ascertain exactly how Title I funds have been spent, the U.S. Office of Education has largely been prevented from making an adequate evaluation of the program.

First, the high rate of residential mobility among American families suggests that some uniformity of curriculum is necessary in order to insure continuity of learning when students transfer from one school to another. Second, the basic skills required for participation in a modern economy should not vary according to the school that one attends. Finally, some common educational experience is required in order to have a citizenry that is informed about major areas of social policy. These factors suggest that a core of common educational needs be outlined for the community schools. This core should be designed so that considerable discretion is left to the community in fulfilling the common requirements.

Perhaps the common educational experience can be satisfied by requiring the community schools to devote a certain proportion of their instructional time to training in the language arts, mathematics, and the sciences. The social studies area is likely to be much more controversial since the common set of social values that has been expounded by the traditional curriculum has had a distinct majority bias.[23]

Even if there were some common objectives among schools, the advocates of decentralization would object to the traditional role of the central school administration: setting down fairly detailed and uniform educational guidelines for children from a wide variety of backgrounds with enormous individual differences and talents. It is believed that these particulars should not be planned by decision makers who are so far removed from the classroom. As Sizer has suggested, " . . . *detailed* decisions concerning the education of a particular child [should] be made at a level close to that child."[24]

FINANCING FOR COMMUNITY AUTONOMY

If community schools are to build their educational programs around the specific needs of their constituents, the decentralized

[23] The traditional social studies curriculum at both the elementary and secondary levels has consistently avoided the many instances in which our country has coerced other nations and minority cultures. While the tyranny of King George III over the American colonies is told and retold, the grossly inhumane aspects of American slavery and our imperialistic ventures in the late nineteenth and early twentieth centuries have been ignored or superficially mentioned. Moreover, while every school child learns of the wholesale slaughter of the buffalo herds, little or no discussion is devoted to the wholesale slaughter of the American Indian and the decimation of his culture.

[24] Theodore Sizer, "Reform and the Control of Education" (processed; Harvard University, Graduate School of Education, 1967), p. 4.

schools must have a great deal more autonomy in planning educational strategies and allocating resources than individual schools have under the present system. The simplest method of achieving autonomous decision making is to give each community school a lump-sum budget that can be allocated in any way the community chooses. The actual limit of the budget for each school would be determined by the criteria set out in the second section of this chapter. While the mechanics of paying the bills and accounting for expenditures would continue to be the responsibility of the central school authority, the specific decisions of allocation would be the responsibility of the governing board of each school.

Budget allocation at the local school level has several strong advantages over citywide budget determinations. Most familiar among these is that no single educational approach can achieve the disparate needs that exist among different groups within large cities. By placing educational decisions in the hands of local governing boards, schools can be much more responsive to the particular demands of their constituents. While this view is appealing, there are other cogent reasons for encouraging autonomy among schools.

Since there is little known about the learning process, schools should continue to experiment and innovate while constantly evaluating the results. The centralized decision-making apparatus of the big-city school boards has emphasized standardization of approaches rather than variety. In fact, the central school board finds it easiest to govern the labyrinth of schools by mandating uniformity among schools along traditional guidelines. But it is irresponsible to promote the traditional approaches when, on the one hand, so little is known about how children learn and, on the other, the specific approach fostered by the big-city school boards has systematically failed to educate substantial numbers of children.

Indeed, the efforts of city school boards to provide compensatory education for disadvantaged children have relied, primarily, on that traditional panacea, the reduction of class size. Most peculiarly, it is expected that the teachers, curriculum, school organization, and educational methods that have consistently failed the disadvantaged child will somehow succeed if only class size is reduced. Needless to say, the schools have continued to fail the disadvantaged child.

The point is that the big-city school board has demonstrated that it is incapable of systematically trying new approaches where old ones have failed. By increasing the number of decision-making units through decentralization, the likelihood of meaningful innovation is much greater than it is under the present monolithic system. There is so much that needs to be known about the advantages and disadvantages of different schooling approaches, and the only way that this knowledge can be gained is by encouraging differences among schools in the way they do things; the present system encourages similarities.

An important by-product of fiscal autonomy among community schools is the existence of a choice of schools for students. Under the present system, pupils are usually assigned to particular schools according to established attendance patterns. Even if students were given some alternatives among schools, the benefits of choice would be mitigated by the citywide standardization of educational procedures.[25]

While most parents will probably prefer to send their children to the school provided by their community, no parent should be coerced into doing so. This tenet is especially important because community schools have been operationally defined upon traditional attendance areas or neighborhoods; yet communities defined in this way are not likely to be strictly homogeneous in the schooling preferences of their populations. That is, within any community there will probably be some parents whose preferences deviate from the educational practices established by the community school board.

Accordingly, a system of alternatives must be established for students whose needs are not satisfied by the particular community schools in their attendance areas. Two types of arrangements are desirable. In a system of autonomous community schools, with the variety of strategies that is expected, students should be given a choice of attending a school in their community or in any other community. Such a provision would recognize that a mutuality of educational interests is only approximated by the neighborhood concept of community. Of course, the transfer of students among community schools would have to be reflected in transfers of budgetary allocations as well.

Second, the central school authority might continue to operate a

[25] The exceptions to this statement are the special purpose schools found in some cities at the secondary level.

limited number of schools as alternatives for students who are dissatisfied with their community schools. These schools would be distributed around the city in such a way that they would be reasonably accessible from all neighborhoods.

These two provisions would give an interesting balance to decentralization and would yield educational alternatives to groups and individual students. Moreover, such a design would foster a modest degree of competition among schools to keep their student enrollments at capacity levels. It has often been suggested that the presence of some competition among schools for students offers the greatest hope for raising the efficiency and effectiveness of our educational system.[26] That is, individual schools would have substantially greater incentives than they presently have for improving the quality and attractiveness of their educational offerings if they were required to compete for students.[27] The decentralization approach offers the possibility of incorporating some of the gains from the competitive model into the big-city schools.

MAKING AUTONOMY OPERATIONAL

To suggest that effective autonomy among community schools can be easily accomplished is to ignore some formidable stumbling blocks: that school principals and other administrators within the school have neither the training nor the experience to assume their new roles; that community school boards will have to function in unfamiliar spheres; that teachers and other professionals must adjust to a new authority, the community school board; and that little is known about the fundamentals of how children learn. The adjustment to a new order is not likely to be smooth. Yet by anticipating the problems of transition and by planning the change carefully, the costs of change can be minimized.

The community school board would be expected to maximize the educational outcomes for its school within the limits of its total

[26] See Milton Friedman, "The Role of Government in Education," in Robert A. Solo (ed.), *Economics and the Public Interest* (Rutgers University Press, 1955), pp. 123–44. For other sources see Henry M. Levin, "The Failure of the Public Schools and the Free Market Remedy," *Urban Review*, Vol. 2 (June 1968), pp. 32–37 (Brookings Reprint 148).

[27] For a discussion of the advantages and disadvantages of a publicly financed free market for education, one that would be paid for by state-financed tuition vouchers that could be used at any "approved" school, see Levin, *ibid.*

budget. Political pressures from within the community and competition for students among communities would be the two principal incentives for pursuing this objective. The board would then select the combinations and types of personnel, materials, facilities, and programs that would enable it to maximize school output. These decisions would depend upon both the preferences of the community and the relative costs and productivities of various strategies for satisfying those priorities.

The problem of sifting through a large number of alternatives and implementing the ones that are chosen will require several capabilities. First, the community school board must become knowledgeable about the relevant alternatives for achieving its goals. Second, there must be broad agreement on the adoption of particular strategies among teachers and administrators as well as among school board members; otherwise new approaches will be doomed to failure. Finally, there must exist a continuing system of evaluation of the strategies that are adopted and a willingness to consider other alternatives if the initial approaches do not live up to expectations within a reasonable period of time.

THE NEED FOR INFORMATION ON ALTERNATIVES

A community school board that is not familiar with the plethora of available educational alternatives cannot bring about effective change. The educational process is so complex that the simple palliatives—such as reducing class size per se—yield few improvements in outcomes. Yet, the view that a representative and concerned school board with little background in education will make knowledgeable decisions is an article of faith held by those who are most disillusioned by the failure of the present system. Indeed, since the only knowledge of the schools gleaned by most individuals is based upon their own schooling experiences and those of their children, the direction of change may be backward to a day when a highly disciplined environment and learning by rote were the standards. School board members have forgotten that in such an environment they might not have been instilled with strong educational motivation and achievement.[28]

[28] Educational conservatism by community spokesmen was noted during the first year of operation of the Adams-Morgan community school in Washington, D.C. See Jacoby, "The Making of a Community School," p. 4.

Several provisions might be made for giving community school boards both the background and the information that is required for sound decision making. First, each community school board could appoint a "resource person" whose responsibility would be to explore various alternatives for achieving the educational objectives. For example, this person might be expected to submit a report to community school board members on alternative approaches to teaching children how to read. Materials, curriculum, and available research findings would be submitted along with a description of each method. Moreover, he would also answer questions about the required resources needed to implement a particular program. In this way, the community school board could obtain some perspective on the various questions that face it.

Given the need for information by all communities, the central school authority should provide an information center that the resource person from each community could utilize. This would take advantage of economies of scale in centralizing the information and materials. It may also be advisable for the central school authority to contract with a local university to provide this service. This latter possibility is perhaps more advisable since many communities question the integrity of the central school board and would not want to depend upon it for information.

PERSONNEL DECISIONS

Teachers and administrators must have a role in school decision making if the community concept is to succeed. Educational outcomes are largely the result of human interactions, of which teachers' attitudes are a prime ingredient. Thus, even the best-conceived plans for change need the support of the teachers and administrators who must carry them out. No single act will antagonize teachers and threaten this needed support more than unilateral announcement of the changes that are expected in educational strategy. Such a process is self-defeating, for change by edict will be met with a resentment by school personnel. It is only when there is broad agreement among all parties that the new policies will have a chance of improving educational outcomes.

Since a community school must have the sympathy of its teachers and administrators, it is suggested that the local school board have substantial discretion over whom it hires. This requires that teachers who are already working in these schools be eligible to apply for positions in other community schools if such teachers are not in sympathy with the policies adopted by their current schools. While community school boards should be able to choose their personnel, some protection must be given to teachers so that they are not harassed or urged to resign on capricious grounds. Moreover, some attention must be given to designing more flexible licensing requirements if individual community schools are to have greater choice in the types of personnel that they can hire. Certainly, the failure of the traditional certification requirements to insure teacher quality is ample basis for changing or liberalizing requirements.[29]

The central school authority's desire to set hiring standards while at the same time "encouraging" community autonomy is likely to provoke continuing conflict between the community and the higher school authority. The community schools should be free to experiment with personnel who do not possess the standard credentials. For example, the Teachers and Writers Collaborative, founded by Herbert Kohl, has achieved outstanding results in "turning on" ghetto children to writing and expressing themselves by getting writers and poets to work with these children in the classroom. Community aides without college degrees—some without high school diplomas—have been found to be an invaluable contribution to instructional programs at many schools. The knowledge of objective requirements for effective teaching is so primitive that schools must be free to hire at least a portion of their instructional staff—perhaps 25 percent—without being bound by the existing licensing requirements.

On the other hand, the complete absence of hiring standards among community schools would permit personnel selection to be capricious at best and nepotistic at worst. It is important to recognize that the decentralization of big-city school districts at the ward level existing at the turn of the century was characterized by personnel selection based upon such criteria as family membership,

[29] Conant, in his extensive review of certification requirements, concluded that none of the rules ". . . have a clearly demonstrable practical bearing on the quality of the teacher, the quality of his preparation, or the extent to which the public is informed about the personnel in the classrooms." James B. Conant, *The Education of American Teachers* (McGraw-Hill, 1963), p. 54.

friendship, and ethnic identification.[30] It was precisely the deleterious effects of nepotism and ward corruption that contributed to the formation of the big-city educational bureaucracies.[31] The conflict between community autonomy and the dictation of personnel standards by higher units of government will not be an easy one to resolve. Major planning efforts must be focused in this direction during the transitional period of decentralization.

Moreover, a new breed of school administrator will be needed, one who can translate the wishes of the school board into ongoing educational programs. Given the uncertain nature of the required training and the typically slow response of universities to emerging social needs, it is not likely that there will be adequate numbers of such administrators in the foreseeable future. Indeed, the demands on the school administrator will be staggering, for he must provide the governing board of the school with continuous information on the strengths and problems associated with the school's operations while at the same time managing those operations.

Foremost among the administrator's duties must be the construction of a systematic scheme of evaluation for the school. Programs that show good results should be identified as early as possible; and others that yield disappointing results, once they have been given an adequate chance to produce, should also be noted. This information along with the evaluative criteria should be presented to the community school board with recommendations for change. In addition, data on evaluation should be provided to the citywide information center so that each community school can also learn from the experiences of the other schools.

On the basis of these evaluations, schools must be willing to modify, adapt, or scrap programs that do not appear to be effective. By basing strategies on a systematic evaluation, the community schools should be able to focus continually on the relevancy and

[30] See Joseph M. Rice, *The Public School System of the United States* (New York: The Century Co., 1893).

[31] The problem of determining selection criteria is a difficult one. For example, many people would frown upon racial hiring policies of any sort. Yet a good educational case can be made for obtaining more black teachers for the predominantly black schools so that the pupils will see role models with whom they can identify in authoritative positions. See Kenneth B. Clark, *Dark Ghetto; Dilemmas of Social Power* (Harper & Row, 1965), pp. 133–39.

general effectiveness of their programs, a focus that does not appear to exist to any significant degree within the present framework.

Because of the initial organizational problems and the lack of experience in operating community schools, it might be desirable for schools to purchase some services from outside contractors. The community school board would plan its educational requirements and compare these with its capabilities. Where the school's proficiencies were least adequate relative to the school's objectives, the school board would solicit bids from private industry, universities, and nonprofit groups for fulfilling those needs. Educational contractors would compete for the particular services that the community wanted to buy, and the most promising proposals would be selected. On the basis of the contractors' performances, such agreements could be renewed, subsequently awarded to another contractor, or the task could be undertaken by the school itself. Given the enormous market potential for firms that can implement programs with successful results, contractors' motives to demonstrate the effectiveness of their approaches would operate to make competition keen among the sellers of educational services. This factor can be made to work to strong advantage for the fledgling community school.

APPENDIX

Title I Aid and Expenditures on Education for Disadvantaged Children

Title I of the Elementary and Secondary Education Act of 1965 authorized grants to the states for subsidizing the education of disadvantaged children. Local school districts were made eligible for suballocations if they had at least 100 disadvantaged children or if at least 3 percent of the total number of children between the ages of five to seventeen were from low-income families as defined by the act. Expenditures for Title I have been about $1 billion a year.

In considering the applications of school districts, the state education agencies were supposed to weigh such factors as size, scope, and quality of the project and its promise of success in meeting the special needs of educationally deprived children. (The tenuous nature of the evidence required to indicate "promise of success" and the weaknesses of subsequent evaluations of the projects become obvious upon reading the state reports.) Other than this broad intention, no provision was actually made for insuring that Title I funds were expended only on eligible children. Indeed, given the fungible nature of Title I aid and present school-accounting procedures, it is not possible to trace the federal dollars to programs exclusively for disadvantaged children. That is, Title I moneys supplement the school budget on the income side and are commingled with other funds on the expenditure side since disadvantaged children receive their compensatory benefits within the general school setting.

Thus, two aspects of Title I aid are of interest. First, Title I suballocations to local school districts represent lump-sum additions to the local budget with no required matching of funds by the local government; that is, Title I aid does not reduce the cost of educating disadvantaged children relative to the costs of providing other goods and services. Second, present school-accounting procedures and a lack of knowledge on what expenditure patterns would have been in the absence of Title I prevent a direct analysis of how local school districts are actually using Title I moneys. These two factors taken together suggest that Title I moneys will have a pure income effect, not only increasing community expenditures on education for the disadvantaged but also increasing community expenditures on education for advantaged children (and on all other goods).[1]

This situation is illustrated by Figure 1(a) which shows a typical community with a budget Y_0 that can be allocated to two goods: education for disadvantaged children, X_1, and education for advantaged children, X_2. I' and I'' represent social indifference curves for the community, each defined as the loci of the various combinations of X_1 and X_2 that would yield equal satisfaction to the community. Consistent with this analysis, I'' represents a higher level of welfare for the community than does I'. Given the prices P_{x_1} and P_{x_2} and a total budget of Y_0, a budget line (line of attainable combinations) can be obtained for the community that is tangent to I', maximizing community welfare for the budget constraint, Y_0. Thus, given

[1] The analysis that follows presumes some knowledge of the theory of consumer preferences. For those who do not have this background we suggest a reading of Paul A. Samuelson, *Economics* (7th ed.; McGraw-Hill, 1967), Chap. 22, or Richard H. Leftwich, *The Price System and Resource Allocation* (rev. ed.; Holt, Rinehart & Winston, 1961), Chaps. IV and V. A more advanced exposition is found in J. R. Hicks, *Value and Capital* (2nd ed.; Oxford University Press, 1946), Chaps. I–III; and a concise mathematical treatment is found in Paul A. Samuelson, *Foundations of Economic Analysis* (Harvard University Press, 1947), Chap. V.

FIGURE I

Effect of Subsidies on Education of Disadvantaged and Nondisadvantaged by Method of Distributing Funds

(a) Title I moneys commingled with community budget

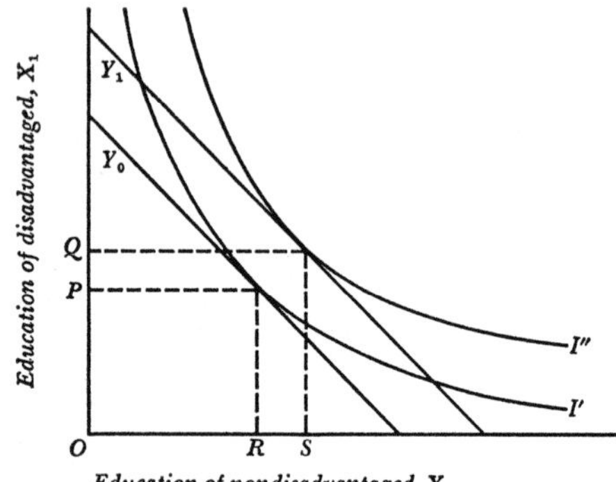

(b) Title I moneys commingled to increase education of disadvantaged

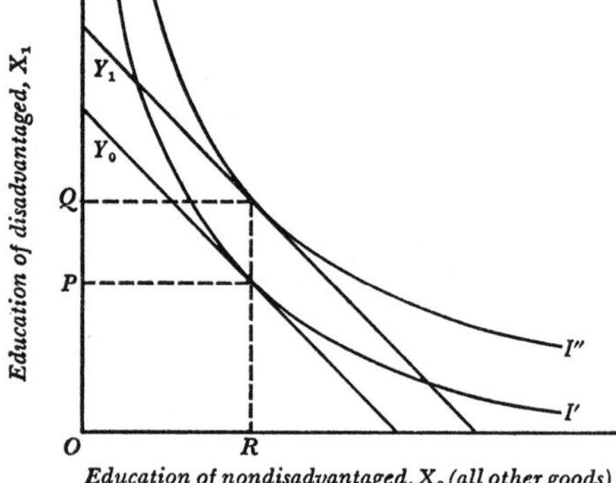

(c) Matching grants-in-aid

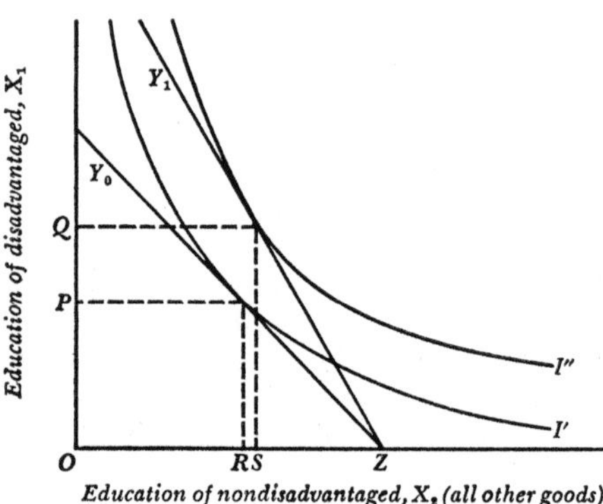

a community budget of Y_0, the community would want to obtain OP units of X_1 and OR units of X_2.

Now, Title I aid is added to the community budget, increasing the budget constraint from Y_0 to Y_1. In no way are the relative prices of the two goods altered. Therefore, the budget line will shift in a parallel manner with a tangency on a higher indifference curve, I''. Community welfare is increased by the consumption of larger quantities of X_1 and X_2. That is, with this augmentation to the community budget of Title I aid, the community will increase education for the disadvantaged from OP to OQ for a net increase of PQ. Thus, it will be able to substantiate on its report to the state some new programs for disadvantaged children. Yet at the same time, the community is consuming additional X_2, education for nondisadvantaged children, having increased the amount of that good obtained by RS. That is, the present form of Title I aid tends to increase the provision of education for other children as well as for disadvantaged children. Indeed, since X_2 should represent all other goods in the community welfare function (both public and private), this finding can be generalized to conclude that Title I aid probably increases the provision of education for the disadvantaged as well as for all other goods. How much of the Title I allocation will actually subsidize education for disadvantaged children will depend upon the income elasticity of that good. Since it appears that Title I aid enables the community to consume more of all goods, it is necessary to examine the conditions under which the community would allocate Title I aid to X_1 alone.

Figure 1(b) shows these conditions. In this case, the community would allocate any increase in income to education for the disadvantaged and would not increase its consumption of any other goods. Thus, all other goods taken together would show an income elasticity of zero, the definition of an inferior good. Indeed, Title I legislation tacitly assumes that this is the existing situation: as community income rises, all of the increase will be devoted to a single good, X_1, education for the disadvantaged. Yet, since virtually all studies of consumption show positive income elasticities for the major components of the "all other goods" category, the assumption can be made that Figure 1(a) is probably a closer approximation to the true situation than is Figure 1(b).

Indeed, common sense would suggest that a matching grant-in-aid would represent a far more efficient means of increasing education for disadvantaged children than does the present lump-sum approach. Figure 1(c) shows this case: the community is consuming OP of X_1, and OR of X_2, with budget constraint Y_0 and relative prices P_{x_1} and P_{x_2}. Now assume that the price of X_1 is reduced by a matching grant-in-aid; that is, for every local dollar spent on education for the disadvantaged the federal government would provide a prespecified matching amount (for example, $1.00). In this case, the budget line or line of attainable combinations would rotate toward the right from its axis at point *Z* since the community could now obtain more X_1 at the subsidized (lower) price, P'_{x_1}. Thus, the effect of the matching grant would be to increase the consumption of X_1 by a relatively large amount, *PQ*. Of course, even this substitution effect might generate some increase in the consumption of X_2 by the associated income effect. However, the point that is demonstrated here is that a matching grant is likely to be far more efficient in increasing expenditure on the disadvantaged than is a lump-sum grant.

HENRY M. LEVIN

Summary of Conference Discussion

Some thirty experts selected from minority communities, urban school systems, universities and professional education groups, as well as the authors of the conference papers, participated in the Brookings Conference on the Community School. The purpose of the two-day meeting was to discuss the characteristics, problems, and future possibilities of the recent movement toward politically decentralizing the big-city schools.

The conference was divided into four sessions, each devoted to a particular aspect of community schools and based upon the set of papers prepared for that meeting. The first session considered the objectives and social aspects of community schools, drawing upon the works of Harold W. Pfautz, Mario D. Fantini, Leonard J. Fein, and Robert C. Maynard. The second session was concerned with the political aspects of decentralization as discussed in the conference papers of Marilyn Gittell, Robert F. Lyke, Rhody A. McCoy, and Michael H. Moskow and Kenneth McLennan. The third session was devoted to the mechanics of decentralization, using the papers of Anthony Downs and H. Thomas James and Henry M. Levin as points of departure. The final session of the conference enabled the participants to summarize their views and draw some tentative conclusions.

What follows is a summary of the conference discussion based upon the transcript of the proceedings. While an attempt has been made to present important viewpoints and to indicate areas of agreement and disagreement, it has not been possible to note each participant's view on every matter discussed. This chapter describes as accurately as possible the development of the conference discussion. Nevertheless, there may exist important conclusions on which some participants would not agree. Thus, where the summary of the discussion indicates broad agreement on particular issues, this does not mean that every conferee was in accord; rather it suggests that a majority, and usually a substantial majority, of the participants were in agreement. An attempt has been made to present any minority views that had ardent support.

Objectives and Social Aspects of Community Schools

The conferees grouped the objectives of community governance into two broad categories: making the schools more responsive to the needs of the populations that they serve, and fulfilling the special needs of black Americans. Actually, these two categories overlap substantially, but it was conceptually desirable to separate them for purposes of discussion.

As described by one participant, the first goal represents a reaction to the clumsy and insensitive administration demonstrated by citywide school authorities. Under the existing centralized system of administration, principals, teachers, and parents have found attempts to improve their schools frustrated by cumbersome procedures and regulations that protect the status quo. The school systems are so large that they cannot consider themselves accountable to particular schools or parents, especially if those schools serve children whose parents lack political muscle. Since departures from tradition must be approved by the central school administration, bold and imaginative proposals for change are throttled by the lack of decision-making power in individual schools and classrooms. In fact, the central school board's obsession for procedural order above other considerations has encrusted the schools with a drab and uniform educational approach despite the variety of educational situations and student needs that exist in the large cities. To the degree that many of the methods, curricula, and personnel have not been appropriate and have failed to give minority children the skills and attitudes that the schools claim as objectives, the failure has become institutionalized and systematic.

The inefficiencies and rigidities evident in the existing approach have been documented by so many novelists and journalists that many people take them for granted. One participant told of city schools that had waited two years for textbooks that could have been received within two weeks if they had been ordered directly from the publishers. Other examples were also given. Many city schools have reported storerooms full of unused scientific equipment and library books without having programs, laboratories, and libraries to make use of these materials. At the same time, other schools have the programs and physical facilities, but lack the equipment. In the schools of some cities a simple request for stationery or paper clips must be approved by a dozen different signatories before the supplies are forthcoming.

One researcher who attended the conference stated that a large proportion of teachers in city schools are systematically assigned to teach subjects for which they lack preparation. Thus it is common for teachers with training in social studies and physical education to be teaching courses at the secondary level in mathematics, sciences, and foreign languages, and substantial numbers of them are also assigned to elementary classrooms.

Further, the choice of textbooks and curriculum can rarely be modified by a teacher no matter how useless or deleterious they may be to the pupils. One incident that was described by a conference participant took place recently in a junior high school with an all-black enrollment. A young, white teacher was harassed by her principal with support from the office of the central school board for introducing the Negro play *Raisin in the Sun* into her English class and for encouraging and supporting her pupils' efforts to produce a student newspaper. Her attempts to introduce relevant activities were criticized as violations of the "required" curriculum. That she had succeeded in getting her students excited about their English classes was ignored in favor of administrative uniformity. There is evidence that many of the better teachers leave schools partly because of such frustrations. In fact, many conferees attributed the general failure of compensatory education programs to the inability of the big-city school bureaucracies to adapt to the needs of the sizable groups of black children.

Thus, the participants agreed that a major objective of school decentralization in the large cities is to make the schools more responsive to the particular populations they serve by making them accountable to the communities from which they draw their enrollments. The unwieldiness of the present, highly centralized administration prevents this accountability. It is expected that if the schools are answerable to a local governing board, the learning environment for the children involved will improve. Educational benefits would result from both direct and indirect effects of community governance.[1] The direct impact of decentralization on the schools would be derived from the ability of each community to select the curricula, materials, programs, and personnel most appropriate to the specific needs of its students. Experimentation and innovation could then lead to school environments that were more receptive to students and more successful in stimulating intellectual and emotional growth than are the present schools. In addition, decentralization would allow the schools to handle logistical problems more efficiently by obtaining textbooks and other supplies in appropriate quantities at the time they were needed. Decentralization could also enable the schools to employ outside consultants on specific problems, utilize new types of personnel such as artists and writers, and contract out certain services that can be supplied more efficiently by private firms.

But in addition to these direct effects, it was suggested that the learning process could be enhanced indirectly by a healthy metamorphosis of community attitudes toward education. That is, the participation of parents and other members of the community in running the schools would lead to a closer relationship between the school and its constituency—a situation that is not possible under the present bureaucratic structure. Educational researchers suggest that parental involvement in the schools leads to favorable attitudes toward education among offspring; yet under the present system, the school often appears to be an impenetrable and alien fortress to the community and the parents. The inability of parents to have significant influence in modifying rigid and anachronistic school policies has produced frustrations and hostile attitudes that are easily transmitted to their children. Several participants asserted that if

[1] For a discussion of these reforms, see the chapter by Mario D. Fantini.

school were responsive to the educational needs of the community, parents would show greater respect for the schools and a more receptive attitude toward education, and eventually an improvement in the attitudes and performances of the students.

Decentralization and the Black Community

According to the representatives of the black community, the educational rationale for community governance is compelling, but the need for change is even more urgent. Not only did they view the present system as educationally inadequate but they asserted that it is an arrangement that must have discriminatory consequences—that is, the school system can afford to favor white middle-class children at the expense of black children because black citizens lack the political power to do anything about it. In this respect, the schools reflect a type of racism that is ignored by the average white American. Kenneth Haskins, principal of the Adams-Morgan community school in Washington, D.C., has suggested that racism in this sense means ". . . that a public school system that fails poor black children can be tolerated, while a public school system that fails white middle-class children cannot."[2] Many participants maintained that this dereliction could be reversed if the administrations of schools in black neighborhoods were responsive to the large groups of black parents who were concerned and involved in the process of education. It was noted that students in the Adams-Morgan community school showed gains in reading proficiency in the first year under community control. Only a handful of other public schools in the District of Columbia exhibited such improvement over this period, while most schools showed declines.

In addition, it was suggested that black Americans see a new and important educational focus emerging from community governance. The view expressed was that the schools should be held responsible for helping to fulfill the ideals and aspirations of the people they serve. Thus, the constituency of the school must include all the people in the community since the needs of the students cannot be divorced from the environment in which they live. More specifi-

[2] Kenneth W. Haskins, "The Case for Local Control," *Saturday Review* (Jan. 11, 1969), p. 52.

cally, the schools should be expected to promote the sense of self-worth and identity of their students while imparting the ability to influence their own lives. The frequent observation that the schools and the larger society tend to destroy these qualities in black children was considered as reprehensible as the academic failures of the schools. As one participant explained:

> . . . the fulfillment of these responsibilities requires the community school to address itself not only to the academic or cognitive skills, but it must address the affective skills as well with particular attention given to the formation of positive attitudes. Indeed, community schools must be designed to compensate for the second-class treatment of black citizens in other sectors of society by building educational programs that will help black children to succeed.

But more than this, many of the conferees considered community control of schools in black neighborhoods as the beginning of a significant drive toward full equality.[3] This belief is based on the widely held view that as long as black Americans lack political and economic power, they will not be able to improve their conditions. Accordingly, community control of the schools was presented as the leading edge of a political wedge that would begin to redistribute decision-making power to those affected by the decisions. Control of the schools, then, was viewed by these participants as the first step in effecting a more just distribution of political power and a greater degree of self-determination for black citizens. As one participant explained: "Improving the schools attended by black children is an urgent priority, but it seems to me that the bigger issue is one of how large numbers of people who have been effectively disenfranchised begin to find their way toward being a part of the society." When asked how important would black control of their community schools be in alleviating the powerlessness that has hindered black advancement, his reply was that it could be very important:

> While the answers are not in, it seems very clear that this could be an initial step toward more effective control of other institutions in the community, for it is the success patterns of communities which give those communities a sense of a better future instead of futility. Given control of the schools, the community could sense a beginning of political potency. It is this factor which would enhance the community's ability to deal more

[3] For a discussion of this development, see the chapter by Robert C. Maynard.

effectively with other problems such as jobs and housing and which would construct the groundwork for full equality.

A prominent thread that ran through the discussion was that the schools might be a starting place for community cohesion. It was suggested that community schools represent a focus around which political and social structures would emerge for black Americans where such structures are presently lacking. This development was considered particularly important because the factors that link black people today are mainly the negative ones of enduring racial discrimination by white society. While there is a recent emphasis on black culture, the schools represent a tangible institution that can generate a sense of community involvement and black pride. Responsibility for the schools represents a positive experience that can be shared by all blacks as opposed to the negative experience of white racism.

The potential of the school in developing the communal ties that black Americans—and perhaps other Americans—so passionately desire cannot be overemphasized. As Maynard suggested, "An issue has been raised around which many residents can rally as never before and one in which their mutual, or community, interest is most clearly defined." In this sense, it seems that the term black community reflects the common attributes that blacks want to develop and share with each other. It was asserted that control of schools represents a setting within which these latent and somewhat mystical ties might emerge to form a true sense of community—a sense of common purpose and destiny.

Thus, the black American views community control as a way of improving and broadening the educational performance of ghetto schools and, in addition, of improving the status of black citizens. This could be accomplished by breaking down many of the rigidities that characterize these schools as well as by introducing programs, personnel, and materials specifically designed to transform black children into capable young adults. Historical evidence suggests that the school bureaucracies are incapable of carrying out such changes within their present structures. Therefore, community control becomes a necessary method of achieving educational reform.

In addition, many blacks feel that community support for running the schools will provide the nucleus for a community power base; and it is believed that strong and cohesive black communities are the most effective strategy for obtaining an equitable share of power in the larger society.

Political Objectives of Community Schools

While few of the conferees denied the importance of the immediate educational goals of community schools, several reacted strongly to the political aspects. The main criticism seemed to be that the search for political "liberation" of black Americans has no place in the schools. In reply, one discussant asked whether it was the means of obtaining power rather than the ends that were being questioned, for the schools have traditionally claimed the goal of preparing students for a participatory democracy. Courses given throughout the standard curriculum are designed to give students the requisite literacy, knowledge, and common set of values to understand and participate in the political life of our society. But, it was pointed out, blacks and other racial minorities have been excluded from the power structure, and they have been unable to form a coalition or find any other group to represent their needs; the present objectives of the schools have not served them well. The black spokesmen emphasized that the values reflected in the school curriculum are necessary for perpetuating the present distribution of political power, and in no way are new players encouraged to join the game.

Since the black community feels that only self-development will give it the strength to reinforce its demands for a fairer share of representation in the larger society, it appears consistent that the schools in the black community emphasize political goals of black cohesion rather than those of the beneficent democracy. The democratic trappings reflected by the present schools are deceptive to black Americans who still lack political equality and meaningful representation.

Socialization and Racial Separation

A second and related social objection to decentralization that was raised was that it would institutionalize the separation of the races. Presumably, present neighborhoods would be the initial basis of community so that blacks would continue to attend predominantly black schools and whites would attend schools with white enrollments. Yet it was recognized that a major objective of the schools in a democratic society is exposing children to fellow students who are drawn from a variety of social, economic, and racial backgrounds. This goal is part of the socialization function of the schools which prepares individuals to fulfill their interpersonal or social obligations in a multicultural setting. It is believed that exposure to a heterogeneity of cultures, races, and social classes improves understanding and interactions among the various groups and increases social mobility. These end-products are considered prerequisites for a functioning democratic society.[4]

The critics asserted that in this respect the community school would be both socially divisive and antidemocratic. But several participants maintained that for black Americans the concept of the "melting pot" has been an historical myth. At present, blacks live in a separate society, and neither legal remedies nor the putative good will of the white community has been able to give them housing, education, and other social activities in an integrated setting. In the case of the city schools, it was not the blacks who rejected integration, it was the big-city school boards who represent a sizable component of the white community.

But since all of the conferees agreed that a healthy America requires the full economic, political, and social integration of blacks and whites, the real question was how to achieve such a goal. It was asserted that, paradoxically, black cohesiveness appeared to be a more effective strategy than any other existing alternative, and the reason for its promise was a simple one. Our society responds more quickly to the demands of powerful constituencies than it does to those of weak ones, and black community is the basis for black political potency.

However, some conferees argued that the trend toward community governance was a dangerous one. They suggested that large governmental units have done more to break down social inequalities than have smaller ones. Therefore, they saw the movement to-

[4] For a detailed discussion of the socialization function, see the chapter by Harold W. Pfautz.

ward decentralization of schools implying less power for black Americans, not more power. As one spokesman maintained:

> The larger units of government have almost always been the most democratic in our society, the least repressive, and the most stimulating. It was the President of the United States who put troops into Arkansas, marshals into Mississippi, and federalized the National Guard in Alabama to protect students who were entering the schools in those communities.

Other participants replied that the example of the federal government cannot be generalized to lower levels of government. In particular, they asserted that states have been notoriously less democratic than the cities and, they suggested further, that the roles of the federal and state governments in the affairs of local governmental units would still be guaranteed by state and federal constitutions.

The effects of black community in achieving the goals of black Americans on university campuses were cited as an illustration of black cohesiveness. The demands of the newly formed black students' unions for increases in black enrollments, more black faculty and administrators, and courses in Afro-American culture have been met with quick and positive responses at most institutions. In addition, these demands have spurred substantial increases in the recruitment of blacks by professional and graduate schools as well as greater financial aid and counseling services. These gains are particularly relevant because they represent the traditional paths of access to the middle class that have been open to whites but largely inaccessible to racial minorities. Community adherents hold that integration and equality will never come until blacks have the power to pursue such objectives, and that the requisite power cannot develop without black unity and self-government. The disagreement between those who advocated black community government and those who saw progress only through larger units of government was a recurring one throughout the conference.

Community Schools and White Americans

If political decentralization of the schools is necessary for minority students, is it an equally valid response to the educational problems of whites? It was asserted that one of the most serious flaws characterizing city schools, as well as other American institutions, is the assumption that identical treatment of different groups yields the same outcomes for all groups.[5] Many participants acknowledged that, given the different cultural attributes of racial and social groupings, the application of the same educational approach produces unequal results. In particular, the evidence suggests that the traditional approach has been far less effective for black children and those of other racial minorities than it has been for children of the white middle class. If this is so, the same logic must be applied to the choice of remedy; the organizational reforms that are needed to improve the status of black students are not necessarily the most appropriate remedies for curing the educational infirmities of schools serving white populations.

In this respect, it was contended that community control of the schools is more urgently needed by black Americans than it is by whites. Many conferees pointed out that blacks (and other racial minorities) are a special educational case because their exigencies are not represented by the power structure or by the traditional institutional arrangements. The result of this lack of representation is that blacks have been shortchanged in the allocation of school resources, and their needs have been ignored in determining the nature of the schooling experience that is provided for their children. As a result, there exists an enormous breach between the setting in which the black child lives and the schooling that is imposed upon him, a contradiction that tends to undermine his self-worth. In addition, several participants noted that the central school authorities have been insensitive to other major concerns of the black population. For example, sites for new schools have been selected in black neighborhoods without consulting residents of the local area. One result of this callousness is that black residents and businesses have been uprooted despite the availability of suitable alternative sites that would leave housing and other neighborhood buildings intact.

On the other hand, it was asserted that no major contradiction is found between the values represented in the schools and those embodied in the white community at large, and whites already have the political power to protect their school interests. The central school authority is politically sensitive to both school resource de-

[5] For an extensive discussion of the failures of the "universalistic" approach, see the chapter by Leonard J. Fein.

mands and site selection preferences of residents in white neighborhoods. In fact, in these as well as other respects, whites already send their children to community schools. Community advocates emphasized that the very failure of policies to reduce de facto school segregation is a tribute to the power of white neighborhoods to keep black students out of their schools.

The conferees agreed that particular whites might not be altogether happy with their schools, but most white Americans can express their dissatisfactions through political channels or by moving to another neighborhood or school district, and many can afford to send their children to private institutions. The black American does not have the power to command political responsiveness, the necessary income to seek private alternatives, or the wide choice of neighborhoods or communities in which he can obtain housing and better schools for his children. Locked into his community and locked out of city hall, the black American's only hope for improving his schools appears to be through direct governance of them.

The Redistribution of Power

It was easier for the conference participants to outline the objectives of community control than to draw a blueprint for the redistribution of power. The major difficulty was the absence of an analogous situation that could be used as a prototype. To deal with this problem, the conferees searched for an applicable model for decentralization, and then sought to define the relevant power relations. The procedure was to (1) describe the present situation; (2) select the areas of control required for meaningful community governance; (3) identify the conflicts inherent in the redistribution of power and the grounds for negotiation; and (4) indicate the probable strategies of the parties in protecting their interests.

THE PRESENT DISTRIBUTION

The big-city schools are officially governed by two major entities: the state government and the citywide school board. The state government maintains substantial control by requiring local school districts to meet a variety of personnel and curricular requirements in order to receive accreditation and state financial aid. In addition, the citywide school boards have their own sets of regulations, requirements, and mandates. While states and city school boards appear to govern the schools, this is more true in letter than in spirit; for like most governmental units each represents a constituency.

At the state level, the constituency is primarily composed of the professional educators rather than a broad base of citizenry. Indeed, the power of the educators to predominate in the decision-making arena can be traced to the political influence of their professional associations, especially the National Education Association and its state affiliates.[6] Through powerful lobbying efforts in the state capitals and close relationships among professional associations, colleges of education, and regulatory bodies, the various arms of the educational profession have exerted enormous influence on legislation and on the activities of the state departments of education. In many states, the principal officers of the departments of education are selected directly from the ranks of the state associations, that is, from the ranks of the professional educator.

At the local level, these interests have been supported by negotiated agreements with teachers and supervisory personnel that severely limit citizen influence on the operations of the schools. The parents, on the other hand, have no such powerful representation, nor do the students or other elements of the larger society. Parental interests are usually channeled through the professionally diluted parent-teachers' associations. The rules and regulations at both the state and city levels prevent strong parental influence in molding school policies.

It was pointed out by several discussants that as long as the outlook of the professional bureaucracy coincides with that of the citizenry it is supposed to serve, professional control can be consistent with the needs of the larger society. It is this tacit assumption that underlies the educator's assertion that his experience and training enable him to know best how children should be schooled. But in the case of black and other minority children, the approach of the professional educators has not been productive. Despite the acknowledged failure of the ghetto schools, few substantial changes have

[6] For the significant role played by the "educational establishment" in determining school policies and particularly licensing requirements for personnel, see James B. Conant, *The Education of American Teachers* (McGraw-Hill, 1963).

been effected by the official governing bodies of the schools—the states and the city school boards—or the educators who administer, supervise, and teach in those schools. In fact, spokesmen for the black community suggested that attempts at so-called compensatory education have had greater success in increasing the number of jobs for the professionals than in improving the education of racial minorities. For a variety of reasons the big-city school boards have not responded to demands for fulfillment of the needs of black students.[7] Thus the black community seeks to alter the present balance of power by taking direct responsibility for the schools that black children attend. The new arrangement would give the community a large measure of autonomy in the operation of its schools, and a new balance of power would emerge among the decentralized schools, the various levels of government, and the professionals who staff the schools.

A GOVERNING BOARD FOR THE LOCAL COMMUNITY

The emergence of the community as a factor in governing the schools implies that each local district would elect a representative school board that would have substantial powers in influencing school practices. It is useful to describe what is meant by the local community and to identify its spokesmen in the power arena. Conference participants generally referred to the community as an entity that was composed of the students and their parents as well as other local citizens who reside within a designated geographical area.

To provide a governing board, each community would hold elections, and it was hoped that these elections would be characterized by extensive voter interest and participation. One immediate obstacle to such participation is that most neighborhoods lack the political structure desirable for such elections since, traditionally, communities have not had the power to govern their schools or other local institutions. Without this broad political structure, the skeptics felt that voter participation would be so low that a few powerful persons could gain control of the schools in order to achieve their own purposes.

[7] The many reasons that city school boards are unresponsive to minority groups are discussed in the chapter by Robert F. Lyke.

While several observers of community politics saw this outcome as a short-run possibility, they did not think it would continue in the long run. They suggested that the representative nature of the local governing board would be reasonably assured if large segments of the population within the community had a strong interest in the schools. Since schools directly affect the lives of many families and the local governing board would be the first major elective effort of the community, the residents would not be indifferent to election outcomes or community school practices.

It was emphasized that in several cities where decentralization plans have already been proposed, the opposition to community schools by professional organizations has tended to unify the black community and create a broad base of community support. The conflict has made the local populations aware of their stake in governing their local schools and has increased the level of community participation. Ironically, it appears that the opposition to community schools may serve as the most effective device for democratizing the governance of the local school districts.

THE AREAS OF CONTROL

While most of the conference participants shared the view that black communities should have a greater measure of authority in the governance of their schools, there was considerably less agreement on how this should be done. Community advocates asserted that in at least three primary areas the local governing boards would require virtual control: personnel, curriculum, and allocation of the community school budget.

As they explained it, the need of the community to select teachers, administrators, and other staff who were sympathetic with the objectives of the community is straightforward. The effectiveness of the local school board in changing the schools will depend to a great extent on the cooperation and proficiency of the school staff in carrying out such changes. Accordingly, personnel must be chosen with particular emphasis on community needs.[8] As one participant pointed out, " . . . if the local district is bound by existing practices (central examination and assignment of staff) it cannot significantly

[8] For a discussion of some of the considerations in selecting personnel, see the chapter by Rhody A. McCoy.

increase its powers in the vital area of who shall staff the schools." Thus, local selection implies that there must be some modification of existing examination and assignment practices. These modifications are most important in the selection of administrators, for the administrator of the community school must identify and be identifiable with community concerns rather than citywide concerns.

Spokesmen for the community schools also advocated local autonomy in designing curriculum. They suggested that the community school must have the freedom to make changes in educational approaches, instructional materials, and educational objectives in order for school programs to be more closely related to the experiences of their students. They emphasized that curriculum control does not mean that the community school board should discard all the traditional practices but that the community schools should have the power to modify and reconstruct the curriculum where necessary to improve its effectiveness and to strengthen its contribution to the self-worth and dignity of the students.

The third area of local control considered necessary by community spokesmen was the freedom to allocate the budget. If community school boards were given their own budgets but were required to distribute them in traditional ways, the ability to alter the present schools would be seriously constrained. That is, if the proportion of the budget for teachers' salaries, materials, and so on and staffing ratios were specified, the local school board could not radically depart from existing practices. The power to allocate the budget is especially crucial to directing the operations of the schools, for as one participant put it: "You cannot have control of personnel or curriculum without the control of finances."

Control of the budget, personnel, and curriculum are of primary importance within each community. Other areas of control have substantial implications beyond community borders as well. These include the drawing of boundaries for delineating communities, the distribution of financial resources among local school boards, the selection of new school sites, and the timing and nature of new construction. It was recognized that each of these functions must ultimately be determined by a higher level of government, for example, the city school board; yet, provision should be made for the local school boards to negotiate with the central authority on each issue.

The drawing of school boundaries was shown to be of vital interest to the community because of its direct impact on the size and nature of the constituency of the local district. The boundaries of the local school area will be a major determinant of the power structure in the local community. That is, the gerrymandering of local district boundaries could undermine or reinforce the cohesion and strength of particular groups in governing the schools. Several discussants stressed the view that blacks and other minority groups would be wary of the process for setting boundaries since school attendance areas in many cities have often been engineered to keep minority students out of "select" schools. For example, the boundaries for a well-known high school in one of the largest cities have been drawn in such a way that white neighborhoods three miles away are served by the school while black students living within five blocks of the school are assigned to another attendance area.

The criteria for distributing financial resources among decentralized school districts would also be of crucial interest to the local districts. All communities would vie for a share of the city's total school funds which derive from the city's own sources as well as from state and federal aid. Therefore, local communities must be given an opportunity to demonstrate their relative needs and to share in determining the allocation of the central budget among the various communities. This representation at the central level would be especially important for protecting the interests of the black community, since these have been traditionally slighted in the distribution of funds. Furthermore, much of the aid that is receivable from state and federal governments is specifically intended for schools with children from low-income families; thus the minority communities have a particular interest in the proper allocation of these moneys.

Spokesmen for the black community emphasized that site selection for schools and new school construction also have a direct effect on the welfare of local communities. The optimal location of new schools would combine accessibility to community residents with minimum disruption of housing and local businesses. Thus, in order to insure that community priorities are taken into account, the local governing board must also have the power to negotiate with the central school authority on site selection. Participants noted two other aspects of new school construction that concern local communities: school design and the choice of building contractors. Several conferees suggested that since each local district would be characterized by different educational needs, these differences should be reflected in the school building. To accomplish this, provision could be made for the community school board to submit its requirements to the architects and planners with the final choice of building plans subject to negotiation. Representatives of the black community suggested that black contractors be invited to submit bids for such construction, and that the contractor who is chosen be required to hire substantial numbers of black workers. It has been a source of deep frustration to black citizens to see publicly financed construction in their communities being undertaken by white contractors and a white labor force while black men are loitering on street corners without employment.

CONFLICTS IN THE REDISTRIBUTION

Having established the areas of community concern, the conferees turned to the problem of achieving a redistribution of power. It was recognized that in the decentralization of authority some would lose power and others would gain. Therefore, it was useful to specify the interests of the parties involved wherever such interests were apparent and to suggest the nature of the conflicts that would arise (and have been arising).[9]

At least five groups have demonstrated interests in any attempt to decentralize the big-city schools. These are the local community, the administrators, the teachers, the city school board, and the state and federal authorities who represent the larger society. The positions of the state and federal governments were least clear, so the conference focused its attention on the priorities of the other groups. On the basis of subsequent discussion it became apparent that the goals of administrators and school boards were also difficult to characterize, except for the reluctance of both groups to relinquish any of the power that they possess. On the other hand, there was much more evidence available on the views of the teachers, so the teacher-community conflict became the prime topic of discussion.

[9] For an extensive discussion of the redistribution of power, see the chapter by Marilyn Gittell.

In focusing on the position of the teachers, it was important to recognize that they do not represent a monolithic body with a single view on school decentralization. Both the American Federation of Teachers and the Urban Task Force of the National Education Association have issued statements supporting greater community power, but in fact the teachers' views on community control vary substantially from city to city. As an example of this diversity, the teachers' union in Washington, D.C., strongly favors community control, while in New York City the local branch of the same union has been less than enthusiastic about this development.

Given the variety of views among teachers, the conferees recognized the dangers of generalizing about their attitudes and goals. Yet there were a number of aspects that could be discussed. One of the more intriguing questions was whether the teachers would be better or worse off under community control. Obviously, the final answer to this question would depend upon the specific nature of the decentralization arrangement, but the conferees were able to suggest certain insights.

In some ways it appeared that teachers would benefit from decentralization. Moskow and McLennan provided evidence that teachers favor "central negotiations for salary and fringe benefits and decentralized negotiations for most decisions involving working conditions and instructional programs. In areas such as teaching load, class size, and procedures for textbook selection, a relatively large number of respondents favored negotiations at the school level."[10] Thus in many respects, the teachers thought that they would have a more effective voice in determining their working conditions and the educational programs if decisions were made at the community level.

Traditional bargaining theory implies that the teachers might also be better off with regard to salaries and fringe benefits if their professional organization or union negotiated with decentralized school boards rather than the central school board. Ordinarily, when a union bargains with many individual firms in an industry it uses a "whipsaw" technique to secure better benefits than could be obtained by dealing with a single organization representing all

[10] See the chapter by Michael H. Moskow and Kenneth McLennan.

firms. By bargaining on a community-to-community basis, the teachers' union could first select that school from which it expected the best settlement. That settlement would then serve as a basis for getting more from each subsequent decentralized school board. As one expert suggested, the union would say: "Well, we got $8,000 in District 1. Now you have to sweeten that a bit. We have to do a little better here." Eventually, the decentralized districts might join together and bargain for salaries on the central level.

But whether this technique would be as successful with schools as with business firms was questioned by some participants. Each firm in a multifirm industry would be under pressure to settle quickly because it would fear losing its share of the market if it were shut down by a strike. But no such competition exists among schools for children who live in the ghetto. If the schools were forced to shut down, the students would return when they reopened. In the meantime, the community would probably tutor its children in "freedom schools," as several communities have done in the past under similar conditions. Moreover, since schools are not union shops, the effectiveness of whipsawing would be reduced. In some city schools, the union membership is so low that a strike would barely affect school operations. In fact, one experimental community school experienced a decline in union memberships from over 90 percent of its teaching staff before community control to only about 20 percent two years after the change in governance.

The conferees thought that a more serious source of conflict is the issue of job security. Teachers have asserted that if the community were to have unfettered control over personnel, they would have no protection against arbitrary and capricious firings. Representatives of the community schools replied that they seek only the power to transfer unsatisfactory teachers out of their local districts, just as the central school board has the authority to transfer teachers from one school to another.

The teachers' representatives pointed out that the transfer analogy was misleading because under a decentralized plan another local governing board would have to accept the teachers who were dismissed. That is, while the central school board presently has the power to transfer teachers among schools within its jurisdiction, it would not have the power to transfer them from one community school to another under decentralization. Indeed, community control of personnel is imcompatible with centrally directed transfers among local districts.

The participants unanimously agreed that there must be a review procedure to avoid arbitrary or capricious dismissals. But in order to develop such a mechanism, the parties to the dispute must agree to bargain and discuss methods of adjudicating personnel issues. One suggestion from a community school representative was the creation of a local body that would rule on all teacher-related matters. This committee could be composed of three groups: teachers' representatives elected by all the teachers of the local district; a personnel committee of professional educators; and the members of the local governing board. It is clear that establishment of an acceptable procedure by which personnel matters would be handled is prerequisite to a stable decentralization plan.

It was noted that personnel problems would be more serious during the transition from centrally to locally administered schools than they are likely to be in the long run. At the inception of decentralization, community schools would inherit most of their teaching staffs. Inevitably, this staff would include teachers whom the community would not have accepted if given a free choice, and many of these teachers would have tenure in the school system. On the other hand, the local school board would select all new appointees and would probably evaluate them carefully before granting tenure. In addition, the process of self-selection among teacher applicants to each community suggests a strong coincidence of interests between new appointees and the community.

But the need for establishing adjudicatory procedures to handle conflicts between local governing boards and professional associations was deemed by virtually all of the conferees to be of utmost importance. Many of the goals of the decentralized districts probably cannot be achieved without modifying the existing agreements between the central school authority and the representative professional organizations. In this respect, the teachers and supervisory personnel are likely to view the present provisions as "hard-won gains," and will not want them eliminated when the bargaining begins. The surrender of any established right or procedure will be accompanied by the demand for a new concession that is at least of equal value, a *quid pro quo.*

However, conferees representing both professional organizations and community interests expressed the opinion that most of the issues, if not all, are negotiable. The teachers' viewpoint was that ". . . while local communities should have an effective share of power, neither the local community, nor the teachers, nor any other group should have untrammeled authority in the areas of personnel, finances, or curriculum. There must be a requirement for consultation at the very least, and there must be a more stringent set of requirements where the things being safeguarded are more important." Community representatives agreed that bargaining and compromise are possible, but the community must seek to protect not only its interests in personnel, curriculum, and finances but also the rights of students, school boundaries, new construction, the allocation of state and federal aid, and any external standards that would be imposed upon local school districts. If the affected interests can be brought together to discuss these issues, it was agreed that, ultimately, many of the conflicts could be resolved.

While several of the big-city school administrators expressed interest in decentralization, the design and implementation of the plans puzzled them. The issue is further complicated because neither the school boards nor the superintendents have as much independence as they require to drastically change the schools. Contracts with teachers and supervisory personnel, state requirements, and meager finances all protect the status quo. In this respect, it appeared that the central school board and its administration would play a rather weak role in the decentralization plan. This weakness suggested that a power vacuum might develop at the local level with the central school authority being the least able of all of the parties to have an influence on the changing arrangement.

Then who would design the decentralization plans, and how would they be enacted? The only realistic answer seemed to be that the final design would be forged by political forces at both the city and state levels. Such matters as school boundaries, site selection, new construction, finances, personnel standards, and other aspects affecting the limits of local determination would be "up for grabs."

The principal contestants for these powers are the incumbent professionals and the challenging members of the minority communities.

One participant predicted that the strategies of the professionals would be traditional in that they would use their influence to exert pressure on state legislators, state departments of education, and city school boards. These efforts—particularly at the state level where massive funding is involved—would be aimed at forestalling decentralization plans or, alternatively, at promoting decentralization while denying the community any powers that might threaten professional control.

Opposing the professionals would be black and other minority Americans seeking community control. Their goal would be to establish a system of control that would grant full autonomy to the decentralized school districts. They would also press for the right of decentralized school boards to negotiate with state and city governments on all major school issues that affect their districts.

Most of the conferees agreed that the battle at the city and state levels would be an uneven match because the local communities have neither the organization, the political representation, nor the finances to air their case, and because there is little fervor among state legislatures to disturb traditional power arrangements. Thus the conference participants focused the discussion on how black and other minority Americans might take their case to higher councils of government in order to achieve potent representation.

Several participants saw this problem as the major weakness in the community control strategy. Their point was that power within a neighborhood is less important than a voice in the larger society, for the educational codes are written and enforced primarily at the state level, while financial resources are drawn from district-wide, state, and federal sources, not neighborhoods. Community control with meager finances and no state accreditation could be self-defeating. In particular, the advocates of larger governing units viewed the insular nature of decentralized school districts as a fatal political weakness. Other conferees were slightly more sanguine. They asserted that minority communities could obtain the necessary political support at higher levels of government by developing proper alliances with other interest groups. For example, if community schools were made part of a package that also benefited large segments of the white middle class, the decentralization proposals could receive substantial support. But representatives of the black communities were pessimistic about the establishment of a meaningful coalition between blacks and substantial segments of the white middle class. One spokesman suggested that the failure to form a coalition became clear in the civil rights movement:

The white middle class had very little to lose from desegregating a hot dog stand, and you saw how much effort was required to carry that out. You are now talking about giving up areas of power that have traditionally resided with the white middle class, and you are talking furthermore about placing it in the hands of black communities. What we are discussing is a form of countering racism, and we have never developed a coalition in this country that has been able to solve that problem.

Other conferees insisted that there must be coalitions if black Americans are to attain effective control of their schools, but the black representatives maintained their position. One pointed to the myth of an alliance with the liberal-left labor movement:

When the thrust of the black movement was against Mississippi sheriffs, the liberal part of the American labor movement had little difficulty in supporting that kind of movement. But the moment you began to talk about eroding traditional power bases such as construction unions, teachers' unions, and other professional organizations, you came to the end of the line. There are no alliances, and this is what black communities have been warning the whole society for a long time.

But that analysis was declared misleading by one conferee who suggested that the failure of traditional alliances does not mean that no coalition can develop. Rather, he asserted, the coalition would be an unusual one composed of unacquiescent blacks on the one hand and inconvenienced whites on the other. That is, as long as blacks can enforce their demands by making it more costly for whites to ignore them than to support them, the basis for this unusual alliance exists.

To come aboard into this coalition whites don't have to benefit positively by a *quid pro quo* in the form of more funds for air pollution or some other good thing for which they will give blacks better schools or public welfare benefits. Rather, whites simply have to be inconvenienced by persistent and organized protests, picketing, and disruptions. The costs and inconveniences caused by these threats and protests can usually be avoided by negotiating with and fulfilling the blacks' demands.

The spokesman went on to suggest that it is precisely this kind of situation that has increased the level of public assistance benefits in some cities, and it appears to be the prototype of a coalition that will press for giving blacks control of their schools. No agreement was reached on the troublesome question of coalitions.

The Mechanics of Decentralization

The success of decentralization will depend largely on how it is applied. The conferees agreed that substantial planning would be necessary to assure a structure that would achieve the community schools' objectives. In addition to the need for establishing a negotiating mechanism among the parties involved, the conference participants indicated that at least two other areas of the decentralized structure required careful planning: finances and evaluation.

FINANCING COMMUNITY SCHOOLS

Determining the best means for assuring the effective financial autonomy of community schools was considered a crucial determinant of the workability of a decentralized scheme. Many of the conferees were attracted to a simple financing mechanism.[11] Since decentralized school districts are too small to raise their own revenues, the provision of fiscal resources would continue to be a function of the central school authority. The central school board would provide each local school board with a lump-sum budget, which would then be allocated at the discretion of the local board. Financial accounts and accountability would remain with the central school authority, but the actual disbursements for each school would be authorized only by the local governing board for that school. On the basis of this decision-making power, the local governing boards would construct their programs and purchase the necessary components to implement them, a course of action that is not permitted under the existing system.

Most of the conferees agreed that the freedom to allocate a lump-sum budget is essential to enable local school boards to control the operations of their schools. At least 80 percent of the funds presently distributed to the schools are earmarked for salary and maintenance

[11] See the chapter by H. Thomas James and Henry M. Levin.

costs with built-in requirements for specific types of personnel. In many cases these requirements are tantamount to forcing schools to waste money on redundant or useless resources while pressing needs are left unsatisfied because of a lack of funds. For example, some state and city authorities have library funds that must be expended on library books. The situation described by a school administrator is often a tragi-comic one:

> Let us say there is $20,000 for library books which I must order from a state-approved library list for a school that doesn't have a library. You know good educators want library books for kids and so the books are ordered and they are stacked up in rows of boxes. They get mildewed and damaged, since most of our schools do not have substantial facilities for storing such materials in a warm, dry place. Once they become damaged, you would like to give them away; but you can't. The law requires that you throw them away. Yet we are constantly told that one of the reasons that poor children are not able to read is because they lack books in the home to stimulate their latent skills.

Even the representatives of teachers' organizations agreed that the lump-sum budget with local autonomy of expenditure was desirable, but they asserted that the teachers would want to negotiate on how the money was spent.

There was also substantial agreement with the proposed guidelines for determining the amount of the lump-sum allocations to each local school board. The central school authority would distribute funds according to the function (comprehensive or special purpose) and level (elementary or secondary) of the school. Secondary schools are more costly than are elementary schools. Most important, schools with large numbers of educationally disadvantaged children would receive larger allotments per student than schools whose student bodies were more advantaged. This provision recognizes that it is necessary to provide added school resources for those children who need the greatest amount of assistance in order more nearly to achieve equality of opportunity among pupils drawn from different races and social classes.

One participant suggested that a reasonable method of fulfilling these criteria would be to require the central school authority to distribute its own resources among local school districts so that each local board would receive the same basic allotment per student. State and federal moneys would be used to augment local funds according to the needs of local districts. The higher levels of government would then be responsible for financing the additional resources required for compensatory education, a role consistent with the goals of the larger society to equalize educational opportunity.

But stating the criteria and mechanisms by which decentralized schools might be financed ignores a major obstacle, the politics of school finance. Many of the conference participants suggested that the big-city schools are already beset by financial woes, and the decentralized arrangement would accentuate these difficulties. Their logic was that if blacks were able to control and operate their own schools, there would be a tendency to ignore even further the financial requirements for those schools. That is, the resources forthcoming to support the schools under a central bureaucracy would be greater than those made available to support schools that were governed and administered by the black community. One participant saw a parallel between the financial support of community schools and that of public housing:

> Originally public housing was conceived of as a program to help low-income people. Increasingly, low-income housing became occupied by black families, so the focus of public housing shifted from an emphasis on the poor to an emphasis on the elderly. The elderly represented a predominantly white clientele. Subsequent efforts to refocus the housing program on the poor have all but halted new investment in public housing. To generalize this phenomenon, it appears that any service which becomes dominantly occupied by Negro recipients will be cut down in funds by the white majority.

This pessimism was underscored by many of the other conferees who considered the inability to achieve strong financial support as the greatest potential weakness in achieving an effective decentralization plan for black schools.

One participant noted, however, that there is at least one aspect of a decentralized plan that would counteract this tendency of financial neglect of black-controlled schools. If each school were given a lump-sum budget, fiscal discrimination against ghetto schools would be obvious. Under the present accounting system, school-by-school expenditures are not computed or reported, thus inequities are not visible. Indeed, the educational system masks the financial shortchanging of schools attended by blacks and less-advantaged students. Despite the publicity given to compensatory education programs, the discussant claimed that there is ample evidence that white middle-class schools in the large cities are receiving greater financial support than are similar schools with black and disadvantaged enrollments. But if a lump-sum budget were reported for each school, the hypocrisy of preaching compensatory education for the poor while implementing it for the middle class would become obvious. The visibility of lump-sum resource allocation patterns would provide a measure of social accountability and would tend to dampen much of the *sub rosa* fiscal discrimination against schools in poor and black neighborhoods.

Several of the conferees felt that the main problem of the city schools is obtaining adequate financing regardless of the school organization. They maintained that heavy reliance on the declining local tax base, too little state and federal support, and rising price levels combine to limit the ability of the big-city schools to improve their educational services. Examples were given of city schools that were being forced to shorten the length of their school year by several weeks because of lack of funds. In many cities emergency funds cannot be found to obtain such basic items as textbooks, and the students must simply share those that are available. To document the relative impoverishment of the city schools, it was stressed that despite the higher costs of educating disadvantaged children, many large cities are able to spend only half as much per student as their suburban neighbors.

The conferees agreed on the urgent need for increased state support for the city schools. For several decades, specialists in school finance have been clamoring for greater reliance on a state income tax to finance the schools. More recently, legal scholars have charged that the present fiscal disparities in school support within states violate the equal protection clause of the Fourteenth Amendment to the Constitution. This legal observation is serving as the basis for a number of suits in which city school districts are suing their states to require them to shoulder the major share of school expenditures and to finance particular schools according to the needs of the students. Thus, the resources needed to approach equality of educational opportunity would be judged by educational outcomes, a criterion that implies greater resources for the urban disadvantaged.

While virtually all the participants were willing to accept the premise that the city schools are underfinanced, few felt that additional finances alone would solve the educational problems of black citizens. Additional support might simply be distributed according to the present distribution of power and the less-powerful constituencies—poor blacks in particular—would continue to receive an inequitable portion relative to their dire educational needs. In fact, even when the central school administration has spent additional dollars on programs for black children, the results have been less than encouraging because most of the money has been applied to strategies that have failed in the past. The feeling among many participants was that community-run schools would utilize additional resources more effectively to improve their operations than have the citywide bureaucracies. Thus, it was concluded that a substantial promise of educational improvement for black students must include structural reform—for example, community control—in conjunction with an infusion of funds.

EVALUATION OF COMMUNITY SCHOOLS

The conferees then turned their attention to the second major aspect that should be built into the decentralized design—evaluation. In order for local communities to exercise significant control over their schools, they must be able to evaluate the performance of their schools. This process requires that at least two ingredients be present: available information on the results of present educational strategies and knowledge of alternative strategies and their probable outcomes. The community and its elected officials need these data to exert a positive influence on school outcomes.

Under the traditional system, the operation of the schools has been left to the bureaucracy, and little information on these two factors has been made available to outsiders. Indeed, such data have rarely been collected even for internal use, for the schools have usually lacked the incentive for self-evaluation. The present system of evaluation is process-oriented, concentrating on pupil-teacher ratios, facilities, expenditures, and other input measures as indices of quality, rather than measuring the achievement of objectives. The result of this orientation is that the community-controlled schools will not inherit a well-developed system for either measuring or disseminating information on educational outcomes. Consequently, the burden of building information and evaluation systems will fall on the decentralized schools. The conference participants discussed how this might be accomplished.

School evaluation was one of the most controversial subjects pursued at the meeting. In general, the differences in viewpoint reflected the larger controversy on whether the schools should be evaluated, how the assessment should be constructed, and who should be responsible for evaluation. Of these three problems, only the last two are of concern to the planners of school decentralization, since the concept of evaluation appears to be an integral part of local control.

In the discourse on what criteria should be used to evaluate community schools, there were several areas of agreement. First, there was broad accord that the analytical or applied tools needed to measure objectively and precisely the many outcomes of schooling are unavailable. While there are standardized testing instruments for assessing the acquisition of cognitive skills, they are characterized by cultural biases that make them particularly unsuitable for use in schools attended by racial minorities. Furthermore, instruments that can accurately measure such affective traits as self-worth, motivation, and other attitudinal characteristics are even less reliable. No one was pessimistic enough to suggest that relevant measures could not be developed, but there was a strong consensus that, at present, adequate educational barometers do not exist. Yet most of the conferees agreed that an evaluation based on rough guidelines of performance was still superior to no evaluation.

Several compelling reasons were advanced for delegating the responsibility for evaluation directly to the decentralized districts. The most important of these was that decentralization and responsiveness to community needs suggests a diversity of goals among the various community schools. Since each community would formulate different objectives for its schools, the applicability of an externally imposed and universal assessment system seems questionable. Second, each community would have more at stake in evaluating what it was doing than would higher authorities. With this kind of incentive, it is important that each local district build an evaluation function into its own structure, a function that would involve all the personnel as well as the local school board. Finally, it appears that many school personnel favor evaluation on a decentralized basis. Moskow and McLennan found that the teachers showed strong preferences for delegating teacher evaluation to the local school level. In fact, it was suggested that evaluation was one issue on which teachers' organizations and community boards could reach an agreement:

> Under such an agreement the teachers would participate in setting the evaluation guidelines and, perhaps, procedures. While the resulting mechanisms might vary greatly from community to community, the teachers as well as administrators and board members would share in the evaluation process.

It was suggested that there is at least one possible alternative to self-evaluation. Under the alternative strategy, local school boards would purchase evaluation services from either universities or private educational contractors. The governing board could set the objectives and perhaps the criteria for evaluation and the outside group would design appropriate measures and procedures to implement the assessment.

The conferees considered the subject of school evaluation to be so complex that they could not suggest a readily applicable evaluation system. This impasse implied a paradox: how could local citizens effectively influence their schools without a systematic assessment of the programs? While some communities might be able to develop useful performance information, others might not. What other forces, then, might be brought about to encourage schools to evaluate their operations, to release information on outcomes, and to pursue more productive strategies?

One suggestion was to require schools to compete with other schools for students so that there would exist incentives to fill particular educational needs.[12] Using this approach, public resources would be allocated to the schools according to the size of their enrollments. This arrangement would encourage schools to offer the best possible schooling in order to keep clientele. In addition, schools would have an incentive to provide information on their operations to the parental "market" in order to attract new pupils.

[12] See the chapter by Anthony Downs.

In a sense, this approach parallels that of the private schools, which must give parents enough information to convince them that the schooling offered is worth the price.

But many conferees objected to the market analogy for community schools, saying that choice of a large number of schools violates the whole organic concept of the school-community nexus. One critic felt:

> . . . that the competitive plan raises the question of whether the redistribution of power to black Americans can best be accomplished by increasing individual choices or group choices. I would argue that the liberation of the oppressed black depends more upon maximizing group choice; and this goal can be more nearly accomplished by black control of community schools in a geographical area than by focusing upon plans that lead to mobility outside of the site area.

A further question was raised by several participants who thought that competing schools might hoodwink parents through deceptive advertising and promotion. They suggested that the publicity campaigns of schools would concentrate on image-building rather than on concrete educational evidence.

But at least one organizer of a group of privately run schools disagreed. He felt that privately run and competing schools receiving public support may represent the only way of breaking out of the present pattern of failure. Under this approach, private schools that tailor themselves to particular groups of children would emerge and would receive public funding. This arrangement already exists in some states for educating children whose needs are not met by the public schools, such as the brain-injured or emotionally disturbed. Since it can be demonstrated that the needs of disadvantaged children are not being met by the public schools of many large cities, there seems to be a precedent for a system of publicly financed private schools to fill the needs of such children.

On the basis of this discussion, most of the conferees agreed that some competition among schools for students would yield substantial educational benefits. Middle-class parents already have a choice of schools through residential mobility as well as through the increasingly exercised option of sending their children to private schools. Many of the participants felt that disfranchised minorities and other low-income people should also be given a choice. The conclusion was that a good evaluation system may take a long time to construct. In the meantime, " . . . we ought to let poor people select among schools on the basis of their own impressions just as the rich do, but let's give them some choices."

Accordingly, the participants focused on a way of implementing a measure of competition even among community schools. Parents would be given the choice of sending their children to the local community school or to any other community school that had openings. Resources would be transferred among schools according to their enrollments; the schools that were more successful in attracting students would receive larger lump-sum budgets. In addition, the central administration would continue to maintain schools strategically located around the city so that they would be accessible to all students who wanted to attend them. Thus community schools would not only compete for students among themselves, but they would also compete with schools operated by the citywide school board. The result of this plan is that parents would be given alternatives, and all schools would be required to "stay on their toes" in order to retain and attract students. In this way, the negative aspects of monopolistic schools could be countered on both a community and a citywide basis.

Interestingly, those conferees who were administering community-controlled schools were especially enthusiastic about this competitive plan. One administrator explained that this arrangement would reward creativity and imagination, characteristics not rewarded under the present system. Thus, ". . . the principal would be encouraged by the very nature of the relationship—competition—to excel in his job. From the viewpoint of the system the results would be very beneficial, for the present single bureaucracy breeds sameness, not the diversity which is talked about as being desirable." He concluded that the able administrator would welcome such an approach because he does not require a captive audience to survive. Many conferees agreed that this form of competition might be the best way of insuring that decentralized schools would fulfill their promise.

Conclusions

The final session of the conference enabled the participants to summarize their thoughts, with explicit liberties granted to those who would predict future developments. Speaker after speaker expressed concern about the rapidly deteriorating situation in the black community in general, and in the black schools in particular. Their point was that if something is not done soon the situation would reach the bursting point. School vandalism and disruptions are on the upsurge, and the patience of community moderates is being sorely tested.

Yet what alternatives are available for improving black schools, and can the schools be improved without changing the powerlessness of the ghetto citizens? Many participants saw community control as the only solution. They had no faith in school bureaucracies that preached integration and compensatory education but practiced neither to any extent. It was suggested that, at the very least, community control might protect minority children from the grosser forms of discrimination that are practiced by our public school systems. But in addition, it was asserted that no substantial upgrading of black schools can take place without the introduction of powerful agents of change. The agent of change that is lacking under the present system is parental and community involvement, and it is now time for the community to try its hand at building schools that will succeed.

But while there was substantial endorsement of community control as the major, prospective educational solution, and the only one that aims to counter the powerlessness of the black community, the prognosis was not one of unrestrained optimism. The major stumbling blocks, as viewed by many of the conferees, were the political hurdles. One astute participant explained:

> That black schools are underfinanced at the present time is recognized by those in attendance here as well as by other educational experts. Now this is the situation that we face when the schools are operated by predominantly white school boards and administrators. When the control shifts to blacks there will be even less of a willingness to finance. I don't use this as an argument against community schools because I think that the gains in terms of promoting self-identity, success models, and so on are even worth this cost.
>
> The question is, what sort of forces or pressures can lead to a greater use of tax resources and the allocation of those revenues to low-income areas? I don't see them. I have no faith in the coalition concept because I think that the only types of coalitions that are presently possible are those be-

tween middle-class blacks and whites. Such an alliance could add funds for a small proportion of blacks, but it would have little or no impact on the majority of blacks, the poor, and powerless.

This participant saw no emerging forces to change his analysis.

The other participants agreed that both political support and the workability of decentralization are crucial elements that will go far to either promote or doom community control. But bearing in mind that the education of minorities is a national problem, the conferees agreed that immediate steps must be taken. The frustrations leading to demands for community control of the schools are ever present, and the movement is increasing in tempo. As one black stated:

> There are no alternatives. If this advanced society can't deliver effective educational services to black children—and I would deny that this is the most complicated technological question faced by this country—then what hope is there for equality in other parts of this land? Now maybe the point we have got to recognize is the need of the black community to say we are going to find in our cohesiveness the answer to this problem. Perhaps we are talking about a machine that just seems to grind on relentlessly, destroying children in its path. Maybe that's what the whole thing is all about, stopping that damn machine.

Perhaps community control of the black schools is a way of redirecting the machine. Most of the conferees agreed that it is worth the effort and that all of our expertise and proficiencies should be exerted to make it succeed. Many participants left the conference with the feeling that the alternatives are indeed meager.

Conference Participants

ANTHONY DOWNS *Real Estate Research Corporation*
NORMAN DRACHLER *Superintendent of Schools, Detroit*
MARIO D. FANTINI *Ford Foundation*
RONALD EVANS *Intermediate School 201 Principal, New York City*
JOSEPH FEATHERSTONE *The New Republic*
LEONARD J. FEIN *Harvard-MIT Joint Center for Urban Studies*
GRAHAM FINNEY *Deputy Superintendent of Schools, Philadelphia*
MARILYN GITTELL *Queens College Institute for Community Schools*
KARL D. GREGORY *Wayne State University*
H. THOMAS JAMES *Stanford University*
GEORGE JONES *National Education Association*
HERBERT KAUFMAN *Yale University*
HENRY M. LEVIN *Stanford University*
ROBERT F. LYKE *Princeton University*
SIDNEY MARLAND, JR. *Institute for Educational Development*
ROBERT C. MAYNARD *The Washington Post*
RHODY A. MCCOY *Brooklyn Demonstration School District*
KENNETH MCLENNAN *Temple University*
MICHAEL H. MOSKOW *Temple University*
JOSEPH A. PECHMAN *Brookings Institution*
HAROLD W. PFAUTZ *Brown University*
DAVID SELDEN *American Federation of Teachers*
JOHN SIMON *Yale University*
VICTOR SOLOMON *Congress of Racial Equality, Harlem*
DAVID SPENCER *Intermediate School 201 Planning Board, New York City*
GILBERT Y. STEINER *Brookings Institution*
ANTONY WARD *East Harlem Block Schools*
BENNETTA WASHINGTON *Office of Economic Opportunity*
CHARLES E. WILSON *Intermediate School 201 Complex, New York City*

Index